Luminos is the open access monograph publishing program from UC Press. Luminos provides a framework for preserving and reinvigorating monograph publishing for the future and increases the reach and visibility of important scholarly work. Titles published in the UC Press Luminos model are published with the same high standards for selection, peer review, production, and marketing as those in our traditional program. www.luminosoa.org

The publisher gratefully acknowledges the generous contribution to this book provided by the AMS 75 PAYS Endowment of the American Musicological Society, funded in part by the National Endowment for the Humanities and the Andrew W. Mellon Foundation.

The publisher also gratefully acknowledges the generous contribution to this book provided by the Curtis Institute of Music, which is committed to supporting its faculty in pursuit of scholarship.

Instruments for New Music

Instruments for New Music

Sound, Technology, and Modernism

Thomas Patteson

UNIVERSITY OF CALIFORNIA PRESS

University of California Press, one of the most distinguished university presses in the United States, enriches lives around the world by advancing scholarship in the humanities, social sciences, and natural sciences. Its activities are supported by the UC Press Foundation and by philanthropic contributions from individuals and institutions. For more information, visit www.ucpress.edu.

University of California Press
Oakland, California

© 2016 by Thomas Patteson

This work is licensed under a Creative Commons CC BY-NC-SA license. To view a copy of the license, visit http://creativecommons.org/licenses.

Every effort has been made to identify the rightful copyright holders of material not specifically commissioned for use in this publication and to secure permission, where applicable, for reuse of all such material. Credit, if and as available, has been provided for all borrowed material either on-page, on the copyright page, or in an acknowledgement section of the book. Errors or omissions in credit citations or failure to obtain permission if required by copyright law have been either unavoidable or unintentional. The author and publisher welcome any information that would allow them to correct future reprints.

Library of Congress Cataloging-in-Publication Data

Patteson, Thomas.
   Instruments for new music : sound, technology, and modernism / Thomas Patteson.
      pages cm
   Includes bibliographical references and index.
   isbn 978-0-520-28802-7 (pbk : alk. paper)
   isbn 978-0-520-96312-2 (ebook)
   1. Musical instruments. 2. Music and technology—History. 3. Electronic musical instruments—History. 4. Music—Philosophy and aesthetics. I. Title.
   ML460.P347 2016
   784.1909'04—dc23

                        2015028397

25 24 23 22 21 20 19 18 17 16
10 9 8 7 6 5 4 3 2 1

For Audrey and Felix

Contents

List of Illustrations	ix
Acknowledgments	xi

1	Listening to Instruments	1
2	"The Joy of Precision": Mechanical Instruments and the Aesthetics of Automation	18
3	"The Alchemy of Tone": Jörg Mager and Electric Music	52
4	"Sonic Handwriting": Media Instruments and Musical Inscription	82
5	"A New, Perfect Musical Instrument": The Trautonium and Electric Music in the 1930s	114
6	The Expanding Instrumentarium	152

Notes	169
Bibliography	209
Index	229

Illustrations

1. Excerpt of the piano roll for Hans Haass's "Intermezzo" (1927) / 21
2. Juxtaposition of a painting by Fernand Léger and a drawing of a drilling machine (1923) / 23
3. Technical illustration of the Welte-Mignon reproducing piano / 29
4. Cover of "Musik und Maschine," special issue of *Musikblätter des Anbruch* (1926) / 35
5. Oskar Schlemmer's costume sketches for the *Triadic Ballet* / 43
6. Schematic representation of the *Triadic Ballet*'s overall structure / 45
7. Paul Hindemith composing on a piano roll (ca. 1926) / 46
8. An artist's rendering of Lee de Forest's Audion Piano (1915) / 61
9. Technical draft of Jörg Mager's crank-operated electric instrument (ca. 1924) / 62
10. Léon Theremin and Jörg Mager (1927) / 67
11. Jörg Mager and an assistant in the laboratory (1927) / 69
12. Jörg Mager's notation system for the division of the octave into seventy-two equal intervals / 77
13. Jörg Mager playing the three-manual Partiturophon (ca. 1930) / 79

14. Photoelectric cells / *95*
15. Diagrammatic representation of sound-film playback / *96*
16. Oskar Fischinger, detail from *Ornamente Ton* (Ornament tone) display card, circa 1932 / *110*
17. Rudolf Pfenninger at work on his "sonic handwriting" / *111*
18. Friedrich Trautwein with the first model of the Trautonium (ca. 1930) / *118*
19. The electroacoustic laboratories of the Radio Research Section (1928) / *122*
20. Paul Hindemith's sketch for the first movement of *Des kleinen Elektromusikers Lieblinge* / *124*
21. "The Orchestra of the Future??" from the 1932 German Radio Exhibition / *126*
22. The Trautonium on the cover of *Radio-Craft magazine*, March 1933 / *127*
23. The Telefunken-Trautonium, also known as the Volkstrautonium / *128*
24. One of the few known advertisements for the Volkstrautonium / *131*
25. The three-voice Trautonium (ca. 1936) / *138*
26. The five-voice Partiturophon (ca. 1934) / *147*
27. The inventor as hero. Bust of Jörg Mager by Heinrich Jobst / *151*

Acknowledgments

This book would not exist without the involvement of many wonderful friends and colleagues. Those I name here are only the foremost.

Instruments for New Music began as a PhD dissertation at the University of Pennsylvania, where it was researched and written from 2010 to 2013. To my advisor, Emily Dolan, who patiently shepherded the project from its humble beginnings, I owe my sincerest gratitude. Committee members Carolyn Abbate, Jeffrey Kallberg, and John Tresch saw the project through to completion and offered invaluable guidance along the way. I am also deeply grateful for the kindness and warmth of Penn music department faculty and staff Lawrence Bernstein, Alfreda Frazier, Maryellen Malek, Jairo Moreno, Carol Muller, Guy Ramsey, Timothy Rommen, and Margaret Smith Deeney.

In the process of revising the dissertation into a book, many people have offered both general critiques and pointed readings of particular passages: my thanks to Peter Donhauser, Edward Jones-Imhotep, Cindy Keefer, and Deirdre Loughridge for lending their eyes and minds to this project.

Douglas Kahn, in addition to his extensive feedback on the text, provided counsel and encouragement every step of the way, for which I cannot thank him enough.

Thanks as well to Jonathan Coopersmith and Paul Bryan at the Curtis Institute of Music for their help in securing financial support for the publication of this book, and to Curtis library staff Michelle Oswell, Emily Butler, and Molly O'Brien for their help during the final stages of research and writing.

The staff at University of California Press was wonderfully helpful in guiding me through the process of turning my manuscript into a book: sincerest thanks to Bradley Depew, Zuha Khan, Aimée Goggins, Rachel Berchten, and above all my editor, Mary Francis. My copyeditor Barbara Armentrout and my indexer Suzanne Bratt showed remarkable patience and thoroughness in putting the manuscript through its final paces.

Finally, I'm grateful to my parents, my family, and my wife, Audrey, and my son, Felix, for their love and support over the years. I couldn't have done it without you.

Thomas Patteson
Philadelphia, May 2015

1

Listening to Instruments

Music is of the imagination,
but the imagination is of the sound
and the sound is of the instruments.[1]
—Robert Donington

The demand for new instruments resounded at the dawn of the twentieth century. "Suddenly," Ferruccio Busoni declared in his 1907 *Sketch of a New Aesthetic of Music,* "one day it became clear to me: the development of music is impeded by our instruments. [. . .] In their scope, their sound, and their performative possibilities, our instruments are constrained, and their hundred chains shackle the would-be creator as well."[2] In his *Art of Noises* manifesto of 1913, Luigi Russolo denounced the symphony orchestra as a "hospital for anemic sounds" and called for new ways of exploring the unlimited domain of acoustic phenomena. Edgard Varèse declared in 1916, "We have a great need for new instruments. [. . .] I refuse to submit to sounds that have already been heard. I seek new technical means which can allow and sustain any kind of expression of thought."[3] Two years later, the Russian composer Joseph Schillinger foresaw the perfection of instruments through the "electrification of music" and asserted that from then on, "the development of music will go hand in hand with science."[4] Summing up these sentiments, the American physicist John Redfield wrote in 1926 that "the music of any age depends upon the kind of musical instruments which that age possesses. *Composers can go no further than the possibilities of the instruments for which they write.*"[5] Among the many messianic visions of artistic renewal in the early twentieth century, these proclamations were distinguished by their technological emphasis. While others sought rejuvenation in folk traditions, popular music and American jazz, classical and baroque genres, or constructivist approaches to composition such as the twelve-tone technique, for these musicians the only solution was "a fundamental change of the sonic apparatus itself"—a new instrumentarium.[6]

The call for new instruments did not long go unanswered. During the fifteen-year span of the Weimar Republic (1918–1933), which held sway between the end of the First World War and the Nazi seizure of power, Germany and its neighbors buzzed with technological experiments in music. Mechanical instruments such as the player piano, originally intended to reproduce the popular hits of the day and immortalize the interpretations of great performers, were refunctioned as superhuman machines capable of realizing musical designs unplayable by ten fingers. Electric instruments offered performing musicians new interfaces and sound-generating circuitry, opening up unexplored worlds of timbre and tone. Finally, recording media such as gramophone records and optical sound film were used not to capture but to *produce* sound according to the composer's wishes, generating musical possibilities beyond the bounds of familiar instruments. From the mid-1920s until the fall of the Republic—and even, to a lesser extent, during the Nazi period—these new instruments stood at the center of the furious artistic debates of the day. Concerts and festivals provided public forums for the technologies and their enthusiasts, music journals published dispatches on the latest developments and dedicated special issues to the topic, inventors demonstrated their creations throughout Europe, and composers both obscure and established set out to create music for these devices. The instrumental innovations of the early twentieth century were not merely isolated experiments but rather part of a systematic, wide-ranging investigation into the technological foundations of sound and its implications for the art of music.[7]

A hundred years later, musicians take for granted what for Busoni and his ilk was a daring proposition. From a purely quantitative standpoint, the ways of producing, manipulating, and disseminating sound have grown exponentially in the last century. Out of a potentially infinite catalog of possibilities, consider just a few examples: ubiquitous university courses and curricula in "electronic music" and "music and technology," the massive consumer market for synthesizers and other electronic instruments, and the proliferation of computer-based interfaces of all kinds, from highly abstract computer music languages to the plethora of apps for cell phones and tablets. But it is not only the sheer number of instruments now available that is significant; it is how these devices—digital, analog, and "acoustic"—reshape the fundamental parameters of the art. Instruments make music in a double sense: they create the sounds, but they also forge connections to the aesthetic, social, and metaphysical realities that give these sounds meaning, charging them with the current of human significance. What music is depends, to a large degree, on what instruments can do. The realization of this fundamental interdependence between music and technology is a legacy of the inventions, debates, and performances whose story I tell in this book.

Some of these things will be familiar from the history of what, since about 1950, has been known as "electronic music," which has been explored at great length in both general and specialist sources. Indeed, this history is by now so well-trodden that it has almost attained the status of a myth. By this I don't meant simply something that is not true; I mean a sort of history by osmosis, a common or vernacular understanding that seeps into public consciousness from various sources of information. (Most historical knowledge is, in this sense, mythic.) *Instruments for New Music* is a product of both my fascination with electronic music and my discontent with its conventional history—my sense that the very concept of electronic music is too limiting and actually forecloses new perspectives on the relationship between sound, art, and technology in twentieth-century culture.

Perhaps the most basic characteristic of the myth of electronic music is the way it maps onto the chronology of the twentieth century. The exhaustion of the orchestra, the visionary artist stifled by the lack of appropriate tools, the appeal to a distant future in which composers' dreams could at last be realized—these tropes form the pillars of this historical narrative. The career of Varèse, in particular, is the touchstone here: after composing a number of groundbreaking works that stretched the limits of the orchestra, his frustration with existing instruments led him to abandon composition in the late 1930s. Only after World War II, with the availability of magnetic tape and the founding of the first studios for electronic music, was he finally able to attain his ideal of absolute artistic control.[8] This story, as told and retold by music historians, neatly bisects the twentieth century into an early period of prophetic speculation and a later phase of genuine artistic accomplishment. Consequently, everything that came before the emergence of electronic music around 1950 is consigned to a "pre-history" of dubious value: if these earlier events are considered at all, they are often relegated to the role of anticipating or foreshadowing later developments. In this book, I try to understand the technological endeavors of the early twentieth century in their own terms. Only then, I believe, can we begin to figure out how these activities relate to the bigger historical picture, not as predecessors or preludes, but as integral elements of modern culture.

There is another problem. The very concept of electronic music too often implies that in the twentieth century music somehow *became technological*, and it highlights modern sound apparatus at the cost of obscuring the material foundations of music throughout history.[9] (In an odd way, in many contexts "electronic music" has become vaguely synonymous with "music and technology.") Further, the myth of electronic music conflates the technological changes undergone in the twentieth century with a particular, admittedly hugely important branch of technology: namely, electronics. Consequently, phenomena such as the unique inventions of Russolo and Harry Partch or the refunctioning of traditional instruments through unconventional playing techniques are typically explained as appendages to electronic music, rather than being seen as manifestations of an overarching category of activity. Electronic music, in short, offers too narrow a conceptual framework to encompass the far-flung technological extensions of twentieth-century music. What is needed, and what I hope this book will provide, is a greater sense of continuity both between musical instruments new and old and between technology and the human conditions within which it exists.

Indeed, the biggest problem with the story of electronic music is the way it tends to be told in isolation from the larger history of twentieth-century culture. The progression from the first electronic instruments to tape machines to synthesizers and computers is depicted as a natural unfolding of technological forms; history becomes a timeline of inventions and innovations, laid out with all the taxonomical neatness of a scientific exhibit. But the history of instruments, when properly told, concerns not just the objects themselves but also what they promise, portend, and make possible. The controversies surrounding the movement for new instruments in the early twentieth century both echoed and influenced the broader debates about the role of technology in modern society: musicians' deepening engagement with technology, far from being merely a search for "new sounds," constitutes one of the primary vectors through which music in the twentieth century opens out into other fields of thought and action, from aesthetics to politics, science, and philosophy.

My purpose in this book is not to champion a kind of technological reductionism—throwing back the curtain to reveal the machines behind the music. The technical and aesthetic threads of music are intertwined through and through: instruments are "technologies of enchantment."[10] Like all artifacts, they are products of human brains and bodies, shot through with imagination, will, and desire. The study of instruments need not represent a challenge to traditional humanistic concerns; on the contrary, it could help resuscitate aesthetics in its radical, original sense: the science of perception and feeling.[11] This means, on the one hand, that technologies cannot be fully comprehended apart from the human contexts in which they emerge. On the other hand, the study of art must encompass the material means of cultural production. Tracing the contours of what has been called the *instrumentality* of music is not a question of exposing aesthetic experience as the subjective by-product of an underlying material reality, but rather of grasping how the spell of art is technologically cast.[12]

DRAMATIS PERSONAE

There was no common musical aesthetic uniting the various figures brought together in this book. While they shared a vision of the radical reform of music through modern technology, they were motivated by distinct and sometimes mutually antagonistic objectives.[13] They disagreed about the kind of instruments worth pursuing, about the musical potential even of given devices, about how the new instruments fit into existing habits of music making, and about the role of technology in culture at large. In short, the movement for new instruments was not a monolithic project but rather an arena in which different worldviews collided. The underlying motivation for the disparate undertakings recounted in the following pages was the search for new musical possibilities, new foundations of creative work. The technological enthusiasm of the age was driven by a kind of musical fundamentalism, a desire to bypass worn-out means of expression and get one's hands on sound itself. New instruments allowed the artists of the time to explore the outer limits of artistic possibility. As one observer noted in 1927, "The boldest artists are groping in the dark of an unexplored space. What they discover there is difficult to measure with the old yardsticks; it is absolutely otherwise. . . . Whether it is a dead end or the path to a new century, a narrow, arduous borderland or a vast, fertile country, no one can say." Significantly, the examples given of these "threshold" phenomena were all technological experiments: the investigation of the continuum between tone and noise, the division of the semitone into quarter tone and smaller values, and the mechanical reproduction of music.[14]

Technology in twentieth century music is typically associated with modernism in its antiromantic, scientistic, and "objective" tendencies. Likewise, the technological enthusiasm of the Weimar period was understood at the time as a manifestation of the "New Sobriety" *(neue Sachlichkeit),* which stood for a down-to-earth, unsentimental attitude toward art and society. Many of the figures in this book—among them Hans Heinz Stuckenschmidt, László Moholy-Nagy, and Rudolf Pfenninger—saw the new instruments as embodiments of modern values such as clarity, order, and control. They embraced a rigorous, quasi-scientific ideal of music in opposition to the image of the inspired artist inherited from the nineteenth century. But this matter-of-fact mindset was by no means universal among advocates of the new instruments. Others, such as Jörg Mager, Oskar Schlemmer, and Oskar Fischinger, wove modern technology into a poetic and visionary worldview. In the language of expressionist aesthetics, they sought to "project themselves into the cosmos" and extend the scope of their experience to a superhuman scale.[15] Embracing the machine as a means of spiritual transport, they gave themselves over to "technological sublime," in which the artifacts built to control natural forces become objects of the fascination and awe that those forces once evoked.[16] Such unlikely alliances between mysticism and modernity were probably what the philosopher Ernst Cassirer had in mind when he bemoaned the "romantics of technology" who exalted inventions that they did not understand.[17] Cassirer and other critics feared that the newest technologies offered an up-to-date guise for dangerous antimodern attitudes.

The split between what might be called "machine modernism" and "machine romanticism" reflected a broader duality in the early twentieth century between an infatuation with modern life and an idealistic quest for alternatives to a disenchanted reality. This opposition was illustrated in Oskar Schlemmer's colorful characterization of the bifurcated artistic culture of the Bauhaus in the early 1920s: "On the one hand, the influence of oriental culture, the cult of India, also a return to nature . . . communes, vegetarianism, Tolstoyism, reaction against the war; and on the other hand, the American spirit *[Amerikanismus],* progress, the marvels of technology and invention, the urban environment."[18] In short, there were two broad strains of technological enthusiasm: one embraced technology as the embodiment of the modern Zeitgeist, while the other saw it as a way to transcend profane reality and reach a state of timelessness or ecstasy.

Just as the new sound technologies brought together artists of opposing aesthetic positions, so too did they throw open the gates separating the various forms of art. One of the most remarkable effects of the technologization of sound was to draw music into the synesthetic gyre of the early twentieth century. This multi- (or inter-)media impulse, too, belonged to the spirit of the age: the painter Paul Klee spoke for many when he dismissed the hallowed distinctions between the arts laid down in Gottfried Lessing's classic eighteenth-century aesthetic treatise *Laoköon* as "learned nonsense."[19] Indeed, one of the primary reasons why music historians have overlooked the technological undertakings of the Weimar period is that very few of the movement's major figures were professional musicians. Stuckenschmidt, for example, though trained as a composer, made his mark as a critic and impresario. The Hungarian painter and photographer Moholy-Nagy was one of the central theorists of technological experimentation in the arts, and his writings exerted a foundational influence on the search for new instrumental modalities in the 1920s. The choreographer Oskar Schlemmer, who taught alongside Moholy-Nagy at the Bauhaus, developed an abstract, puppetlike form of dance and costume design whose musical equivalent he sought in mechanical instruments. The inventors Jörg Mager and Friedrich Trautwein, though at best amateur musicians, were able to envision new forms of music on the basis of their electroacoustic investigations into sound. Finally, the pioneers of optical sound film after 1930—Walter Ruttmann, Oskar Fischinger, and Rudolf Pfenninger—were all filmmakers by training, and they translated their skills in that medium to a new form of music-making based on cinematic techniques such as splicing and montage.

The intermingling of artistic media points toward another overlooked aspect of Weimar-era experimentation: virtually all the new instruments of the period were based more or less closely on existing forms of media technology. As the mass-media empires of broadcasting and recording rose around them, the musicians and artists of the Weimar Republic sought to seize the industries' tools and turn them into instruments for new music. Moholy-Nagy provided a catalytic jolt to the movement with his 1922 essay "Production-Reproduction," published in the Dutch art journal *De Stijl*.[20] Here he formulated what would become the credo of like-minded artists: a turn from merely *reproductive* applications (duplication, dissemination) to generative or *productive* uses—that is, the creation of new forms of art that exploited the unique capabilities of modern technologies.

Artists of the period did not universally oppose media as means of communication—indeed, most believed that recording and radio transmission had great potential as instruments of mass enlightenment—but they resisted what they saw as the one-dimensional function of modern technologies in propagating existing forms of art. In some cases, turning media into instruments was simply a question of deliberate artistic "refunctioning": for example, inscribing directly onto recording formats such as player piano rolls or optical sound film. In the case of early electric instruments, however, the relationship to existing media technologies was more remote, and thus the act of repurposing was more technically involved: radio components, intended to receive signals, could be cobbled together in new configurations to create and control electrically generated tones. One contemporary observer wrote that electric instruments, "whose technical components are familiar from the domain of radio electronics, do not want to be an ear, but rather a voice."[21]

For many of the protagonists of this book, then, the new instruments became a vehicle for technological critique: they reimagined media not as passive transmitters of preformed content but as tools whose function and meaning were determined by their users.[22] From the standpoint of the later technological history of the twentieth century, Moholy-Nagy's duality of production-reproduction anticipates the emerging categories of *instruments* and *media:* tools of artistic expression, on the one hand, and means of communication, on the other. Media scholar Jonathan Sterne has argued that the conventional distinction between musical instruments and reproductive media has long failed to do justice to reality: instead of a hard line between the two, history shows a continuous flow between "productive" and "reproductive" sound technologies.[23] The distinction between media and instrument, in short, is not embedded in the objects themselves but emerges from patterns of use. Technologies do not impose upon their players a uniform technique but rather, at most, inbuilt tendencies or inertial forces—attractors, so to speak, in the phase space of creative possibility.

TECHNOLOGY IN THE BALANCE

While the search for new instruments was buoyed by an attitude of what might be called technological euphoria, this optimistic mood was by no means universal in the early twentieth century. The early twentieth century was a time of profound technological anxiety in European culture, and the movement for new instruments both reflected and shaped broader debates about technology writ large. The origins of this debate reach back into the second half of the previous century, as engineers and scientists sought to raise the cultural standing of their professions by showing how material progress benefitted not only the body but also the mind and spirit. One of the foremost protagonists in this project was the German physicist Hermann von Helmholtz (1821–1894). Helmholtz viewed his research as a bridge between the older tradition of the humanities, or *Kulturwissenschaften*, with their qualitative and holistic orientation, and the ascendant natural sciences, which were highly specialized and analytically oriented.[24] Incidentally, Helmholtz was also a pioneering researcher in acoustics whose findings were hugely influential for many early-twentieth-century experiments in sound technology. In his book *On the Sensations of Tone*, first published in 1863, Helmholtz attempted to synthesize the two domains of music and natural science—in his words, to "connect the boundaries of two sciences, which, although drawn toward each other by many natural affinities, have hitherto remained practically distinct—the boundaries of *physical and physiological acoustics* on one side, and of *musical science and aesthetics* on the other."[25]

Helmholtz's work was a touchstone for many of the figures in this book, on account of both its groundbreaking insights and its ambitious project of bridging art and science. But this was just one manifestation of a larger effort by German intellectuals to demonstrate the underlying unity of technological progress and humanistic culture. In his 1877 book *Principles of a Philosophy of Technology*, Ernst Kapp challenged the conventional understanding of technology in terms of mechanisms and depicted tools as "organ projections," or extensions of the human body: for Kapp, the hammer was a synthetic fist, spectacles were externalized eyes, and the telegraph was an artificial nervous system.[26] By envisioning technology as an organic outgrowth of humanity rather than an extrinsic, alien force, Kapp and other scientifically inclined intellectuals challenged the technophobic bias in German culture and helped foster a sympathetic attitude toward technology by framing it in terms of the natural, the spiritual, and the creative.[27]

This project gained steam with the advancing industrialization of Germany and the rise of a new, scientifically trained class of professionals around the turn of the century. The engineer Max Eyth asserted that technological objects should be viewed as products of the human spirit no different from works of art. A device that turns electricity into light, Eyth suggested, is as noble a creation as a novel or a poem. He described the urge to invent in terms typically reserved for the inspiration of the artistic genius:

> The cause of all invention [...] is the *creative* impulse in the spirit of man, the *pleasure* of making, the *joy* of producing. It is the same force that drives the artist and the poet to his creation, without want, without necessity, but inexorably; the Promethean spark than lives in man, the divine in us, that makes the animal into a human being and gives the human his affinity to God.[28]

Another engineer-philosopher, Eberhard Zschimmer, argued that the cultural value of technological creations was to be found not in the artifacts themselves, but in the expressions of human will that they embodied. Through the painstaking labors of his craft, the inventor undertook a quest for freedom through the mastery of the physical world: "Because we are born into chains in nature, thus there awakes with the spark of spirit the idea of freedom over nature: *the idea of technology.* Every new invention is a new stage in the freedom attained by humanity through the progress of technology."[29] Zschimmer and others sought to bridge the apparent chasm between the mechanical and the organic by portraying inventors as creative figures—artists in the medium of technology, so to speak.

But this effort to make a place for inventors and engineers in the cultural pantheon was by no means unopposed. For many, and especially for the cultural elite that had been steeped in the humanist tradition of the nineteenth century, technology symbolized all the ills of the modern age. This techno-skeptical attitude found its most influential voice in Oswald Spengler's pop-intellectual treatise *Decline of the West* (1918–1922), which presented a gloomy narrative of European civilization sputtering toward its inevitable doom at the hands of its own devices. In Spengler's pessimistic vision, the technological and materialist obsessions of Western, "Faustian" culture had created a world drained of human meaning and understood solely in terms of scientific manipulation.[30] Just as nature had been brought to heel by its human creatures, Spengler suggested, humanity would soon be subjugated by its own mechanical progeny. The sociologist Max Weber sounded a similar note in his lecture "Science as a Vocation," written, like Spengler's book, during the final days of the First World War. Weber proclaimed that the techno-scientific mindset of European modernity had led to the "disenchantment of the world." Humanity's experience of awe before the unfathomable workings of nature had given way to the blasé arrogance of universal knowledge and mastery.[31]

This simmering discontent with modernity found expression in a diffuse intellectual tendency known as "philosophy of life" *(Lebensphilosophie)*. Rooted in the writings of thinkers such as Wilhelm Dilthey, Henri Bergson, and Friedrich Nietzsche, this was an eclectic cocktail of ideas that included disgust with the supposed superficiality of regnant scientific materialism, a concern for unity and synthesis over the analytic mindset of nineteenth-century positivism, and strikingly proto-environmental critiques of industrialization and the destruction of the natural world.[32] Although *Lebensphilosophie,* above all through its associations with philosophers such as Nietzsche and Ludwig Klages, eventually became tainted through piecemeal appropriation by the Nazis, it was no monopoly of the political right. Apprehension about the fragmented, chaotic nature of modern life was felt across the ideological spectrum, and none were immune from what historian Peter Gay called the "hunger for wholeness."[33]

The fear that modernity posed a threat to humanistic culture was especially acute in musical circles. The valorization of technology in the early twentieth century challenged a widespread suspicion that the modern, disenchanted world of science was fundamentally incompatible with the expressive domain of art—epitomized, according to aesthetic consensus, by music. Music was the sanctum of an endangered subjective "inwardness," whether conceived as religious awe, emotional expression, or metaphysical transcendence. Over the course of the nineteenth century, the concert music tradition came to represent a refuge from the noise and chaos of modernity, a safe haven for the spiritual values threatened by industrialization and the emergence of mass society. The technological enthusiasm of the early twentieth century thus signaled an ominous incursion of modernity into one of the last bastions of humanist culture.[34]

Defenders of musical tradition, though often skeptical of the new technologies, felt compelled to take them seriously. No less an authority than Curt Sachs, a prominent music historian and one of the founders of the modern discipline of organology, turned his attention to the new instruments and their significance for the music of the modern age:

> Today [in 1927] [. . .] we find ourselves again at a critical, decisive point. Lauded and lamented, young composers are taking up the new expressive means offered by the record industry and its relatives. We ourselves have witnessed the maturation of these technologies: the development of the Edison

phonograph to the Gramophone and the little music box to the [Welte-]Mignon Organ has played out in our own time, and today were are astounded witnesses to tone production through electrical currents.[35]

For Sachs, as for many others, the dawning instrumental revolution represented an epochal shift in the relationship between spirit *(Geist)* and technology *(Technik)*—in other words, between musical ideas and their means of realization. Sachs was troubled by the possibility that the "technique of the instrument builder," not the "mind of the composer," could gain the upper hand in the unfolding of music history.[36] In the new instruments, he perceived the danger of technology run amok, unchecked by a higher principle.

In 1926, the critic Adolf Weissmann published a book entitled *Die Entgötterung der Musik (Music Come to Earth)*, in which he explicitly counterposed the romantic concept of art and the effects of modern technology: "We find ourselves in the midst of radical upheavals in the domain of art, and it is music, perhaps, which plays the greatest part in them. Nothing of the kind has ever happened before. [. . .] Music's descent to earth [*Entgötterung*] need not be its ruin; but its conformity to this new world of machinery cannot but change its very core."[37] For Weissmann, modern technology was a declaration of war on the nineteenth-century ideal of art. Automobiles and airplanes collapse distance and endanger the artist's "splendid isolation," while economic pressures force him to think of ephemeral successes and scorn the quest for immortality through timeless works. The result is the uprooting of romanticism, a process begun in the nineteenth century and completed by the Great War.[38] Weissmann expressed the conflict between technology and human freedom in terms of the struggle between musician and instrument: "Mind devised the machine; now the machine fetters and drives mind. [. . .] At the piano, man, as a musician, still wrestled with the machine. He could once dominate it by giving it a soul. Now the machine is ready to subdue him."[39] As he recognized, music in the early twentieth century had become the site of a proxy battle over technology and its role in modern society.

INSTRUMENTS AND THE FUTURE

Thinkers such as Sachs and Weissmann, with their skeptical attitudes toward the new technologies, represented the old guard of an increasingly embattled humanistic tradition opposed to the "materialist" values of emerging industrial society. It was the engineers' gospel of Helmholtz and company—technology as a harbinger of human freedom—that formed the deep cultural substrate of the utopian visions of the early twentieth century and that united the otherwise contentious band of characters featured in this book. In the domain of music, one of the earliest and most influential advocates of this ideal was the Italian-German composer and writer Ferruccio Busoni (1886–1924). Busoni was the primary vector through which the technological enthusiasm of the early twentieth century entered into the bloodstream of European classical music. It was his writings, and above all his widely read 1907 treatise *Sketch of a New Aesthetic of Music (Entwurf einer neuen Ästhetik der Tonkunst)*, that laid the intellectual foundation for the technological experiments of the 1920s and '30s. More than any other figure, Busoni was the patron saint of the movement for new instruments.

For the purposes of this book, the critical idea of Busoni's *Sketch* was that compositional thought had outstripped the potential of available musical technologies: instruments had become the limiting reagents in the chemical reaction that fueled the progress of music. For Busoni, the constraints imposed by traditional instruments were not only technical but also emotional and associative: no amount of skill can allow the composer to escape "the tremulous ardor of the cello, the hesitant entry of the horn, the timid shortness of breath of the oboe, the showy loquaciousness of the clarinet."[40] Crucially, however, the exhaustion of the symphonic instrumentarium was at once a crisis and an opportunity for radical renewal: "It may be that all the possibilities of traditional instruments have not yet been exploited," Busoni wrote. "But we are certainly well along the way of the path toward exhaustion. Where then do we turn our gaze, where does the next step lead? The answer, I believe, is abstract sound, unbounded techniques and technologies *[Technik]*, tonal limitlessness. All efforts must push in this direction, in order to bring about a new, virginal beginning."[41]

Remarkably, in light of the scope of his later influence, Busoni said very little about actual technologies in his book. He dilated at some length on technical novelties such as new scales and systems of tuning but mentioned only one new instrument, the Telharmonium of the American inventor Thaddeus Cahill, and described it in rather impressionistic terms. (Busoni's misunderstanding of Cahill's instrument had ramifications in the later development early electronic instruments, as shown in chapter 3.) He hailed the Telharmonium's "scientifically perfect sound" and declared that "only a long and diligent experimentation, an ongoing education of the ears, will render this unfamiliar material pliable for the coming generation, and for art."⁴² It was Busoni's ability to link the transcendental imagery of musical idealism with the real technological prospects of the age that enabled his writing to cast such a powerful spell on the later course of twentieth-century music.

Even as his book went through two highly successful editions, Busoni's views provoked spirited opposition. The most prominent challenge came from the German composer Hans Pfitzner, whose 1917 pamphlet *The Danger of Futurism (Futuristengefahr)* doubled as a soapbox for his nationalist and antimodernist views on contemporary music.⁴³ "Futurism" for Pfitzner—the term appears nowhere in Busoni's book—signified Busoni's contempt for tradition and reckless enthusiasm for novelty. He accused Busoni of dismissing the entire history of music as a mere prelude that must be "annihilated root and branch" in order for the music of the future to be born. The product of Busoni's vain quest for utopian systems of musical organization was at best idle speculation, and at worst artistic nihilism:

> In general [Busoni's] expositions degenerate into dreams and prophecies of as-yet nonexistent developments and the future musical theories that will lead to them, and—of course, not unrelated to this—a more implicit than overt negation of everything that has come before. [. . .] Strange! Busoni disavows what is right at hand, but he believes in what is nonexistent!⁴⁴

For Pfitzner, who saw himself as a defender of the German classical-romantic tradition, Busoni's vision of the music of the future was simply unrecognizable as the art of Bach, Beethoven, and Brahms: "It appears to me that if Busoni's dreams were to be realized, the result would be no new aesthetic of music, but an entirely new art," he wrote, "if indeed there could be an art that has nothing in common with what we now call music, aside from the vibrations of the air."⁴⁵ Pfitzner believed that great art can emerge only from the inextinguishable well of creative inspiration and never from the development of new instruments or techniques.⁴⁶ The origin and essence of music is *Einfall*, or inspiration; instruments are merely the external means of clothing the musical idea in acoustic form. Pfitzner argued that because music, unlike the other arts, lacks a preexistent material with which to work, composition is a purely spiritual act. In his words, "the composer has nothing in the external world as material, but rather only his feelings. He creates ex nihilo." The alternative to this belief in inspired creation is "a regression to the workmanlike primitiveness of earlier times, when the concept of the 'composer' had not yet emerged in its pure form."[47] For Pfitzner, the notion that music was somehow dependent on technology was an affront to all practitioners of the art.

In his response to Pfitzner's attack, an open letter bearing the title "The Future of Music," Busoni offered a defense of his musical aesthetics couched, appropriately enough, in a technological metaphor. Just as those who first dreamed of human flight could not envision the machines that finally fulfilled that ancient wish, Busoni could not foresee the course that the new music would take. Instead, he hoped to lay the foundation for future developments whose precise contours were unimaginable from the standpoint of the present. In a final gibe at Pfitzner, who had compared his antagonist's speculations to the science fiction novels of Jules Verne, Busoni reminded his adversary "how much technical fantasy in these books has now become fact."[48]

As the confrontation between Busoni and Pfitzner demonstrates, the question of instruments and their role in music was bound up with larger debates over music's place in the trajectory of history and artists' competing loyalties to past and future. While Pfitzner worried that musical tradition would be sacrificed for the sake of a "new music" of questionable value, Busoni believed that the survival of the art could be ensured only by a radical technological intervention. Here, as elsewhere, debates ostensibly about technology turned out to revolve around other matters, from the possibility of progress in art to the relationship between forms of art and the society in which they exist.

Busoni's speculative vision would exert a powerful allure for the composers, inventors, and critics of the Weimar Republic. The dominant mood of the movement was, quite literally, "futurist." For the protagonists of the search for new instruments, the success of their endeavor was to be measured not only by its immediate impact on contemporary musical life but also by its distant and unforeseeable ramifications. This attitude resonated with the optimistic progress-thinking typical of the technological discourse of the time. The philosopher Ernst Cassirer, writing in 1930, declared that "technology is ultimately concerned not with what *is,* but with what *could be.*"[49] The journalist Frank Warschauer argued that historicist thinking, which tries to understand the present on the basis of the past, must give way to a "science of the future" that understands the present on the basis of its teleological arc: "The path of technology, according to everything we know, is perfectly straight. We need only follow its trajectory in order to see where it leads, and indeed, must lead. To recognize the character of technification, it is necessary to look to the future. Only then can what is happening in the present moment become clear."[50] This notion of a technologically conditioned sense of futurity corresponded to a tendency in the broader pan-European avant-garde toward theoretical speculation, polemics, and imaginative brainstorms. Many modernists seemed to be more concerned with creating systems, techniques, and processes for making art than with producing finished works. Artists saw themselves in relation not to a historical lineage from the past but to future developments in which they hoped to play a generative role.[51]

For all his invocations of a distant future in which his prophecies would be vindicated, Busoni's musical utopia did not have to wait long. In 1906, a year before *Sketch of a New Aesthetic of Music* was first published, Lee de Forest patented his Audion triode, the invention that would come to symbolize the birth of the electronic age. No longer would gigantic spinning dynamos be needed to generate sufficient electric charge to create a synthetic tone; now this could be done by the compact, lightweight, and eventually mass-producible vacuum tube. Ironically, while engineers increasingly fancied themselves as inspired visionaries, many artists aspired to the sublime rigor of science: Musicians of the period spoke of their work in terms of "discovery," "investigation," and "research." The musical possibilities they contemplated were no mere thought experiments—they were real potentialities engendered by the shifting technological basis of sound production.

Still, the product of the techno-aesthetic fusion foretold by Busoni was bound to be something new and volatile. Pfitzner's crotchety admonitions about the "dangers of futurism" would eventually gain a certain retrospective validity: the vertiginous effects of the new instruments would indeed change music into "an entirely new art," as he had warned. By introducing the machine into the studio, composers exchanged the limited but stable instrumentarium of the nineteenth century for the bewildering possibilities of modern technology. As we will see in the following chapters, the new instruments offered a devil's bargain: their powers were vast but also unpredictable and uncontrollable. Neither imperiously dictating musical reality nor obediently channeling their masters' wishes, they were "tricksters" whose mercurial nature belied their apparent fixity as material objects.[52] Rather than expanding compositional possibilities in a linear and predictable way, the instrumental innovations of the early twentieth century scrambled conventional aesthetic categories, destabilized the boundaries between the arts, and reshaped the relationship between past, present, and future in artistic consciousness. As Busoni's progeny would discover, the marriage of music and modern technology would have implications unforeseen even by its most radical advocates. To a greater degree than ever before, music and technology would enter into a mutually catalytic relationship, impelling each other toward exhilarating and unsettling new possibilities.

2

"The Joy of Precision"

Mechanical Instruments and the Aesthetics of Automation

> It is not the automaton that plays the flute; it is the mechanic, who measured the wind and set the fingers in motion.[1]
> —Jean-Jacques Rousseau

On the evening of July 25, 1926, an unusual concert took place in the small Black Forest town of Donaueschingen, Germany. Presented as "original compositions for mechanical instruments," the event featured three pieces by Ernst Toch, six "Polyphonic Études" by Gerhart Münch, and two works by Paul Hindemith, all written especially for a model of piano called the Welte-Mignon, which played automatically by means of a pneumatic mechanism activated by a spinning paper roll. The finale was an experimental stage performance called the *Triadic Ballet,* with costumes and choreography by the Bauhaus teacher Oskar Schlemmer and accompaniment for mechanical organ by Hindemith. A contemporary account captured the strange scene as the music began:

> The hall was illuminated by unseen sources. It was absolutely quiet as Hindemith wound up the device. [. . .] The piano began to play: music like an étude, toccatas with otherwise unplayable harmonic progressions, with a speed that could never be approached even by the most virtuosic of players, with an exactitude of which a human could never be capable, with a superhuman sonic force, with a geometrical clarity of rhythm, tempo, dynamics, and phrasing, which only a machine can produce. [. . .] The piano finished the composition and there was an uneasy pause. Should one applaud? There's no one sitting there. It's only a machine. Finally a quiet applause, growing louder. Calls of "da capo." And sure enough, the piano played it again, without hesitation, as precisely as the first time.[2]

This concert, and its successor the following year, presented a collection of original compositions written not for a human performer to play, but for the mechanical piano itself. These pieces, though written by a handful of different composers, shared certain stylistic traits. They were all miniatures in scale, with the longest piece clocking in at a mere four and a half minutes. A brisk or very fast tempo and a medium-to-loud dynamic level were dominant throughout most of the compositions. In terms of genre, the pieces tended toward either preclassical contrapuntal or ornamental models. This predilection for polyphonic forms, on the one hand, and quasi-improvisatory showpieces, on the other, was typical of the modernist style of the mid-1920s.[3]

In Hans Haass's *Capriccio Fugue,* the fugal subject is presented straightaway, the entries of the voices rapidly accumulating to a densely layered polyphonic haze. The audible structure of the piece quickly disappears amid a bewildering sequence of *trompe l'oreille* effects—cloudlike agglomerations of tones, trills, parallel motion in several octaves at once, and cascading scalar passages. Haass exploits the Welte-Mignon's capacity for breakneck speed not only in the general prestissimo pace of the music but also in particular passages where the succession of tones surpasses the temporal resolution of the human ear. At these moments the listener can no longer register individual pitches but instead perceives only tonal blurs and smears, effects that are almost entirely dissociated from the conventional timbral palette of the piano.

At the other end of the spectrum is the fourth of Gerhart Münch's *Six Polyphonic Etudes,* a strikingly understated example of the Welte-Mignon's technical capabilities. Entitled "Fugato," the piece presents three distinct registers of activity spanning the entire range of the piano: a sparsely populated bass zone, a somewhat more active middle register, and an upper voice proceeding in shuffling pairs of notes (dotted-eighths followed by sixteenths). Each voice seems to go about its business more or less unaware of the others, with the upper two parts tracing meandering downward paths that reach their nadir and then abruptly "reset" to the top of their range. Because the repeated patterns in the middle and upper voices are slightly out of phase with each other, the musical motion is at once audibly cyclical and subtly disorienting. Just after the midpoint in the brief "Fugato," each of the voices is doubled at a different interval, creating an effect of harmonic blurring that amplifies the piece's ambiguous finish: instead of concluding, it simply cuts off midphrase.

The 1926 concert in Donaueschingen was the first public manifestation of a short-lived but intense engagement with the artistic potential of new instruments. For a brief span in the middle of the decade, the "mechanical music" phenomenon transfixed the German musical intelligentsia. In flurries of articles in musical journals, untold hours of labor in composers' studios, and a handful of concerts, this movement ran its spectacular course, bringing technology and its role in modern music to the forefront of European consciousness. In 1927, as the mechanical vogue had already begun to fade, Hindemith wrote that "no other aspect of musical life has been so hotly disputed in recent times as that of music made by mechanical instruments."[4] By separating performance from the presence of musicians, the advocates of mechanical music challenged conventional aesthetic assumptions and raised unsettling questions about the technological mediation of musical expression, eliciting debates that would continue to reverberate through the remaining years of the Weimar Republic.

MUSICA EX MACHINA

The machine—as symbol and reality—captivated the imagination of early twentieth-century Germany. Between unification in 1871 and the outbreak of World War I in 1914, the country embarked on a rapid process of industrialization that transformed it into a technological and economic superpower. Modern technology—from airplanes and automobiles to film and photography—came to represent a revolutionary force that promised, for good or ill, to reshape life in all its dimensions.[5] After the war, Germany, along with the United States and the Soviet Union, was among the countries that most eagerly embraced the new marvels of the machine age: from the Ford-style production line to radio broadcasting, modern technology promised to usher in a new world of prosperity and progress.

Though the arts had shown the influence of modern technologies since even before the turn of the century, beginning around 1920 the "machine aesthetic" began to surface everywhere. The French architect Le Corbusier's manifesto *Vers un architecture* featured photographs of biplanes, ocean liners, automobiles, and grain silos alongside the examples of modern architecture, while the anthology *Buch neuer Künstler* interleaved reproductions of contemporary abstract art with images

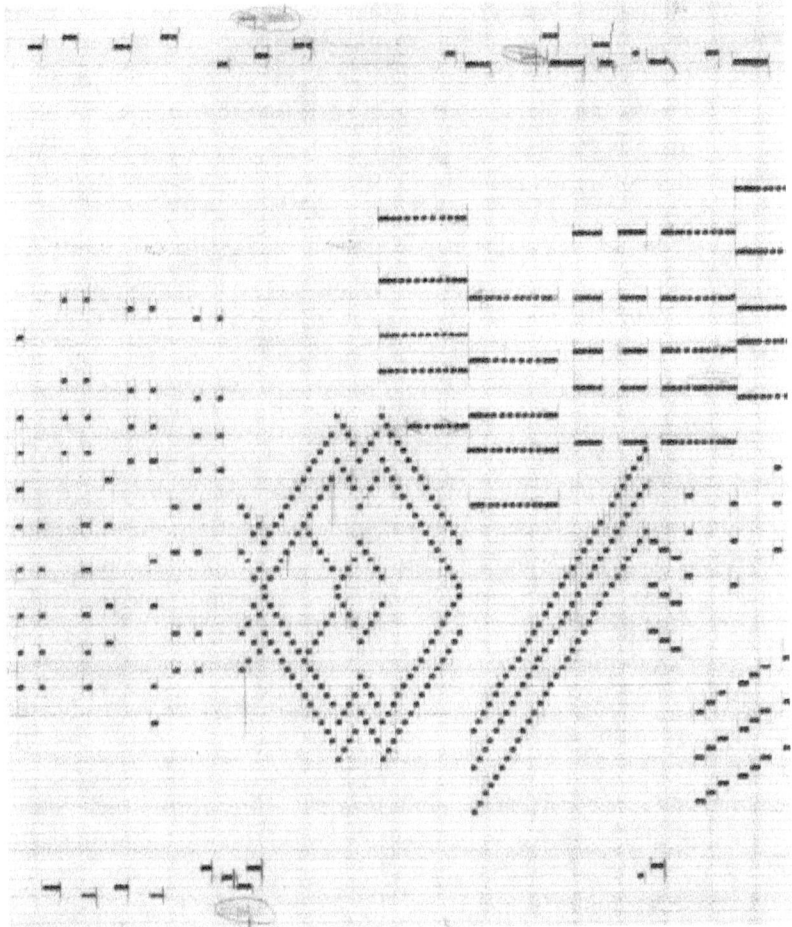

FIGURE 1. Excerpt of the piano roll for Hans Haass's "Intermezzo" (1927). The horizontal axis represents time, the vertical pitch. Source: Jürgen Hocker, *Faszination Player Piano: Das Selbstspielende Klavier von den Anfängen bis zur Gegenwart* (Bergkirchen: Edition Bochinsky, 2009), 234.

of power tools, cogwheels, and ventilators.[6] In Germany, the foremost exponent of this spirit was the art school known as the Bauhaus, which was founded in the immediate aftermath of the war by architect Walter Gropius. In 1923, Gropius gave a lecture entitled "Art and Technology: A New Unity," which signalled the school's program of synthesizing fine arts and industrial techniques of production. For Bauhaus artists, the beauty of the machine symbolized the modern spirit: simplicity over convolution, efficiency over ornament, universal over particular. Instead of expressing a willful artistic personality, the machine was thought to manifest an unconscious and collective creative impulse. Oskar Schlemmer explained: "If today's arts love the machine, technology, and organization, if they aspire to precision and reject anything vague and dreamy, this implies an instinctive repudiation of chaos and a longing to find the form appropriate to our times."[7]

Music, too, fell under the spell of the machine aesthetic. Many composers cultivated an unnuanced, "mechanical" style in reaction to the nineteenth-century ideal of music as a seismograph of psychological fluctuations. Examples of this new tendency began to turn up soon after the war. Stravinsky, who would become the foremost exponent of the antiromantic animus of the 1920s, could think of no higher compliment for a performance of his Concertino for String Quartet (1920) than to compare the motoric regularity of the ensemble to the clatter of a sewing machine.[8] Hindemith directed the performer of the "Ragtime" movement from his Piano Suite op. 26 (1922) to "play this piece very wildly, but always firmly in rhythm, like a machine," and American composer George Antheil's piano technique was described by one observer as "a mixture of frenzy and precision. [. . .] A machine seemed to be playing the keys."[9] While the piano seemed especially suited for the musical approximation of the machine, the orchestra could serve the purpose as well, as in the musical steam engine of Arthur Honegger's famous *Pacific 231* or Alexander Mosolov's *Zavod*, in which heavy percussion and obsessive repetition evoke the industrial frenzy of a steel foundry.

As these examples demonstrate, however, there was an important difference between the machine aesthetic in music and in the visual and plastic arts. New technologies had revolutionized the productive basis of many of the other arts: architecture had been fundamentally altered by modern building materials such as steel and sheet glass, painting reflected the naturalistic influence of photography, and the new medium of cinema emerged directly from contemporary technological developments. In music, by contrast, the link to the machine was still only metaphorical. The classical instrumentarium had remained largely unchanged since the middle of the nineteenth century, and some modernist musicians chafed at what they felt to be unbearable technological constraints. They sought not merely to evoke or imitate machines through music but to use machines to make music. As the critic Erich Steinhard argued, "For several years now Stravinsky and other young composers

Léger

Bohrmaschine

FIGURE 2. Juxtaposition of the painting *La ville* (1919) by Fernand Léger and a drawing of a drilling machine. Source: Ludwig Kassák and László Moholy-Nagy, eds., *Buch neuer Künstler*, (Vienna: Ma, 1923; repr., Baden, Switz.: L. Müller, 1991).

have been writing unsentimental, motoric, physiological music, which is meant by design to be played 'cold.' It is simply a logical consequence that one should now entrust such mechanical music to a machine, or even—perhaps for the first time this century—authorize original compositions for machines."[10] The idea of mechanical music as it emerged in the 1920s, then, was to move beyond the mimetic suggestion of the machine in human performance to the actual production of sound by mechanical means.

Although both its advocates and its critics often regarded mechanical music as a symbol of modernity, the phenomenon long predated the twentieth century. The oldest sense of the term referred to automatic instruments such as music boxes, orchestrions, and automata, devices that belong to an important and underappreciated chapter in the history of European music. In the seventeenth century, the Jesuit scholar Athanasius Kircher described the basic mechanism of early automatic instruments as the "phonotactic cylinder." A spindle made of metal or wood is turned by means of a gear system driven by water pressure, gravity, or some other force. The spindle is bedecked with tiny pins that are precisely placed so as to activate an adjacent row of metal tongues or a similar sounding element. Provided the entire mechanism is turned at a consistent pace, it is capable of reproducing the relationships of pitch and rhythm as they are encoded in a typical musical score. Pinned wheels and barrels fitting Kircher's description were used as early as the eighth century A.D. By 1700 (around the time of the invention of the pianoforte), keyboard instruments such as organs, virginals, and spinets were being outfitted for automatic reproduction.[11]

In the middle of the eighteenth century, the composer Johann Joachim Quantz noted that "with skill a musical machine could be constructed that would play certain pieces with a quickness and exactitude so remarkable that no human being could equal it either with his fingers or with his tongue."[12] Quantz thought that such a machine could only excite astonishment, a sensation that would soon wear off once listeners understood how the mechanism worked. In his view, mechanical instruments ultimately served to highlight the aesthetic primacy of live performance, which could be attained only by human musicians. But such dismissals did nothing to dampen the rage for mechanical instruments. Guidebooks such as *La Tonotechnie ou l'Art de noter les cylindres*, published in 1775 by Marie-Dominique-Joseph Engramelle, provided detailed instructions on the practice of encoding music on pinned cylinders.[13] So great was the cachet of automatic instruments in the eighteenth century that the triumvirate of Viennese classicism—Haydn, Mozart, and Beethoven—all wrote original compositions for mechanical devices, treating them as entirely worthy means of realizing their musical conceptions.[14]

The nineteenth century was a golden age of mechanical instruments, from the dainty jangle of the music box to the elaborate symphonic simulation of devices such as the orchestrion.[15] Among their most famous creators was the inventor Friedrich Kaufmann, whose numerous instruments were displayed in his "Acoustic Cabinet" in Dresden. Astonished critics wrote that "the machines appear to be a living being, thinking and feeling," and marveled at the automata's "wonderful and spiritual" performance. Applying a musical Turing test, one observer even declared that "one totally forgets that one is hearing a machine here."[16] Such devices continued to be built and enjoyed through the century, although they faced continuous skepticism from those who perceived mechanical instruments as a threat to music's purportedly nontechnological essence.

With the emergence of the gramophone and phonograph in the early twentieth century, mechanical music took on a new meaning. Critics of the new recording technologies now used the term as a slur. Gramophone records, one German critic claimed, offer nothing but "a soulless jingling, an ugly tone, bereft of all sensual charm"; instead of enjoying the music, gramophone listeners merely marvel at the mechanism that plays it.[17] Such attacks were echoed on the other side of the Atlantic as well. In a 1906 article entitled "The Menace of Mechanical Music," American bandleader and composer John Philip Sousa decried "these talking and playing machines" that threaten to "reduce the expression of music to a mathematical system of megaphones, wheels, cogs, disks, cylinders, and all manner of revolving things, which are as like real art as the marble statue of Eve is like her beautiful, living, breathing daughters."[18] Thus, in the early twentieth-century *mechanical music* came to mean essentially "recorded music"; though the term was still used to refer to the products of older devices such as orchestrions and music boxes, it more often referred to newer ones such as gramophone records. In both cases, the expression had a decidedly negative connotation. For most people who invoked the phrase, "mechanical music" meant at best a shoddy substitute for the real thing and at worst a technological perversion of the natural order. The emergence of a new concept of mechanical music would accordingly demand a complete revision of the term's historical meaning. The instrument that made this possible was the mechanical piano, also popularly known as the player piano.

THE PLAYER PIANO

The automation of the piano began in the late nineteenth century, with devices called—confusingly, in light of later developments—"piano players." First developed in the 1870s, the piano player typically took the form of a cabinet on wheels which was rolled up to the piano when in use. In order to store a greater amount of musical information than was allowed by the older cylinder and its variants, the notes were encoded as tiny perforations on a spooled paper roll. As the holes on the roll passed over a component called the tracker bar, air was let into the vacuum chamber, and the difference between the atmospheric pressure of the outside air and that in the chamber generated the force required to trigger a set of wooden "fingers," one for each of the piano's keys. The machine's "feet" likewise activated the piano's pedals.

By the turn of the twentieth century, the piano player had been almost entirely replaced by the player piano, in which the playback mechanism was built into the instrument. Here, again, the machine was not entirely automatic: only the pitches and their rhythmic relations were encoded on the roll, while the "player-pianist" controlled other aspects of the reproduction, such as tempo and dynamics, via dials and also operated the instrument's pneumatic pump by means of a foot pedal.[19] Unlike many other mechanical instruments, the early versions of the player piano were not designed for passive listening. Creating an artistic rendition of a given roll required manual skill and close familiarity with the score, though indications were often printed on rolls to guide the novice player. These instruments thus occupied a place between the traditional piano and fully mechanical devices such as music boxes and gramophones: they enabled domestic musicianship but demanded much less skill than traditional piano playing.[20]

A new kind of mechanical playback arrived in 1904, when the Welte Company in Freiburg introduced the world's first "reproducing piano," the Welte-Mignon—so called because the original model was a compact cabinet unit without a keyboard. In contrast to earlier player pianos, the Welte-Mignon was capable of fully automatic playback. Even the pneumatic pump at the heart of the instrument, previously operated by a foot pedal, was now electrically powered. (For this reason, the Welte-Mignon and similar instruments were sometimes called "electric pianos," adding another layer of potential terminological confusion: their motive force was electrical but not the sound they produced.) As its name suggests, the reproducing piano also had a different purpose than the earlier, semi-automatic models. These devices were designed to record and faithfully re-create the performances of the world's great keyboard virtuosi. Using the same basic technology as the earlier player piano, it could capture every movement of a pianistic performance and later reproduce it down to the slightest nuance. The instrument was envisioned as an alternative to the gramophone, which in the early twentieth century was incapable of convincingly reproducing the sound of the piano.[21]

The recording of pitch and duration on the Welte-Mignon was relatively straightforward. Each key of a specially built "recording piano" was affixed with an electrical contact. These contacts were connected to an external recording apparatus, which contained a paper roll and eighty-eight quills or ink wheels attached to electromagnets, as well as two additional quills for the pedals. When a key was struck on the piano, an electrical circuit was closed, activating the appropriate quill in the recording mechanism, which left a line of ink on the paper roll for as long as the key was held down. Because the roll turned at a constant speed, rhythmic relations were captured in the spacing of the markings along the roll. After recording, the roll was punched by hand, following the indications left by the ink markings.[22] (The Welte-Mignon could also capture dynamics in the recording process, although the technique is still the subject of speculation. The company closely guarded the secret of the dynamic recording process, and all of the recording pianos were destroyed when the Welte factory in Freiburg was bombed during World War II.[23]) Unlike the gramophone, which registered the actual vibrations of sound, the Welte-Mignon recorded a set of directions for the later reproduction of music; in this, it anticipated later technologies such as the Music Instrument Digital Interface (MIDI) of the 1980s.

For the advocates of mechanical music, the fully automated piano represented the inevitable final stage of a lengthy process of technological evolution. In this view, the very design of the piano lent itself to the quantification of its motions. As Arnold Schoenberg argued, the piano and other instruments had already been "mechanized" to such an extent that the removal of the human agent required no great technological or conceptual leap:

> The objections touched off by the rather provocative expression "mechanization of music" collapse when one realizes how much mechanization has taken place in our most important instruments. Do not merely compare the piano with the violin: on the piano, even apart from the mechanism proper, the system of levers, the tones themselves are ready-made and unalterable,

whereas on the violin each tone, according to its pitch, has first to be produced. Or compare the organ with the horn. *On the organ the player in reality carries out a manual movement which has nothing whatever to do with sound-production, merely giving the signal for it to happen.* But think simply of the clarinet's keys, the horn's valves, the harp's pedals, the guitar's frets, and finally the very scroll of the violin, and then decide whether we can do without the mechanical element in our tools for producing sound and whether it has made music worse. It is sentimental to wail about mechanization and unthinkingly believe that spirit, so far as it is present, is driven out by mechanism.[24]

Converting the reproducing piano into an instrument of mechanical music, then, required only that one bypass the recording process and compose directly onto the medium by punching holes in the paper roll by hand. With this relatively simple modification, the piano—since the time of Beethoven the veritable icon of soulful expression—was rewired into the perfect musical machine.

Perhaps the first musician to attempt to compose directly onto the piano roll was the Italian-German composer and pianist Ferruccio Busoni. Around 1907–08, Busoni sketched an original work for the Aeolian Pianola, the famous American brand of player piano whose name would later become synonymous with the instrument in its manifold forms. Busoni left this piece, entitled simply "Für die Pianola," incomplete, but even as a torso, it provides an intriguing counterpart to the technological speculations in his *Sketch of a New Aesthetic of Music,* which he wrote contemporaneously.[25]

The first substantial explorations of the compositional potential of the player piano took place in 1917, when the British music critics Edwin Evans and Ernest Newman published articles in *The Musical Times* speculating about the possibilities of music specially conceived for the instrument. Evans predicted that mechanical instruments would liberate composers from the limitations of physical technique, allowing them to "write direct [sic] for this improved mechanism, thereby freeing themselves from all the mechanical restrictions appertaining to the use of ten fingers, which at present limit the number, rapidity, and distance of the notes used."[26] Inspired by Evans's ideas, Ernest Newman wrote an article entitled "Piano-Player Music of the Future" later that year. Newman asserted that "the piano-player is not simply an old-style pianoforte sounded by pneumatics instead of by the hand: it is a *new musical instrument,* from which we shall never get the best possible results until composers learn the peculiar resources of it and how to exploit these."[27] He argued that composers of keyboard music had

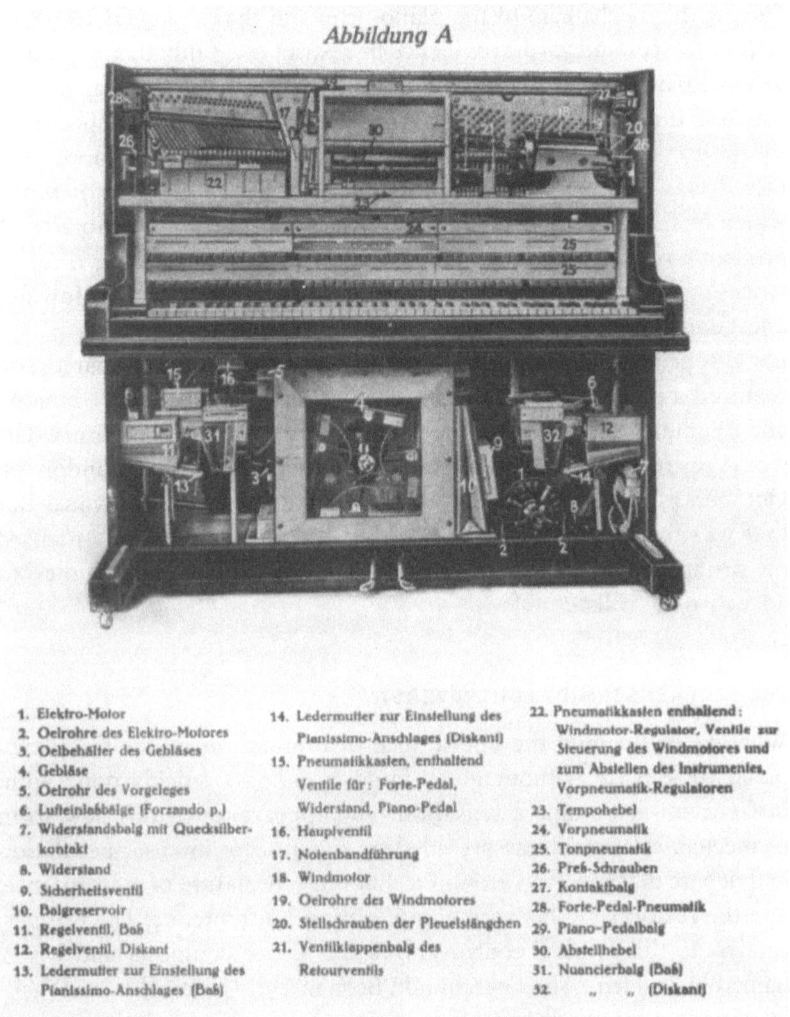

Abbildung A

1. Elektro-Motor
2. Oelrohre des Elektro-Motores
3. Oelbehälter des Gebläses
4. Gebläse
5. Oelrohr des Vorgeleges
6. Lufteinlaßbälge (Forzando p.)
7. Widerstandsbalg mit Quecksilberkontakt
8. Widerstand
9. Sicherheitsventil
10. Balgreservoir
11. Regelventil, Baß
12. Regelventil, Diskant
13. Ledermutter zur Einstellung des Pianissimo-Anschlages (Baß)
14. Ledermutter zur Einstellung des Pianissimo-Anschlages (Diskant)
15. Pneumatikkasten, enthaltend Ventile für: Forte-Pedal, Widerstand, Piano-Pedal
16. Hauptventil
17. Notenbandführung
18. Windmotor
19. Oelrohre des Windmotores
20. Stellschrauben der Pleuelstängchen
21. Ventilklappenbalg des Retourventils
22. Pneumatikkasten enthaltend: Windmotor-Regulator, Ventile zur Steuerung des Windmotores und zum Abstellen des Instrumentes, Vorpneumatik-Regulatoren
23. Tempohebel
24. Vorpneumatik
25. Tonpneumatik
26. Preß-Schrauben
27. Kontaktbalg
28. Forte-Pedal-Pneumatik
29. Piano-Pedalbalg
30. Abstellhebel
31. Nuancierbalg (Baß)
32. „ „ (Diskant)

FIGURE 3. Technical illustration of the Welte-Mignon reproducing piano. Source: Jürgen Hocker, *Faszination Player Piano: Das Selbstspielende Klavier von den Anfängen bis zur Gegenwart* (Bergkirchen, Ger.: Edition Bochinsky, 2009), 96.

always had to exert considerable effort to overcome the limitations of their instruments, from the elaborate ornamentation that compensated for the quickly decaying tone of the harpsichord to the use of the sustain pedal as a "clumsy third fist" which allowed the piano to emulate the rich sonority of the nineteenth-century orchestra. In order to fully exploit the technical capabilities of the instrument, it was necessary to "forget the mechanism of the pianoforte, and the ten fingers to which it has pleased a niggard Providence to restrict us." Only then would "a genuine piano-player idiom of composition" begin to take shape.[28]

Later that year Evans sent out requests for original compositions to about twenty composers throughout Europe. Among those contacted was Igor Stravinsky, who submitted his *Étude pour pianola*, which he had already begun when Evans's letter arrived.[29] More compositions trickled in over the next several years, including original works by Alfredo Casella, Eugène Goosens, Herbert N. Howells, and Gian Francesco Malipiero.[30] As the Aeolian was a player piano, not a reproducing piano, these pieces were not fully automated and required a player-pianist to apply the necessary adjustments of tempo and dynamics according to directions supplied by the composers. The works were premiered in a concert at Aeolian Hall in London on October 13, 1921, following an introductory lecture by Evans. But that was the last most people heard of the music. Aeolian, a focused on profit above artistic novelty, apparently didn't even bother to advertise the rolls.[31]

THE STUCKENSCHMIDT CONTROVERSY

Whereas in England the appearance of original music for the player piano took place without much fanfare and was quickly done with, in Germany it became a sensation. The appearance of this new form of mechanical music was preceded by a period of intense speculation and debate that revolved around technology, the nature of performance, and the relationship between composers and interpreters. The primary catalyst in this musical controversy was a young composer and writer named Hans Heinz Stuckenschmidt. Born in 1901 in Strasbourg, Stuckenschmidt established himself early in the 1920s as a tireless provocateur for the cause of modern music, organizing concerts, publishing widely in major journals, and earning notoriety as a polemical but perceptive observer of the contemporary musical scene.

In August 1924, Stuckenschmidt published a short article entitled "Mechanization of Music" in the Hungarian modernist journal *Ma* (Today). This was the opening salvo of a barrage of writings in which Stuckenschmidt introduced a new concept of mechanical music into contemporary discourse. In the following two years, this essay was printed in various slightly modified forms in no fewer than six different periodicals in Germany, Austria, Czechoslovakia, and the United

States.³² With deliberate sensationalism, Stuckenschmidt set out in these articles to champion the mechanization of music as an inevitable and welcome development. In his view, the nuance and unpredictability of human performance were nothing but defects. "The performer's character, his momentary feelings, his private opinions are quite irrelevant to the essence of the artwork," he wrote. "The more 'objective' the interpreter, the better the interpretation."³³ The ideal musician is not an interpreter at all but rather an "administrator" (*Verwalter*) of the composer's directions. Thus, musical machines such as the player piano and the gramophone could be used to capture definitive performances of canonic works once and for all, rendering new interpretations superfluous. Furthermore, Stuckenschmidt declared, in light of the economic crisis of the early 1920s, performances of classical music had become untenable luxuries. Mechanical reproduction thus ensured the survival of this music, as the interpretation of existing works could be entrusted once and for all to new technologies such as the player piano and gramophone. "In the foreseeable future the musical instrumentalist will be only the stuff of legend," Stuckenschmidt proclaimed. "Today's instruments will fill the cabinets of antique collectors."³⁴

Stuckenschmidt's crusade against meddlesome interpreters was in part a reaction to the perceived liberties taken by interpreters in the early twentieth century, which went beyond nuances of tempo and dynamics. Recordings of performances from this period reveal that it was not uncommon for pianists to improvise entire passages "in the spirit" of the notated music. For example, three different Welte-Mignon recordings of Liszt's "Liebestraum" show three different endings: one player shortens the piece by a full ten measures, another repeats the final bar, and a third adds a bit of extemporized music.³⁵ Stuckenschmidt's position represented the leading edge of a new emphasis on fidelity and the supposedly inalterable form embodied in the score, a view that would become second nature over the course of the twentieth century.

But the idea that mechanical instruments would replace musicians as performers of existing music was the less provocative of Stuckenschmidt's assertions. His more radical notion was that new compositions could be written for mechanical instruments, conceived specifically for their performative capabilities and free from the conventions and limitations of human musicianship. "The real significance of these machines," he wrote, "lies in the possibility of authentically writing for them. [. . .] One can compose directly [for the piano roll], as one used to compose in notes, with all imaginable nuances, with tempi, dynamics, and phrasing of mathematically exact determination."[36] Though these statements echo the earlier proclamations of the Britons Evans and Newman, Stuckenschmidt was likely unaware of their work. Rather, he was channeling the ideas of the Hungarian visual artist László Moholy-Nagy, whose writings of the early 1920s had sketched the theoretical possibility of creatively refunctioning reproductive media such as the gramophone.[37] (Moholy-Nagy's influence on the movement for new instruments is traced in greater detail in chapter 4.) Stuckenschmidt's innovation was to apply Moholy-Nagy's idea to the musically more viable medium of the player piano: "With this method," wrote Stuckenschmidt, "one can have any number of tone-masses strike at once; one can increase the volume and speed of the music over the natural limits of human technique. In a word, one will be able to realize entirely *new and hitherto unknown phenomena of sound,* whose effects can be confirmed and determined to the last detail by the composer himself."[38] Instead of creating the illusory presence of "live" music, the player piano could be used to eliminate the performer altogether, to create music "directly and authentically." In Stuckenschmidt's view, this way of working fulfilled composers' long-held desire for absolute creative autonomy. Like painters or sculptors, they could now produce complete and self-sufficient works, free from the interference of artistic middlemen.

Not surprisingly, given their provocative tone, Stuckenschmidt's essays unleashed a firestorm of criticism in the musical press. The composer Heinz Pringsheim threw down the gauntlet in a parodic account of mechanical music that presents a humorous parallel to the description of the concert quoted at the beginning of this chapter:

> The concert of the future: in the middle of the stage stands the beautiful new Flettner Rotorophone: the bell rings; with solicitous care the "orchestral servant"—the most important personality, so to speak the Furtwängler of the dawning golden gramophone age—puts the authentic record in place and sets the mechanism in motion; a reverentially listening audience, in festive garb, fills the rows of the concert hall into the furthest corners.[39]

Pringsheim argued that the essence of music lies in the act of performance: "What is music," he demanded, "if not the content of music making? [. . .] Why go to a concert, when there's no longer an artist to see?" This irreducible basis of music justifies even the reviled cult of the virtuoso, which Pringsheim traced to the "unconscious recognition [. . .] that the musical work is according to its primary definition the *object of the music-making person,* whose ideal type is honored and deified in the performing artist." All efforts to counteract this are based on the mistaken notion that music is a "purely abstract matter."[40]

Other critics lined up to attack Stuckenschmidt along similar lines. The composer Heinrich Kaminski demanded, "Is it necessary to state the obvious, that the musical human being is a membrane (physically, psychically, and intellectually), and thus an indispensable factor of the genuine creation of music?"[41] Another, Heinz Tiessen exhorted, "Would the composer really be served by his work merely being *heard* by armchair listeners? No! The composer wants to be *played,* and the lively actions of an artist who actively champions his work cannot be replaced with the most perfected mechanism, even if it spoke with the tongues of angels."[42] Erwin Stein likewise insisted that music is inseparable from playing *(musizieren).* It is not a matter only of acoustics but of artistry, in which the presence of the performing musician is indispensable. For Stuckenschmidt's critics, then, music was indissolubly connected to the living human being who performed it. Mechanical reproduction estranged music from its origin in human gesture and reduced it to a meaningless play of sounds. Pringsheim brought the matter to its polemical crux: "Does music exist in order to be heard," he asked, "or in order to be *made?*"[43]

For Stuckenschmidt, however, the notion that the presence of the performer was somehow essential to music was nothing more than a baseless superstition. "For you," he admonished his critics, "the human being is the primary factor of music. For us the tones are all that matter. It has not yet been demonstrated that music is made of anything other than 'rhythms and intervals.'"[44] The mechanical piano was the technological proof of Stuckenschmidt's musical materialism. Every note the pianist plays is reducible to three factors: the instant of attack (its temporal relation to other notes), the duration, and the speed with which the hammer hits the string (loudness). Each of these can be captured on the piano roll and mechanically reproduced, or even created by hand without any performance. There are quantifiable mechanical actions, and there is the resulting acoustic phenomenon, and that is all:

> Ten more or less trained fingers set the keys in motion. The manner of these motions is determined by the mind of the player. But in the moment they are executed, they have ceased being mind and soul. They are now mechanical, controllable, concrete. They can be captured, recorded, filmed, as it were. One would be hard pressed to find a soul in there. Of course, the spirit of

the player is contained in these motions. But it is transformed, materialized. [. . .] Every expressive nuance that the pianist creates by the movement of the keys can also be achieved and captured by mechanical means.[45]

Denying the primacy of the performer, Stuckenschmidt identified music with the physical manifestation of sound, whatever its provenance. Adopting a tone of hectoring sarcasm, he assailed his critics: "We have learned that music is something that is perceived by the ears. But ears respond only to acoustic phenomena, that is, to tones. Thus [. . .] it seems clear that you have an entirely different understanding of music than we do: something that is not acoustic, which one doesn't hear—which is perhaps perceived with the eyes, the nose, or the other senses."[46] Thus, a debate ostensibly concerning a technological matter—the suitability of the mechanical piano both as a replacement for conventional musical interpretation and as a medium for original compositions—turned out to hinge on questions of what might be called musical phenomenology. While his critics insisted that the ritual and social character of concert performance were essential to genuine musical experience, Stuckenschmidt redefined music as a purely acoustic phenomenon. The human musician, previously the indispensable vessel through which tone is borne into the world, was for him merely a potential distraction.

MUSICAL MATERIALISM

Stuckenschmidt's assault on the verities of classical music, however outrageous to his critics, was consistent with many of the radical cultural currents of the time. The controversy around mechanical music was only a single front in a wider war between the deeply rooted humanism of German culture and the burgeoning new order of modern technoscience. Stuckenschmidt's campaign against musical traditionalists paralleled the efforts of the Vienna Circle, a group of scientists and philosophers who sought to replace the "metaphysical and theological debris of millennia" with a modern worldview rooted in radical materialism.[47] By subjecting intellectual discourse to rigorous logical analysis, they hoped to root out the fruitless speculation that occupied much contemporary philosophy. The group's mission bore a striking resemblance to Stuckenschmidt's polemics:

> [We seek a] neutral system of formulae, a symbolism freed from the slag of historical languages. Neatness and clarity are striven for, and dark distances and unfathomable depths are rejected. In science there are no "depths"; there is surface everywhere: all experience forms a complex network, which

FIGURE 4. Cover of "Musik und Maschine," special issue of *Musikblätter des Anbruch* 8, no. 8–9 (1926).

cannot always be surveyed and can often be grasped only in parts. Everything is accessible to man; and man is the measure of all things.[48]

In a 1929 recruitment flyer, the members of the Vienna Circle sounded the alarm against the creeping irrationalism that threatened to halt the progress of modern society: "We live in a critical spiritual situation! Metaphysical and theological thought is taking hold in certain groups; astrology, anthroposophy and similar movements are spreading. On the other side: ever more conscious efforts for a scientific worldview, logical-mathematical and empirical thought."[49] Like Stuckenschmidt, the members of the Vienna Circle saw their position vindicated by inexorable trends in technological development. The mechanization of the world through industrial mass production would once and for all replace meaningless "metaphysical ideas" with the strictly materialist logic of cause and effect.[50]

Another striking analogue to mechanical music was found in the tendency known as the *neue Sachlichkeit,* or the "New Objectivity."[51] Popularized by the art historian Gustav Hartlaub as the title of a 1925 exhibition of contemporary paintings in Mannheim, the phrase denoted an attitude of sobriety and matter-of-factness deliberately opposed to the volatile aesthetic of expressionism, which dominated German culture in the prewar years and remained influential in the early 1920s. The artists associated with the New Objectivity rejected the earlier movement's lurid distortions and transgressive outbursts in favor of the dispassionate, often jaundiced reportage of the world around them. A 1925 comparison of expressionist and "post-expressionist" tendencies in painting included some dualities whose relevance could easily be extended to music: "excessive" versus "rather strict, purist," "dynamic" versus "static," "monumental" versus "miniature," "warm" versus "cool to cold," and "like uncut stone" versus "like polished metal."[52] Hartlaub's term was quickly imported into musical discourse, where it signalled the predilection for clear, transparent textures, an omnipresent motoric pulse, and mostly flat or terraced dynamic levels—in short, the total negation of the late romantic *espressivo* of Mahler or Strauss. The apparent affinities between the New Objectivity and Stuckenschmidt's notion of mechanical music were widely noted. "The ensouled human as interpreter always represents a danger to the *neue Sachlichkeit*," wrote the composer Fidelio Finke in 1928. "The ideal interpreter of this art is the machine; not one that hasn't yet been invented, but rather one of those already existing devices, which the uncomprehending accuse of lack of nuance."[53] The musicologist Curt Sachs even claimed that the New Objectivity was an "exact parallel" of the mechanical tendency in music.[54]

One of the earliest musical applications of the term appeared in Heinrich Strobel's article "Neue Sachlichkeit in der Musik," published—coincidentally—in July 1926, the month of the first concert of mechanical music in Donaueschingen. Strobel saw the new tendency exemplified in the works of Stravinsky, Reger, Busoni, and Hindemith and in the twelve-tone compositions of Schoenberg, which embodied "the striving for absolute clarity and formal consolidation, the joy of perfected handiwork, playful insouciance, and 'objective' forming."[55] In this music, according to Strobel, "expression" gives way to "construction," and the channeling of subjective feeling is replaced by the rational organization of aesthetic forms. Strobel elaborated on the new attitude in his 1928 monograph on Hindemith:

> It is no longer a question of "capturing in music" events or feelings. One constructs something with tones that is most comparable with a building. Real "creativity" lies not in the desire to "express," but the desire to "form." The ordering, constructive work of forming is the actual "content" of music. That it is nonetheless a kind of "expression" is self-evident—but it is not an

"expression" that can be interpreted in terms of feeling (sorrow, joy, lament, contentment, etc.), but rather expression in a higher, spiritual sense, independent of the ego—an ordering and forming.[56]

Around the same time, the influential Viennese critic Paul Bekker—one of the leading journalistic advocates of modernist composers such as Schoenberg and Ernst Krenek—laid out an explicitly materialist musical poetics that echoed Stuckenschmidt's earlier arguments and forged a direct link between music and the visual arts. "No art has been made into an object of metaphysical speculation to a comparable extent to music," Bekker declared. "Every popular aesthetic boils down to the belief that music is a kind of magic, a miracle, a revelation."[57] In opposition to this irrational view, he argued that the musician finds ready-to-hand material equivalent to that of all other artists. The material "formed" by the composer is "an absolutely real material, a material that is in a scientific sense exactly as objectively and organically determined as stone, wood, canvas, or paint [. . .] a material with which one can experiment, which one can analyze and measure. This material of music is *air,* and the tools of music with which we are familiar, human voices and instruments of all sorts, are tools for working on this material." Thus, artistic creation is not an act of "invention" *(Erfindung)* but rather of "forming" *(Gestaltung).* [58] Bekker's language recalls the so-called formalist aesthetics of the highly influential nineteenth-century music critic Eduard Hanslick, and indeed, in the responses to mechanical music, one frequently encounters allusions to Hanslick's definition of music as "tonally moving forms." Paul Stefan, editor of the Viennese journal *Musikblätter des Anbruch,* made the connection quite explicit, stating that "it has been asserted that a generation for which music is nothing more than tonally moving forms [. . .] must necessarily arrive at mechanization."[59] In a 1923 essay in the same journal, Bekker had drawn a connection between the new music of the postwar period and Hanslick's aesthetics, noting, "This formalist art [. . .] presupposes the unimportance of the emotional and subjective, thus a predominantly collectivist, typical, and objectivizing kind of intellectual orientation."[60]

As this passage makes clear, mechanical music and the aesthetic discourse that accompanied it were by no means isolated from the ideologically charged atmosphere of the postwar years. Slogans such as "Objectivity," "Construction," and "Purity" served as highly charged double entendres signalling conjoined political and aesthetic attitudes. In the international avant-garde movements of the early 1920s, such as De Stijl, the Bauhaus, and Soviet Constructivism, radically abstract approaches to art were frequently joined with more or less overt appeals to left-wing politics.[61] Indeed, as Peter Galison has argued, the modernist quest for "transparent construction" was implicitly political: by breaking down their materials to fundamental units and passing them through the sieve of formalized technique, modern artists hoped to cleanse their work of unwanted historical resonances and traces of parochial nationalism.[62] Hannes Meyer, the Marxist architect who took over leadership of the Bauhaus in 1928, declared in a manifesto entitled "Die neue Welt" ("The New World"), "*Pure construction is the mark of the new world of forms.* The constructivist form knows no fatherland; it is stateless and the expression of an internationalized way of thought."[63]

Stuckenschmidt's point of entry into the politicized art world of the Weimar Republic was the November Group, one of the largest and most influential artists' organizations of the time, which he joined in the early 1920s. Occupying positions on the political spectrum ranging from center-left democratic socialism to revolutionary communism, members of the November Group were united less by artistic vision than by a common political orientation.[64] Among their many undertakings was a contemporary music concert series, which included a repeat performance of the Donaueschingen program of mechanical music in Berlin arranged by Stuckenschmidt shortly after he took over the leadership of the musical division in November 1926.[65] After this point Stuckenschmidt's political animus, often only hinted at in his earlier polemical writings, began to emerge more forcefully. Adopting the generically leftist language of the international avant-garde, he declared that the "hypertrophy of individualism" was under attack by a new tendency toward "collectivism, sobriety *[Sachlichkeit],* and objectivity *[Objektivität]."*[66] Writing a year later in the American journal *Modern Music,* he was no less explicit:

> The individualism of an age, now definitely passed, which neglected the universal for the personal, has given place to a more collective attitude. For years our literary and graphic arts were devoted to a hysterical glorification of the ego. [. . .] The individual, with his impulses, tastes, and passions, must be suppressed, for unrestrained individualism has always been productive of bad and useless art. It jeopardizes fantasy, form, and purity of workmanship.[67]

In a retrospective article on the November Group's tenth anniversary published in 1928, Stuckenschmidt derided the notion that "intellectual production can be imagined without connection to the external world." In opposition to such romantic solipsism, Stuckenschmidt asserted his belief in the "materialist doctrine" according to which art is "the expression of a dominant or emerging ideology—for my part, a will to relevance, which seeks to change the world."[68] For Stuckenschmidt, the quarrel over mechanical music reflected the conflict between the bourgeois individualism of the nineteenth century, represented by the expressive, unique, and (as Walter Benjamin would later put it) "auratic" artwork, and technological modernity, represented by the mechanically produced and formally abstract work.[69] Accordingly, the search for deindividuated forms of musical expression was nothing less than the artistic correlate to the socialist-collectivist reorganization of society.

OBJECTIVE MUSIC

The polemical frenzy surrounding mechanical music blurred the distinction between two quite different meanings of the term: first, as a means of replacing the performance of preexisting music; second, and more radically, as a new compositional paradigm conceived from the ground up as music *for* the machine. This ambiguity lurks both in Stuckenschmidt's writings and in the reactions of his critics, where it is often unclear which meaning of the term is at stake. But others were more careful to decouple the "productive" and "reproductive" senses of the mechanical music. In an open letter published in *Musikblätter des Anbruch*, Dietrich van Strassburg accused Stuckenschmidt of overemphasizing the problem of reproduction and neglecting the "more important *creative* problem of a 'mechanistic music,' a compositional technique for machines." Writing before the 1926 premieres in Donaueschingen, van Strassburg lamented the lack of original mechanical music, which he attributed to an internalized sense of bodily limitations: "That there are still today no truly 'unperformable' works is certainly to be explained by the secret control that the thought of technical performability exercises, consciously or unconsciously, upon the act of composition."[70]

Others supported the idea of original music for mechanical instruments but rejected the notion that these instruments could replace human performers. Hindemith argued that "music reproduced by mechanical means has absolutely nothing to do with music as an art of individual performance; the two have merely the external sonic manifestation in common." He insisted that mechanical music should be seen as a distinct form of artistic expression, intended neither to imitate nor to replace traditional music making: "The advantages [of mechanical instruments] lie merely in their absolute unequivocality, their clarity, cleanness, and in the possibility of the utmost precision—qualities that human playing does not possess, but which it also doesn't need."[71] Ernst Toch likewise explained that mechanical music represented no threat to traditional music but rather a new growth comparable to the rings of development encircling an old city center: "The music in question here is not just any music that is reproduced by a mechanical instrument; it is music *for* a mechanical instrument, just like 'music *for* violin and piano' or 'music *for* orchestra'; it is composed in or out of the spirit of the instrument."[72]

For composers such as Toch and Hindemith, the purpose of mechanical instruments was not the reproduction of music conceived for live performance but the creation of a new and distinctive kind of music. Mechanical music, in this strict sense, is not simply music that happens to be played by mechanical instruments but music specifically composed for these instruments and their technical capabilities. What the hand-punched piano roll encodes is not the trace of a performance but a novel aesthetic phenomenon. The rejection of the medium's recording function in favor of what might be called *generative inscription* could be seen as an analogue to the concurrent crisis of representation in the visual arts. Just as the canvas was no longer a medium for the reproduction of visual impressions but rather the source of abstract forms sui generis, a recording medium such as the piano roll or the gramophone record was conceived as a "sound canvas" on which to project musical phenomena with no parallels in the natural world. In the words of the painter Paul Klee, "Art does not reproduce the visible; rather, it makes visible."[73]

For Toch, the unique quality of mechanical music lay in the "coolness" of its sound—not a lack of warmth, he is careful to note, but the tangible presence of a "non-warmth" *(Nicht-Wärme)*. Elsewhere, switching metaphors from touch to sight, Toch invoked the "crystalline clarity, the peculiar hyperclarity" of mechanically produced sound, in which there is no trace of human presence:

> If the rolls are not produced by performance, but rather made by hand, they show an image of the most perfect, geometrical exactitude, and this corresponds to the sonic effect: a degree of precision that can never be attained by human playing; the absolute objectification, the absolute depersonalization of playing. Nothing slips in which is not fixed in the *notes* by pitch, meter, rhythm, tempo, and dynamics. Every trace of spontaneity, sentiment, and impulse is expunged.[74]

At the second concert of mechanical music, which took place in 1927 in Baden-Baden, the program opened with back-to-back performances of two versions of Mozart's F-minor Fantasy (K. 608) for mechanical organ, first from a roll made by the famous British organist Edwin Lemare and then from a hand-punched roll. Toch recalled that upon hearing the first notes of Lemare's performance, he broke out in spontaneous laughter: "Although the cylinder was made from the playing of an excellent organist, the abject powerlessness of the human wrestling with materiality and the unavoidable side effects of the performance shone clearly in comparison to the beautifully free-floating, unlabored, and flawless objectivity of the 'handmade' cylinder."[75]

Toch's reaction gives an insightful glimpse into the unexpected resonances of mechanical sound. He recounted that he had never before been able to shake off the feeling of the "mechanical" when listening to performances of instrumental music: only the singer is truly free of this struggle with material, while from the violin to the winds to the keyboard, instruments show a greater and greater degree of mechanical complexity. But listening to the original Mozart cylinders, Toch had a different reaction: "The insurmountable distance between player and instrument, which even for the best organists remains as the awkward imprint of the machine, fell away, and with it the entire musical sediment of the struggle. [. . .] In hearing this entirely 'mechanical' organ music, I became free for the first time from the impression of the machine. For I heard something serene, unquestionably self-contained and delineated: *mechanical music.*"[76] Thus, at the moment of its technological apotheosis, music slips free of its material constraints; the perfect musical machine attains a state of aesthetic self-sufficiency comparable only to that of its supposed nemesis, the human vocalist.

Toch's anecdote gives witness to a phenomenological shift in which the absence of human performers is reconceived as the presence of a new aesthetic quality. Accordingly, rather than concerning themselves with the capability of performers, composers must now attend to listeners and their perceptual abilities. The critic Erich Doflein explained, "Since playability need no longer be heeded, audibility—the artistic shaping of what is heard—must be cultivated to a greater degree."[77] The disappearance of the human performer collapses the distance between auditors and the musical phenomenon: the spectacle of performance is replaced with the drama of listening itself.

METAPHYSICAL MACHINES

In the eyes of advocates such as Stuckenschmidt, mechanical music was a corollary to the antimetaphysical stance of modern science, an attitude that increasingly permeated daily life as well. But the final performance of the 1926 Donaueschingen festival, a stage work called the *Triadic Ballet*, put a very different face on the mechanization of art. On the stage, three dancers in brightly colored or metallic geometrical costumes performed a series of puppetlike dances, their motions slow and deliberate, animated by a dreamlike seriousness. Offstage and out of sight, a mechanical organ intoned a musical accompaniment, its motoric rhythms seeming to animate the abstract figures onstage. Equal parts formal rigor and vaudeville playfulness, the *Triadic Ballet* was at once a multimedia showcase for the mechanical aesthetic and a bizarre critique of the entire phenomenon.

The work was the brainchild of Oskar Schlemmer, one of the foremost theorists and practitioners of the Bauhaus theater. Beginning in 1921, he led a theater workshop at the school that integrated the conventional elements of dance, acting, and set design with music, painting, and projected lights in a multimedia fusion that exemplified the Bauhaus's characteristic blurring of aesthetic boundaries. Schlemmer hailed the "confusion of artistic concepts" as the sign of an emerging synthesis of all the arts. He saw his theatrical innovations as a continuation of the earlier experimental works of artists such as Viking Eggeling, Alexander Lazlo, and Ludwig Hirschfeld-Mack, who sought to integrate sound, light, and motion in a single creative vision. In his pedagogical activities at the Bauhaus, Schlemmer also exhibited a keen interest in music and sound as aspects of stage performance. He encouraged his students to explore the possibilities of both mechanical and traditional musical instruments and to investigate the various tonal qualities arising from different physical materials.[78]

Like many artists of the time, however, Schlemmer saw the guiding spirit of the age in architecture, which served as a model of "the simplest and most powerful abstraction: the severe and clearly structured form, in opposition to nature."[79] This passion for the abstract shaped Schlemmer's design of the dancers' costumes, which in turn provided the formal impetus for the overall structure of the *Triadic Ballet*. Schlemmer envisioned the costumes as a means of transcending particular, individual human shapes in order to attain ideal universal forms; they were to provide "an intermediary between absolute, (in)human marionettes and

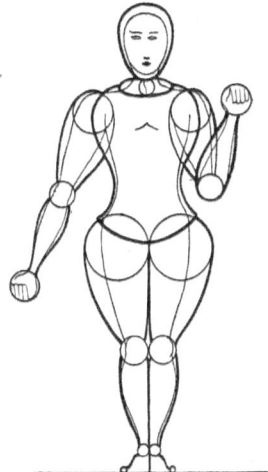 

FIGURE 5. Oskar Schlemmer's costume sketches for the *Triadic Ballet*. Source: Walter Gropius, ed., *The Theater of the Bauhaus*, trans. Arthur S. Wensinger (Middletown, CT: Wesleyan University Press, 1961), 26–27. First published as *Die Bühne im Bauhaus* (Munich: Albert Langen Verlag, 1925).

the natural human form."[80] In his theoretical writings, he distinguished four ways of relating the human form to space. The first is a kind of applied cubism, which maps the parts of the body onto "spatiocubical constructions." The second is guided by the functional laws of the human body and results in a variety of typified shapes approximating natural forms, such as an egg shape for the head and ball shapes for the joints. Schlemmer compared the result to the form of a marionette. The third is based on the laws of motion of the human body, creating shapes based on the dynamic potential of the different body parts. The result is a "technical organism." Finally, the fourth is a "dematerialization" of the body that converts the elements of the human form into symbolic, metaphysical shapes: the hand becomes a star, and the folded arms become a lemniscate, or infinity symbol.

Schlemmer's first ideas for an abstract stage work based on geometrical costumes originated in 1912 and were inspired by Arnold Schoenberg's groundbreaking song cycle *Pierrot Lunaire*. The *Triadic Ballet* was finally premiered in Stuttgart in 1922 and underwent a number of changes and different productions over the following decade.[81] The title of the work alludes not to the musical phenomenon of the major or minor chord but rather to the concept of the triad on a more conceptual level. From the number three and its multiples, Schlemmer derived the organizing principle of the entire work. The *Triadic Ballet* comprises three aesthetic dimensions (costumes, music, and dance). There are three dancers, eighteen costumes, and twelve dances. The work contains three major sections, each further subdivided into a series of short dances. Each section is characterized by a dominant color and mood: the first series is lemon yellow and "jovial-burlesque," the second is pink and "ceremonial-solemn," the third is black and "mystic-fantastic." On the visual plane, Schlemmer conceived an additional organizational triad, each component of which is further subdivided by three: space (height-depth-breadth), form (triangle-circle-square), and color (red-blue-yellow). Finally, the triadic structure of the work had symbolic overtones which were at once metaphysical and political: for Schlemmer, three is the number in which "the monomaniacal ego and the dualistic opposition are overcome, and the collective begins."[82]

Schlemmer originally intended to use the music of three different composers (Stuckenschmidt, Toch, and Hindemith, in that order), mirroring the theme of the triad and the three parts of the ballet, but the job eventually fell to Hindemith alone.[83] Collaboration between Schlemmer and Hindemith had started in 1921, when Schlemmer designed stage sets for performances of Hindemith's short operas *Mörder, Hoffnung der Frauen,* and *Das Nusch-Nuschi* in Stuttgart. (In an interesting parallel to the *Triadic Ballet, Das Nusch-Nuschi* was subtitled "A Play for Burmese Marionettes.") The Donaueschingen performance was the first time the ballet was performed with originally composed music. Earlier versions of the work had used a medley of eighteenth-century and contemporary classical music: pieces by Haydn, Mozart, Debussy, and others accompanied the dance of Schlemmer's forms. Many of the critical reviews of the early production focused on the incongruity of abstract costumes and unconventional dance with traditional and even overtly "classical" music, and Schlemmer himself admitted that the music used in the early productions of the *Triadic Ballet* were determined more by convenience than by aesthetic design. His decision to present the ballet in 1926 with newly composed music for mechanical organ was likely motivated in part by these criticisms.

Hindemith's music for the *Triadic Ballet* consisted of hand-punched rolls for the Welte-Philharmonie mechanical organ (sibling of the Welte-Mignon), which had been introduced in 1912 and in the following years had become a popular choice for musical accompaniment to silent films.[84] This instrument, even more than the reproducing piano, could be seen as the logical endpoint of musical mechanization. Long before

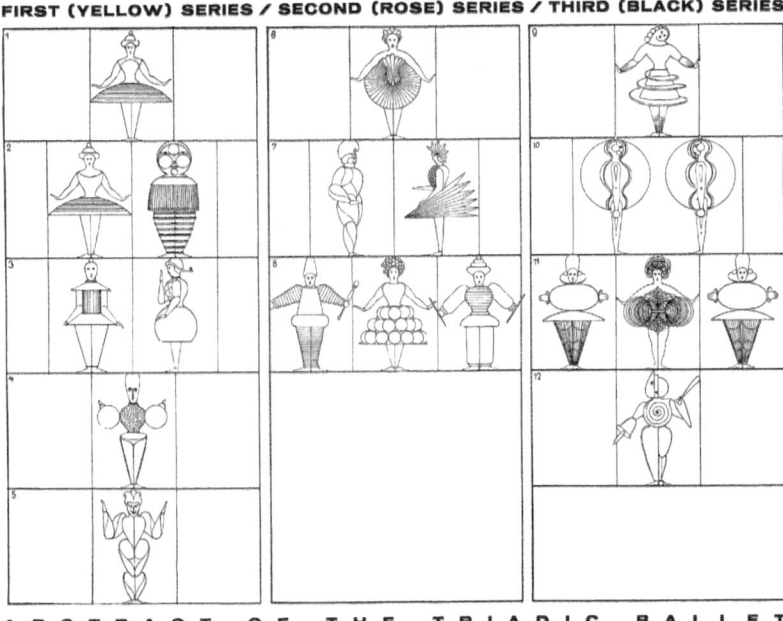

FIGURE 6. Schematic representation of the *Triadic Ballet's* overall structure. Source: Walter Gropius, ed., *The Theater of the Bauhaus*, trans. Arthur S. Wensinger (Middletown, CT: Wesleyan University Press, 1961), 26–27. First published as *Die Bühne im Bauhaus* (Munich: Albert Langen Verlag, 1925).

the twentieth century, the organ had been regarded as a triumph in the technological mastery of sound. According to the critic Eberhard Preussner, the historical study of sound technology could be undertaken on the basis of this mechanical "ur-instrument," whose elaborate apparatus converted the motions of the player into a highly differentiated sonic output.[85] Another writer suggested that the very term *mechanical organ* was redundant, since the instrument was already a triumph of mechanization.[86] For Schlemmer, the Welte-Philharmonie was a natural fit to the spirit of the *Triadic Ballet:* the music-box quality of the mechanical accompaniment, the puppetlike choreography, and the "mathematical and bodily mechanical" costumes combine to create a harmonious whole whose balance and restraint he opposed to the "psychological exuberance" characteristic of contemporary dance.[87]

The Welte-Philharmonie was a rather modest instrument, possessing only five stops plus an automatic percussion mechanism with four drums. Hindemith noted with pride how he had wrested music of great

FIGURE 7. Paul Hindemith composing on a piano roll, circa 1926. Source: Jürgen Hocker, *Faszination Player Piano: Das Selbstspielende Klavier von den Anfängen bis zur Gegenwart* (Bergkirchen, Ger.: Edition Bochinsky, 2009), 205.

variety from such limited means. The character of his accompaniment is typical of the mechanical music genre, favoring sprightly tempos, polyphonic textures, and virtuosic figuration.[88] Schlemmer, however, was not entirely satisfied with the music. Although the mechanical exactitude of the music nicely fit the precise motions of the stage figures, he found that some sought-after synesthetic correspondences—for example, between the costumes' shimmering metallic spheres and the sound of trumpets—could not be fulfilled due to the organ's timbral constraints.[89]

Reviews of the *Triadic Ballet* showed the polarization typical of the time: some critics assailed the work as a mere play of forms and bemoaned the "gimmicks of constructivist intellectuals," while others gushed that Schlemmer's work was "unreal and yet true" and "full of meaning, though words cannot grasp it."[90] Erich Steinhard, whose account of the concert's earlier performances for mechanical piano was quoted at the beginning of this chapter, questioned why, in a world of automobiles, airplanes, and neon signs, the dancers should not themselves be automatons. He drolly noted that the only thing missing was a mechanical audience that automatically whistled and clapped.[91]

Steinhard's jibe was prescient. Schlemmer dreamed of taking mechanization even further, culminating in "plays whose 'plots' consist of nothing more than the pure movement of forms, color, and light."[92] In his view, this "absolute visual stage" was the inevitable outcome of the techno-aesthetic logic of mechanization: "Should the dancers be complete marionettes, pulled on strings, or better, moved about autonomously by a perfectly mechanical precision apparatus, almost without human input, unless by means of an invisible control panel? Yes! It is only a question of time and money, in order to complete the experiment in this fashion."[93] This idea was inspired by Heinrich von Kleist's 1810 short story "Über das Marionettentheater," a literary dialogue about technological mediation framed as a conversation between the narrator and a puppeteer. Controlling a puppet, Kleist's story suggests, is no thoughtless act "like turning the handle of a barrel-organ." In order to gracefully control the marionette, the puppeteer must "transpose himself into the center of gravity of the marionette," performing a kind of virtual dance whose motions are transmitted through the strings to the lifeless figure below. In Schlemmer's twentieth-century spin on Kleist's parable, the choreographer retreats behind the scenes to direct the drama of the mechanical stage, just as, in Stuckenschmidt's vision, the musician is replaced by the composer-technician who controls the instrument from afar.[94]

From one perspective, then, both men pursued parallel objectives: they both sought to rejuvenate performance art—ironically—through the mechanization of performance. Schlemmer, like Stuckenschmidt, viewed the machine not as a threat but as an opportunity for new forms of artistic expression. In a 1926 journal entry, he reduced the technological enthusiasm of the Weimar Republic to a tidy formula: "Not the misery of mechanization, but the joy of precision!"[95] While their critics took for granted the necessity of human presence, Schlemmer and Stuckenschmidt embraced mechanization as a means of reducing performance art to its phenomenal essence. Their goal was not the fetishization of technology but rather a degree of formal purity that the self-consciousness of performers could only impede.

But the two men diverged when it came to the broader meaning of mechanization. For Stuckenschmidt, mechanical instruments were weapons in the struggle between antiquated artistic obscurantism and the modern scientific worldview. Schlemmer, on the other hand, preached a parallelism between technological advancement and spiritual depth. Material progress promised to efface the very distinction between the mechanical and the metaphysical: "Possibilities are extraordinary in light of today's technological advancements: precision machinery, scientific apparatus of glass and metal, the artificial limbs developed by surgery, the fantastic costumes of the deep-sea diver and the modern soldier, and so forth. . . . *Consequently, potentialities of constructive configuration are extraordinary on the metaphysical side as well.*"[96]

Although he was committed to the modernist project, with its emphasis on rational methods and its distrust of intuition, Schlemmer sought to incorporate many of the "spiritual" elements that Stuckenschmidt hoped to banish. For Schlemmer, abstract-mechanical art was directly linked to a higher purpose: the new theater was intended "to serve the metaphysical needs of man by constructing a world of illusion and by creating the transcendental on the basis of the irrational."[97] The machine, crowning triumph of rationality, frees its creator from the limits of rational thought and transfigures humankind into a "mechanistic organism." Or, in Kleist's paradox, "We have to eat again of the tree of knowledge to fall back again into a state of innocence."[98]

MECHANICAL FAILURE

This entire span of activity, from Stuckenschmidt's first salvos to the last original compositions for mechanical instruments, lasted only about three years. After the second concert in 1927, the movement quickly came to an end. The once vast potential of mechanical instruments seemed to be suddenly and entirely exhausted. Stuckenschmidt withdrew from his proselytizing and penned an acerbic critique of the musical influence of the New Objectivity. His motive may have been in part personal: in spite of his central role in the development of mechanical music, Stuckenschmidt had not been invited to write music for the 1926 concert in Donaueschingen concert. Several weeks before the concert, he wrote a letter to Prince Max Egon of Baden, the nominal patron of the festival, claiming he was the victim of inexplicable injustice on the part of the organizers of the concert (among them Paul Hindemith) and asking the prince to intervene on his behalf. Nothing came of it.[99]

Ironically, it was Hans Haass, who composed the most remarkable tours de force of mechanical music, who wrote what could be seen as its obituary.[100] In an article entitled "Über das Wesen mechanischer Klaviermusik," published in October 1927, Haass pulled the rug out from under the movement with a critique of the key notion of musical "objectivity." The meaning of objectivity, he argued, is "complete freedom from all individuality: that is, the exclusion of capricious or involuntary notions on the part of the interpreter as well as (and I stress) the composer himself." Thus, an objective piano music would be one in which "every single note, even the smallest, has a value that is determined to the most precise degree."[101]

But this precision is exactly what the mechanical piano lacks. Haass enumerated several technical imperfections that compromise the instrument's "objectivity": the sensitivity of the paper to humidity, the inaccuracy in the placement of notes upon the roll, and fluctuations in the spinning speed of the roll as the paper accumulates on the spindle. But the real problem, Haass argued, is that devices such as the Welte-Mignon have been designed from the beginning as instruments of *reproduction,* meant to record and re-create the highly individual playing techniques of human performers. The machine is optimized to play what human hands can play: technically difficult passages, such as arpeggios through several octaves and repeated chords, require a greater amount of mechanical energy, in analogy to the increased exertion by a performer playing these passages: "In [certain] cases, increased technical difficulty causes an increase in volume, which a purely objective music within its limits cannot make use of, precisely because this music seeks to avoid the impression of expression."[102] Thus, creating truly objective music with the Welte-Mignon or comparable instruments was, according to Haass, an unattainable ideal.

While Haass tempered his critique by noting that the Welte-Mignon was still capable of playing extremely fast and otherwise unperformable music, his article was an early sign of a growing unease among the advocates of mechanical music. The journalist Hans Heinsheimer anticipated the idea that the piano's limitations were hardwired in an article published in the wake of the 1926 Donaueschingen concert. "The free reign of the musical imagination encounters in the material properties of the piano limitations scarcely different from those of the sound produced by human hands," Heinsheimer declared. "*For mechanical music we require genuinely mechanical instruments.*"[103] In writing directly for the Welte-Mignon, composers had hoped to transcend the limitations of performers, but in so doing, they were brought face to face with the constraints of the instrument itself. Before long, they found that the unique technical affordances offered by the instrument—extreme speed, sustained volume, and sheer mass of musical activity—quickly wore thin.[104] This, too, had been foreseen early on when Hindemith admonished composers of mechanical music against the "senseless accumulation of technical complexity."[105]

In spite of these difficulties and disappointments, one particular use of these technologies still held out promise: the accompaniment of silent films. Mechanical music seemed perfectly suited to this purpose, because it ran at a constant tempo, just like the film reel. Hindemith was the foremost advocate for this application of mechanical instruments: he pointed out the uncanny disjunction between the "dead" filmic image and the "live" music that typically accompanied it and pleaded for original mechanical music written expressly for new films, rather than added as an afterthought.[106] Thanks in part to his influence, the Donaueschingen festival programs from 1927 to 1929 featured a number of works for mechanical piano and organ that were composed especially for films.

But even this relatively modest application of mechanical music proved to be ill-fated: at the Baden-Baden festival in 1927, on the same day as the premiere of Hindemith's mechanical organ soundtrack for the short cartoon film *Felix the Cat at the Circus,* there was a demonstration of the Tri-Ergon sound-film technology by Guido Bagier, a technician for Universum-Film-Aktiengesellschaft (UFA), the premier movie studio in Weimar Republic Germany. That evening, the audience was invited to compare a live performance of Hanns Eisler's music for Walter Ruttmann's abstract animated film *Lichtspiel, Opus III* with the same music recorded onto film via the Tri-Ergon process. Thus, no sooner had Hindemith attempted to salvage a role for mechanical music as synchronized film accompaniment than this function was eclipsed by the newer and more advanced technology of sound-on-film. Why synchronize the film reel with a mechanical organ when the music can now be recorded directly onto the sound track? The programs of the next few festivals featured various configurations of film and music, both live and recorded on sound film, but only one additional piece of film music for mechanical instruments, a collaborative piece for the Welte-Mignon by Hindemith and Werner Gräff for the Hans Richter experimental short *Vormittagsspuk* (Ghosts before breakfast). This was the last known original piece of music for mechanical instruments composed in the Weimar Republic.

The ideal of mechanical music would not be abandoned, however, but pursued in new forms. For the some disillusioned partisans, the gramophone and sound film offered the best of both worlds: like the piano roll, they provided a medium for "direct composition" without the intervention of performers. But they also opened up a new sound world far beyond the confines of the piano, a domain of infinite tonal gradations and undiscovered timbres. Another response to the failure of mechanical music was to turn to the new field of electric instruments that had opened up in the second half of the 1920s. In these instruments, the electrical signal emitted by vacuum tubes was converted into a musical tone, allowing a new degree of control over pitch, dynamics, and timbre. The underlying principle of *elektrische Klangerzeugung* (electric tone generation) promised to expand the domain of sound, albeit with human performers ensconced at the controls.[107]

Meanwhile, a final ironic outcome of the movement inaugurated by Stuckenschmidt was that by the end of the 1920s the term *mechanical music* had exploded into virtual meaninglessness. In the music journals of the time, the phrase became a catchall for contemporary developments in music technology, from radio to gramophone to new electric instruments. On a more technical register, the engineer Peter Lertes, who in 1933 published the first book-length overview of the new electric instruments, used the term *mechanical* as a retronym to describe nonelectrophones, similar to the way the word *acoustic* has been used in the second half of the twentieth century.[108] A few years earlier, the critic Paul Bernhard had drawn a more radical conclusion by declaring that the only nonmechanical form of music was human song, since "all music is made with machines; the throat alone is organic."[109] Perhaps Stuckenschmidt would have been pleased.

3

"The Alchemy of Tone"

Jörg Mager and Electric Music

> Still more revealing would be a history of musical instruments written, not (as it always is) from the technical standpoint of tone-production, but as a study of the deep spiritual bases of the tone-colors and tone-effects aimed at.[1]
>
> —Oswald Spengler

During the same July 1926 festival in Donaueschingen where the sounds of "mechanical music" were unleashed upon the world, an inventor named Jörg Mager demonstrated a remarkable new instrument. He played a curious device consisting of an L-shaped handle that he turned on its axis around a semicircular metal panel; as the handle moved, a connected loudspeaker emitted a keening, disembodied tone that glided and swooped, sounding either out of tune or otherworldly. This device—the Spherophone—was intended to usher in a new kind of music based on microtonal pitch increments discernable to the ear but unattainable by most instruments. Though it was overshadowed by the more sensational concerts for mechanical piano and the Schlemmer-Hindemith *Triadic Ballet,* Mager's demonstration of the Spherophone sent tremors through the audience. The journalist Herbert Weiskopf perceived in the instrument a phenomenon of profound significance for the history of music: "We do not wish to abandon ourselves to utopias," he wrote, "but in this case the oft-misused term 'epoch-making' seems to be appropriate." In his view, the Spherophone promised nothing less than the "alteration of the entire process of musical listening."[2] Paul Hindemith noted that the Spherophone was still in an early stage of development but declared it "the most revolutionary invention in the field of musical instruments" and expressed his eagerness to compose for it.[3]

At the time of his 1926 demonstration in Donaueschingen, Mager's instrument was virtually the only one of its kind in Germany. But by the late 1920s, German inventors were constructing a bewildering array of electric artifacts, experimenting boldly with both playing interfaces and techniques of tone production. These instruments did without the familiar "moving parts" possessed by all instruments hitherto: instead of a plucked string or a vibrating column of air, the motive force was the invisible and nearly inconceivable oscillation of electrons in vacuum tubes. The result was a class of instrument so novel that it would eventually require a new organological category to account for it—the *electrophone*. Around these auspicious devices, there gathered a network of composers, performers, engineers, and journalistic acolytes brought together by glimmering visions of new musical horizons. This movement came to be known as "electric music," and Mager was its most prominent figure.

Although electric music was nourished by the same technological enthusiasm that fed mechanical music, the two movements were in other ways worlds apart. First, electrophones were *instruments* in the colloquial sense—played live by musicians, rather than programmed and later mechanically activated—and so were more readily embraced by a skeptical musical public. While mechanical instruments threatened to make performers obsolete, electric instruments promised musicians new expressive powers, expanding their artistry by acting as "organic" extensions of their bodies.

Second, if mechanical music was a manifestation of the cool, detached sensibility of the New Sobriety, electric music resonated with the apocalyptic spirit of expressionism, the diffuse artistic mood that flourished in the years around the First World War.[4] Expressionist artists believed that progress in art required the destruction of hidebound rules and aesthetic dogma, favored the sublime over the merely beautiful, and rejected the down-to-earth materialism of the modern age in favor of the search for profound depths and extreme experiences. Mager's vision of electric music was a technological manifestation of this temperament: he attempted to burst the bonds of the conventional instrumentarium in order to create a new world of sounds commensurate with the unbounded longings of modern humanity.

Finally, the electric music movement embodied a spiritual attitude toward technology. Mager's instruments were manifestations of the "electromagnetic imaginary," where high technology rubbed shoulders with metaphysical speculation.[5] While H.H. Stuckenschmidt championed mechanical music as an art form suited to the modern, scientific worldview with its distrust of unseen forces, Mager and his allies heard electrically generated tones as manifestations of primal energy, signals from the beyond. In his profile of the inventor for the modernist music journal *Melos,* the journalist Hans Kuznitzky wrote that Mager's instruments embodied the "romantic experience and affirmation of the machine age, the age of technology."[6] Kuznitzky linked Mager's instruments to the "radical abstraction" of Oskar Schlemmer, seeing in the work of both men the glimmering of a "new romanticism [. . .] a mystical immersion in a newly conditioned attitude toward life."[7] Mager's inventions were unified by an overarching utopian vision: he pursued the ideal of a musical instrument that would put at musicians' fingertips the unlimited possibilities of what Ferruccio Busoni called "abstract sound."

MICROTONAL PRELUDE

Jörg Mager was born in 1880 in the town of Aschaffenburg, near Frankfurt in northwest Bavaria, to a mother who was a church singer and a father from a long line of clockmakers. He grew up in modest circumstances as one of thirteen children. Though the family's poverty prevented Mager from attending conservatory, he studied music on his own, originally with the aspiration of becoming a composer. Having settled on the vocations of schoolteacher and church organist, Mager became serendipitously involved in instrument building in the summer of 1911, when—according to his own telling—a heat wave wrenched his church pipe organ badly out of tune. Intrigued by the instrument's strange new harmonies, Mager conducted an experiment in tuning. He procured a set of organ pipes and carefully tuned each by ear to create a quarter-tone scale, interleaving an additional pitch between each of the twelve semitones of the conventional keyboard.[8] With this, he had in his own words "founded quarter-tone research in Germany."[9] Mager eagerly immersed himself in the history and theory of tuning. In the clutch of enthusiasm, he penned a letter to Richard Strauss informing the famed composer of his potentially epochal discovery. Strauss expressed a guarded interest in Mager's undertaking but drily noted that he would continue to make do with the half-tone scale.[10]

Soon after his first experiments, Mager commissioned the construction of a quarter-tone harmonium (a portable reed organ) built to his specifications.[11] The instrument had two manuals, each tuned in twelve-tone equal temperament, but the upper manual was tuned a quarter-tone higher than the lower manual. Quarter-tone intervals were thus obtained by playing the two manuals simultaneously. In Mager's first published writing, the 1915 pamphlet *Quarter-Tone Music,* he set out a subjective but systematic catalog of the various new sonorities of the quarter-tone system. He listed each of the eleven new dyads and provided short characterizations of their sounds. The interval between C and raised D (five quarter-tone steps), for example, is "unruly, pressing for resolution, [of a] robust character," while the interval of seventeen quarter tones (equivalent to a raised augmented fifth) "sounds good; each tone is independent, not fusing together, but standing out."[12] He also catalogued all the new triads of the quarter-tone system, grouping them as variants of the four diatonic types (major, minor, diminished, and augmented). For Mager, this experimental probing served to demonstrate the musical viability of the quarter-tone system: "The research of possible quarter-tone applications is concerned at first with simple progressions and passages. [. . .] One is surprised by how clearly this smallest interval can be perceived by every normal ear!"[13] Mager's harmonium thus represented a peculiar application of instrumental technology: it was something between a conventional musical instrument, which it outwardly resembled, and an instrument in the scientific sense—a device for imparting knowledge about the empirical world.

Mager's microtonal fascination was part of a broader tendency in early twentieth-century music, the aesthetic and technological implications of tuning were the objects of heated debate among scientists, musicians, and intellectuals of the time. As early as 1863, Hermann von Helmholtz had argued in his widely read *On the Sensations of Tone* that tuning systems are based less on the unchanging nature of sound than on the vagaries of human culture. Helmholtz's investigations into alternate tunings helped sanction a number of microtonal experiments in the late nineteenth century, such as the "bichromatic piano" G. A. Behrens-Senegalden patented in 1892.[14] In 1911, the same year as Mager's first experiments with his detuned organ, Arnold Schoenberg mused on the prospect of expanding the scale beyond the limits of twelve-tone equal temperament in his *Harmonielehre (Theory of Harmony).* His attitude toward the matter was highly ambivalent: on the one hand, he acknowledged that the division of the scale in increments smaller than the tempered semitone was likely an historical inevitability; on the other hand, he seemed to dismiss current efforts to make use of these finer intervals and deferred the realization of this goal to a distant future, arguing that experiments in this domain "seem senseless, as long as there are too few instruments available to play them." The necessary instruments would appear, he said, as soon as the "ear and imagination" were prepared: "For it is far more a matter of mind and spirit than of material, and the spirit must be ready."[15] In spite of Schoenberg's skepticism, his discussion of tuning in the *Harmonielehre* became a frequently cited touchstone for microtonal composers and instrument builders.

Around the same time, the German sociologist Max Weber was investigating tuning in his study of the social and historical development of European music from the standpoint of mathematical rationalization.[16] For Weber, the logical endpoint of musical rationalization was the establishment of twelve-tone equal temperament, which replaced the heterogeneous welter of earlier tunings with a unified system based on a single interval. The dominance of equal temperament exhibits the double edge of rationalization. On the one hand, it enabled the uninhibited modulation between keys and the chromatic enrichment of harmony without which postclassical music would be unimaginable: "Only temperament brought [music] to full freedom," Weber declared. But on the other hand, he argued that the leveling of differences between keys and the dominance of the uniform tempered semitone had dulled listening habits and shackled music in "dragging chains."[17] The rationalization thesis suggested that music had been led into a technological cul-de-sac, a closed system whose finite possibilities were rapidly approaching exhaustion. Significantly, Weber's study of tuning predated by several years his renowned thesis of the "disenchantment of the world," which would become a keynote of twentieth-century social theory.[18]

The themes of tuning, disenchantment, and musical rationalization also found expression in contemporary literature. *Syrinx*, a novel published in 1914 by the writer and poet Julius Maria Becker (1887–1949), tells the story of a schoolteacher and church organist named Hamann and his quest to overcome the suffocating constriction of musical expression imposed by conventional systems of tuning:

> We should cry out at the brutality of our scales. They defraud us of the subtlest gradations available to the domain of sound and pin down an infinity to twelve points. They are twelve columns in a river without bridges connecting them; the whole thing is in truth an acoustic fragment with whose

imperfection the world cannot be content. [. . .] Do you know what we have done to the flowing sea of sound? We have run it through a sieve and come up with these twelve drops, which give only a faint idea of the vastness of the primal sea.[19]

In order to tap into the oceanic infinitude of the pitch spectrum, Hamann builds a new kind of organ in which the player, by increasing pressure on the key of his instrument, triggers an electrical mechanism that shortens the length of the corresponding pipe in proportion to the pressure applied, thus creating a continuous, glissando-like transition from one tone to the next. With this instrument, he achieves "not merely a technical refinement of the organ, nor a reform of music all told, but rather a symbolic solution of the secret of the world."[20] *Syrinx* is a remarkable testament to the convergence of technology, music, and metaphysics in the early twentieth century. In spite its seemingly farfetched premise, the novel had a firm basis in reality: Becker's protagonist was modeled on none other than Jörg Mager.[21]

The notion that the musical language of the classical-romantic tradition was incapable of further development became an article of faith among modernist musicians of various stripes in the early twentieth century, one that provoked a wide array of solutions and reactions to the perceived dead end of common-practice tonality. Mager, for example, lamented the depletion of the "gold mines of musical expression," noting that composers such as Wagner, Liszt, and Strauss had already stretched the limits of the chromatic scale.[22] What made Mager's interpretation of the exhaustion thesis unique was its technological spin. Like Busoni, he was convinced that new instruments alone could surmount the impasse music had reached in the early twentieth century. In this, his position was more radical even than that of a composer such as Schoenberg: for Mager, the free circulation of all members of the chromatic scale only highlighted that system's limitations—rattling the cage of twelve-tone equal temperament instead of throwing open the gate. The exploration of new systems of tuning based on intervals finer than the tempered semitone, then, was more than a merely technical matter. In Mager's view, this quest was nothing less than an attempt to ensure the future of music as a living form of art. If the history of tuning had traced a trajectory of disenchantment, Mager suggested that enlightened technologies could reinstate the unspoiled wholeness that had been sacrificed on the altar of musical rationalization. His goal, in short, would be to capture the infinite in an instrument.

ELECTRIC MUSIC

Mager's pamphlet on quarter-tone music was published in 1915, in the thick of the First World War. The inventor was soon called to the front, where he served as a soldier and medic. As a committed socialist, Mager later took part in the Communist uprising in Munich, but after its failure he was forced to flee for Berlin, fearing prosecution for his involvement in the attempted revolution.[23] (According to one unconfirmed legend, he served for three days as minister of culture for the short-lived Bavarian Soviet Republic.)[24]

In the German capital, Mager found himself in one of the major centers of microtonal research in Europe. Ferruccio Busoni, whose influential *Sketch of a New Aesthetic of Music* had proposed the possibility of the division of the whole tone into thirds and sixths, was summoned to the city in 1920 to lead a master class at the Academy of Fine Arts, and his presence drew a number of young composers who were interested in microtonal composition and instrument building.[25] By 1922, the Berlin circle of microtonalists included the Czech Alois Hába, the Russian Ivan Wyschnegradsky, and the Germans Mager, Willi Möllendorf, and Richard Stein. They all were veterans of the microtonal scene: Stein had composed and published quarter-tone music as early as 1909; Mager and Möllendorf had built quarter-tone instruments in 1912 and 1914, respectively; and Wyschnegradsky and Hába had had their microtonal works published and performed. However, none were satisfied with the available means of realizing their music. In the fall of 1922, the five men convened to determine a course of action for the development of microtonal instruments. Although the conference ended without any clear resolution, it was a decisive event for Mager, who by this time had come to see the quarter-tone system as an unacceptable compromise between his ideals and the limitations of conventional instrumental technology. The meeting cemented his decision to abandon acoustic instruments in fixed tuning and instead attempt to gain control of the pitch spectrum by means of electric tone generation.[26]

Mager's electric leap was made possible by the precipitous development of radio equipment in the first decades of the twentieth century, a period of rapid technological change that one historian has dubbed "the dawn of the electronic age."[27] In techno-historical terms, "electric music" was an accidental by-product of the development of radio broadcasting: modern electronics grew out of a little glass bulb originally intended simply to aid in the reception of radio waves. Shortly after inventing the incandescent light bulb in 1878, Thomas Edison had noticed that the cathode inside the bulb generated a mysterious emission that blackened the interior of the glass. This finding, investigated but not fundamentally understood by Edison, was later taken up by John Ambrose Fleming, who discovered that the so-called Edison effect was a process of thermionic emission, in which an electric charge flowed from the heated cathode to the anode. In 1904, Fleming invented the diode or two-element thermionic valve, which found use as a rectifier, converting alternating current into direct current and thus aiding in the conversion of radio signals into audio.[28]

In 1906, the American inventor Lee de Forest added a third element to the diode by placing a tiny wire grid between the cathode and the anode. A relatively small signal passed to the grid would therefore regulate a much larger current between the cathode and anode, thus amplifying the original signal. De Forest's three-element (triode) vacuum tube, which he called the Audion, was later discovered to have the remarkable capacity not only to detect and amplify radio waves but also to create its own electrical oscillations. In January 1913, the American inventor Edwin Howard Armstrong discovered that by directing the output of the Audion tube back into the input, the device's amplification effect could be vastly multiplied, allowing it to detect and render audible even distant radio signals. Most important, for the later development of electric instruments, he found that beyond a certain level of amplification, the Audion began to hiss, whistle, and howl. It was no longer simply receiving and amplifying signals; it was now generating its own.[29] Armstrong's discovery of feedback (also known as regenerative amplification) would have profound implications for the fledgling radio industry, which at the time was capable of only weak broadcasts of extremely limited range. It would set in motion a major technological shift, as the vacuum tube in myriad forms (together with AC distribution systems) replaced the large and unwieldy dynamos as the primary means of generating and controlling electricity.[30] Though audio feedback was generally considered undesirable and uncontrollable, once tamed by the proper circuitry, it would form the technological basis of electric tone generation. Electric instruments, in essence, found a creative purpose for the refuse product of radio broadcasting: "In all of these instruments," a contemporary journalist observed, "it is ultimately a matter of deliberately creating the so-called feedback noise well-known to every radio listener—that bothersome whistling and singing of the loudspeaker—and giving it a certain tonal beauty to rival the sounds of our traditional musical instruments."[31]

Following on Armstrong's work, de Forest discovered that the pitch of the electrically generated tone was governed by the capacitance of the circuit, and thus could be controlled for musical purposes. In an article published in the radio enthusiasts' journal *The Electrical Experimenter,* de Forest declared, "I am able to obtain a succession of musical notes, clear and sweet, of surprising volume, the pitch and timbre of which can be varied almost at will to imitate any musical tone of an orchestra." (Tellingly, he closed the article by assuring his readers that the sounds of his so-called Audion Piano were produced electrically and not mechanically; he was aware that for the general public "mechanical" was all but synonymous with "unmusical.")[32] In 1915, de Forest was granted the first patent for the use of vacuum tubes as tone generators, but he soon abandoned this branch of electrical research, leaving it for others to explore.

It was in this technological context that Jörg Mager undertook his first experiments in electric tone generation in Berlin in the early 1920s. He described the path to his invention in his pamphlet *A New Epoch of Music through Radio,* published on the occasion of the first German Radio Exhibition in 1924. Here Mager put forward a radical vision of radio as a medium for new forms of music, rather than the dissemination of existing works: "The radio firms have indeed energetically championed the *transmission* of music through radio," Mager wrote, "but at the same time they have shown virtually no interest in the far more significant problem of *creating* music."[33] He elaborated this claim in a "Radio Prophecy" published the same year in the journal *Der deutsche Rundfunk:*

> The music of the future will be attained by *radio instruments!* Of course, not with radio transmission, but rather *direct generation* of musical tones by means of cathode instruments! Indeed, cathode music will be far superior to previous music, in that it can generate a much finer, more highly developed, richly colored music than all our known musical instruments![34]

Mager dismissed inventors such as Edison and Marconi as mere technicians who were ignorant of the artistic need for instrumental innovation, while he portrayed himself as an artist-engineer who possessed both the aesthetic sensitivity and the technical know-how required to initiate a new age of music.[35] He denounced the limited use of electroacoustics as a means of musical reproduction through

FIGURE 8. An artist's rendering of Lee de Forest's Audion Piano. Source: Lee de Forest, "Audion Bulbs as Producers of Pure Musical Tones," *The Electrical Experimenter* 3, no. 8 (1915): 394.

recording and broadcasting and called for creative applications of the new technologies—"a higher acoustics, a higher radio." Just as the composers of mechanical music refunctioned automatic instruments as tools for artistic experimentation, Mager envisioned "radio-music without transmission," a Promethean gambit to release radio-electricity from its bondage to technical reproduction and deliver it into the hands of contemporary composers.[36]

Sometime around 1921, using surplus radio components gathered from his job as a factory worker for the electronics manufacturer Lorenz, Mager cobbled together his first prototype electric instrument.[37] It was a simple device in which the pitch was controlled by the rotary motion of a hand crank over a semicircular metal plate.[38] The movement of the crank controlled the capacitance of the circuit, which in turn raised or lowered the frequency of the instrument's tone. A button on the handle closed the circuit, generating a tone for as long as it was held down. As the player turned the crank, the instrument generated a continuous, gliding transition between tones; it was thus perfectly suited to obtain the finest microtonal inflections. Recounting his joy

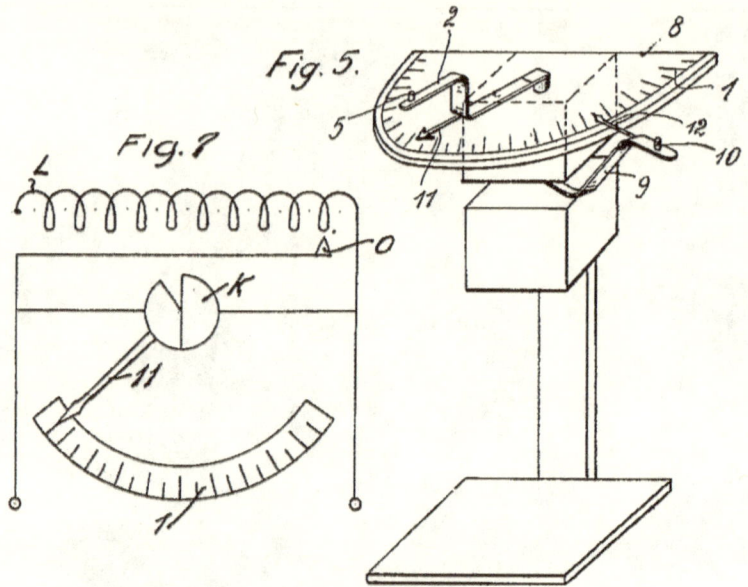

FIGURE 9. Technical draft of Jörg Mager's crank-operated electric instrument, circa 1924. Source: Jörg Mager, "Electro-acoustic Musical Instrument" (US Patent 1,829,099, filed on March 21, 1928 and issued on October 17, 1931).

upon attaining what he called the "ideal glissando," Mager wrote, "Absolute music! The pan-tonal circle lay before me! The ocean of tone in its immeasurability! The *omnitonium,* the musical ideal of all times!"[39]

The question of discrete versus continuous pitch space was a bone of contention among the Berlin microtonalists: although Hába welcomed Mager's instrument, Richard Stein dismissed as "utopian" the notion that music could do without fixed scale degrees.[40] Mager, in his defense, quoted the revered Helmholtz, who had argued in *On the Sensations of Tone* that the stepwise segmentation of pitch imposed by musical instruments such as the piano alienated music from nature, where "gliding transitions" are the rule.[41] The appeal of continuous tonal motion was widespread in the early twentieth century and found expression in the writings and music of Nikolai Kulbin, Percy Grainger, Henry Cowell, and Edgard Varèse. For these figures, as for Mager, the glissando was nothing less than the infinite tonal spectrum made audible.[42]

In its circuitry, Mager's device was closely related to the instrument developed concurrently in Russia by Léon Theremin. Both employed beat-frequency oscillators, a means of tone generation based on the heterodyne principle discovered by the Canadian inventor Reginald Fessenden in 1901, which allowed for the production of a musical tone as the by-product of two inaudible high-frequency vibrations. (As is well known from the study of acoustics, two simultaneous oscillations generate a new vibration whose frequency is equal to the difference between the frequencies of the original two.) Although developed in the context of radio transmission, the heterodyne principle proved useful in many of the earliest electric instruments: by keeping one of the high frequencies constant and allowing the other to be altered through the player's actions, the resulting tone could be controlled with some degree of precision.[43]

The playing interface of Mager's instrument was the product of a technological misunderstanding. Mager, like many others, had been awakened to the possibility of electric tone generation by Busoni's account of the Telharmonium, the massive, dynamo-powered electric instrument built in the first years of the twentieth century by the American inventor Thaddeus Cahill.[44] In his *Sketch of a New Aesthetic of Music*, Busoni described the instrument as "a comprehensive apparatus which makes it possible to transform an electric current into a fixed and mathematically exact number of vibrations" and attributed to it the ability to attain "the infinite gradation of the octave [. . .] by merely moving a lever corresponding to the pointer of a quadrant." But the playing interface described here was completely fabricated: in reality, the Telharmonium was played from a conventional musical keyboard. Busoni, who never saw the instrument in person and based his account on a single article in an American magazine, grafted Cahill's actual invention onto the fantastic product of his own imagination, a "universal instrument" capable of generating any frequency with the turn of a dial.[45] Mager's description of the Telharmonium essentially parroted Busoni's:

> With a lever the tone apparatus is set to the desired number of vibrations. The extraordinary richness of tones enables an extraordinary fullness of harmonies. This great number of tones can be most easily named with the number of their vibrations [i.e., their frequency]: science and art are thus wed in the most ideal manner. The "alchemy of tone" will become a favorite occupation for musical discoverers. All the euphonies thus discovered will be fixed, until laws for the construction of genuine consonances and dissonances have been found.[46]

Both Mager and Busoni transmitted a false image of Cahill's instrument that reflected their own obsession with microtonality. In building a means of continuous pitch control into his first electric instrument, Mager meant to follow Cahill's precedent, but he was in fact creating an entirely new invention, one that sprang directly from his quest for the unlimited "ocean of tone."[47]

Mager originally called this instrument the *Electrophon,* but by 1924, he had rechristened it the Spherophone (*Sphärophon,* from the German *Sphäre,* "sphere," and *–phon,* "sound").[48] He traced the inspiration for this name to the writings of the nineteenth-century acoustician Johann Heinrich Scheibler, who compared the sound of "pure" harmony (intervals in just intonation) to the "song of the spheres."[49] The inventor thus positioned his instrument in the long tradition of speculative organology at the very moment that he committed himself to the new and untested possibilities of electric tone production. For Mager, the music of the future, unleashed by new instruments, echoed the timeless song of the cosmos.

ORGANIC INSTRUMENTS

In an article published shortly after his 1926 debut in Donaueschingen, Mager pleaded for aid in the continued development of his instrument: "If the Spherophone is to fulfill the justifiably high expectations it has aroused, it needs its own acoustic laboratory and practice space. Friends of new music, music administrators, acousticians, press, and patrons, help us to attain this, and there is no doubt that something truly great and valuable will emerge!"[50] Mager's confidence had been bolstered by the encouragement of a number of musical luminaries. Early on he had won the blessing of Busoni, who in June 1922 wrote an impassioned letter to the Swiss conductor Volkmar Andreae asking for 50,000 marks to support the inventor's undertaking. The money need not be a gift, Busoni wrote—it could surely be paid back with interest in the not-too-distant future. "Think about it," he wrote. "Old dreams could be realized—similar to those that inspired men to the discovery of flight. *Da cosa nasce cosa* [out of one thing comes another]—who knows where it might lead?"[51] The prominent musicologist Curt Sachs, professor at the Berlin Academy of Music (Hochschule für Musik), tested the instrument himself and wrote Mager a glowing endorsement.[52] Alois Hába, the Czech composer and alumnus of the Berlin circle of quarter-tone enthusiasts who founded a department of microtonal music at the Prague Conservatory in 1924, also penned a testimonial for Mager in which he praised the inventor's electric instrument and expressed his eagerness to write new music for it.[53]

Even the characteristically restrained Hindemith was intrigued by Mager's instrument. Its ability to generate tones of any frequency suggested to him the possibility of creating synthetic timbres through the superposition of pure tones in harmonic proportions. If this effort were successful, he reasoned, all existing musical instruments would quickly become superfluous. Further, Mager's Spherophone could conceivably be played by mechanical means, thus combining the tonal and timbral possibilities of electric tone generation with the rhythmic and technical potential of automatic instruments. Finally, Hindemith pointed out the economic implications: traditional instruments such as violin and piano were unaffordable for most people, but a Spherophone built to the size of a typical radio receiver—and sold for a similar price—could find a place in every home.[54]

The device that elicited these enthusiastic reactions remained technically quite rudimentary. Mager's instrument was still monophonic—capable of playing only a single tone at a time—and its timbre could not be substantially varied. Weiskopf compared this "primitive" instrument to the ancient monochord, suggesting that the Spherophone, in its very simplicity, marked a new era of music.[55] Like Mager's earlier quarter-tone harmonium, the device occupied an ambiguous position between the acoustic laboratory and the concert hall: the inventor himself described the Spherophone as an "experimental tone-differentiation instrument."[56] But by the time of the 1926 demonstration in Donaueschingen, he had implemented a small but important change to make the Spherophone better suited to live performance. With the addition of a second crank, positioned on the underside of the semicircular plate, the instrument was able to achieve a more conventionally musical transition between tones. Previously, to get from one tone to another, the player had to pass through all the intervening pitches, creating a glissando, or release the button while moving the crank to its new position, introducing a gap of silence. Now the second crank could be moved to the position of the new tone while the first tone was still sounding. By enabling a legato transition between tones, Mager conformed the Spherophone to conventional playing techniques, and thus took a major step toward the mainstream acceptance of his instrument.

A year after the unveiling of the Spherophone in Donaueschingen, Mager showed off his instrument on a much bigger stage, at the international exhibition "Music in the Lives of the People" in Frankfurt. Here the Spherophone shared the spotlight with the eponymous instrument of the Russian inventor Léon Theremin. Theremin's instrument, originally known as the Etherophone and later simply called by the name of its inventor, captivated audiences with its "touchless" playing technique, in which the player controlled the tone by moving one hand within an electromagnetic field around a vertical antenna. Like the Spherophone, the Theremin produced an eerie, keening tone that evoked supernatural images in the minds of many listeners. Theremin had first toured Germany in 1923, and he set up a laboratory and residence in Berlin in 1927, where he made contact with the Soviet government agent Georg Julius Goldberg, who assisted him with publicity and filing patents.[57] (As detailed by Albert Glinsky, Theremin's tour was part of an elaborate effort on the part of Soviet intelligence agencies to gain access to economically advantageous technical information in the capitalist countries of Western Europe.) In Frankfurt, the inventor gave a lecture-recital entitled "New Trails in Musical Creation," which combined an explanation of his instrument, an introduction to playing technique, and short performances of classical chestnuts arranged for piano and Theremin.[58]

The appearance of the two inventors at the same event provided a field day for journalistic devotees of "electric music," who produced a spate of articles playing up the contrast between the two men and their instruments. Mager was presented as an archetypical German romantic, idealistic and impractical, while Theremin was depicted as a suave, theatrical showman.[59] But the hints of rivalry between Mager and Theremin overshadowed the commonality of their projects, which went beyond the technical similarity of their inventions. A witness to the Frankfurt exhibition described the hybrid personality of the typical "electro-musician": "[They were] certainly more than three quarters musician, but through some external circumstance they had ended up in the domain of technology. Delicate, almost hypersensitive natures with many of the marks of Western European decadence—men that one meets almost never in technical professions but very often in the arts."[60] The question of whether figures such as Mager and Theremin were at bottom artists, engineers, both, or neither, would continue to occupy both followers and critics of the electric music movement.

Beyond their shared calling as musician-inventors, both Mager and Theremin staked their careers on the claim that electric instruments could be reconciled with the expressive demands of performing musicians.

FIGURE 10. One of the many journalistic juxtapositions of Léon Theremin and Jörg Mager. Source: *Die Musik* 20, no. 1 (1927): 41.

They and their advocates in the musical press took pains to present these devices as a new kind of humanized, "organic" technology in contrast to the automatic machines of Stuckenschmidt and company. By focusing on the immateriality of electric tone production, they attempted to decouple technology and mechanism and thus accommodate the critiques of mechanical music. Whereas mechanical instruments represented the complete externalization of music from the human being, electric instruments were conceived as technological extensions of the human body; instead of posing an obstacle for musical expression, they enabled direct contact between musicians and their medium. Theremin insisted that his instrument posed no obstacle to the performer's individual expression and had nothing to do with "automatic technology and soullessness."[61] Mager invoked an explicitly biological metaphor to describe the unmediated interaction between the performer and the electric tone: "Through radio-electricity alone is the nerve of music laid bare as through no other means, reacting hypersensitively to the subtlest vibrations of feeling."[62]

These claims were promptly echoed by the inventors' allies in musical press. Indeed, many writings on electric music from this period evince a remarkable consistency almost suggestive of a coordinated publicity offensive. In a 1927 article on the Theremin, Heinrich Strobel, editor of the influential modernist journal *Melos*, wrote: "The player can form and shape the tone material through the movement of his hands, indeed of his entire body. This is a fundamental difference from mechanical music, in which the dead instrument reigns absolutely. It always produces merely a reproduction of a reproduction, unless one—as has happened—composes for the machine on the basis of its characteristic properties."[63] For Strobel, the distinction between electric and mechanical instruments was between an embodied, reflexive, "live" technology and a merely reproductive "dead" one.[64] Likewise, the critic Arno Huth declared that with the demonstration of Mager's and Theremin's instruments, "once and for all it is proven that instruments making use of electric current for tone generation do not numb and kill aesthetic sensitivity but, on the contrary, allow them in the greatest degree to act more directly than before."[65] Another critic wrote, "The most important thing about these instruments is not the use of electricity in service of art—that is, the switching on of soulless tones, the purely mechanical mastery of the sound material—but rather, on the contrary, the much more intimate connection of this sound material with the individuality of the performing artist." The electric instrument, he suggested, is servant and not master. It merely provides the raw material of sound, which is shaped, as ever, by the sensitive touch of the performer: "The tone generation in these instruments is electric, but the playing is artistic, as with every other instrument."[66] Mager's former microtonal colleague, the composer Richard Stein, drew a historical parallel, reminding readers that instrumental music, too, was once seen as a "mechanical, soulless imitation of vocal music." Just as instrumental music had overcome listeners' prejudices, so too would electric music eventually prevail on account of its expanded technical capacities.[67]

One of Mager's most outspoken advocates, the journalist Herbert Weiskopf elaborated on this theme, arguing that electric instruments were not only superior to the mechanical devices with which they were often unfairly grouped, they were in fact more responsive to their players' touch than familiar instruments such as the piano:

> The new manner of tone generation through cathode tubes makes the material so pliable that the difficulties that confronted music making in the form of mechanical obstacles to be overcome have been reduced to a fraction of what they are in other instruments. [. . .] Many musicians fear with every improvement of the instrument through mechanical means an encroachment upon inner musical life. This is by no means the case, however dangerous the word *electricity* may sound to artists. One will readily perceive that this most sensitive of all elements can be influenced through the senses far more easily than the complicated mechanism of a piano. [. . .] Next to the Spherophone,

FIGURE 11. Jörg Mager and an assistant in the laboratory around the time of the Musik im Leben der Völker international exhibition in Frankfurt. Source: "Eine neue Epoche der Musikgeschichte?" *Das neue Frankfurt* 6 (1927): 145.

only singing, the primal ground of all music and its elementary form, would be justified in its existence.[68]

Just as Ernst Toch had compared the aesthetic sovereignty of mechanical music to the sublime autonomy of the singing voice, Weiskopf ventured a counterintuitive convergence of high tech and no tech. Even skeptically inclined critics noted Mager's effort to "let the machine become a higher organism" and "deliver music from the thralldom of instruments."[69] Mager's inventions, though employing the latest technological innovations, promised to transcend materiality and mediation, achieving a directness to rival the inborn ur-instrument of the human voice: paradoxically, sound technology attains perfection in the moment of its disappearance.

TOWARD *KLANGFARBENMUSIK*

Just as he was starting to make a name for himself in German musical circles, Mager set a new technological course for the development of his instruments. In the late 1920s, his focus gradually turned from the microtonal manipulation of the pitch spectrum to the exploration of timbre through electric tone generation. Mager had been grappling for some time with the possibility of using electricity to create new tone colors.

In his 1924 "Radio Prophecy," he noted that "the Spherophone will be able not only to reproduce the *primary timbres* of our familiar instruments but will also enable the construction of *entirely new, uniquely beautiful* tone colors."[70] At the end of *A New Epoch of Music through Radio*, written in the same year, Mager speculated that "perhaps the variation of timbre will one day play an even greater role in music than the variation of pitch; perhaps the coming epoch will be characterized not only by the finer division of the octave but also through more perfect melody of timbres."[71] And finally, in 1926 he explicitly signalled his new orientation when he declared, "Though there are varying opinions on the significance of variegated octave division, there is unanimity in the evaluation of a Spherophone with the most versatile *timbral potential*. And here great prospects beckon."[72]

The quest for the compositional control of timbre links Mager's work not only to the experimental instrument building and idealist musical metaphysics of the nineteenth century but also to the creative approaches to orchestration of composers such as Wagner, Debussy, and Richard Strauss. Although traditional instruments had advanced in many respects to allow the performer an ever greater command of pitch (for example, valves on brass instruments and equal temperament on keyboards) and volume (the steel-frame grand piano), the timbre of a given instrument was essentially hardwired and thus largely closed off to compositional design and performative gesture. For Mager, the manipulation of timbre thus represented the final frontier of instrument building, a problem to which electric tone generation offered the ideal solution.

One of the earliest and most influential attempts to subject tone color to techno-scientific discipline was found in Hermann von Helmholtz's 1863 treatise *On the Sensations of Tone*. In order to demonstrate how timbre could be artificially generated and controlled, Helmholtz built an apparatus consisting of a set of tuning forks tuned to the harmonic spectrum of a low B-flat. Each fork was placed between the two poles of an electromagnet and in front of a tube-shaped resonator that amplified its otherwise quiet tone. When the electromagnets were charged, the tuning forks were set into continuous vibration, their relative volume adjusted by partially covering the cavity of the appropriate resonator. Helmholtz described how he could use this device to construct artificial timbres through the carefully calibrated superimposition of individual sine tones.[73] His primitive additive synthesizer was designed to facilitate the scientific understanding of timbre through the experimental reconstruction of the vowel sounds of human (specifically, German) speech, but its method of tone production could also be employed to generate unique, unheard-of timbres. By isolating timbre as a distinct aspect of sound, Helmholtz demonstrated that tone color was scientifically manipulable, as opposed to God-given and inalterable.

The musical implications of Helmholtz's timbral experiments were recognized even before the turn of the century. An anonymous article published in the *Journal of Instrument Building (Zeitschrift für Instrumentenbau)*, signed only "Technician," explained in 1887:

> To the means music provides for the expression of artistic feeling [i.e., melody, harmony, rhythm, and dynamics], there belongs yet another, which, if it can be freely mastered, will become the foremost: sound *[Klang]*. Indeed, we already know the magic of timbre, which is to music what color and complexion is to painting. But how poor are our current means of calling forth sound in its infinite richness—and why? Because our technical means are insufficient. We know from Helmholtz how sound comes into being, that it owes its existence to the simultaneous sounding of many tones, and we can conclude from this that the timbral element must surpass by far the other elements in terms of richness and inexhaustibility. But as long as we are forced to make use only of the few sounds that we can incidentally create, instead of freely combining tones of any number into sounds, this treasure remains closed to us. [. . .] For we are able to change the mechanical relationships that determine the emergence of tones and overtones only to a limited extent, and not in the rapid alteration that would be demanded by the art of sound; and as long as we lack the means to create tones of any number and volume, the beauties of sound will remain unattainable. The possibility of such a free mastery of tone generation seems to rest upon the use of electricity in the creation of tones, and when we perceive in the example of the telephone how electricity makes possible the reproduction of so many sonic variables, our hope for the free mastery of sound must naturally affix itself to electricity. [. . .] The free generation of sound appears enabled by electricity, and with the application of electricity in music this art will enter into an entirely new phase of development.[74]

While the technical possibility of electrically generated tone-colors was known in the late nineteenth century, the aesthetic motivation for such a technique would emerge a bit later. In a speculative passage at the end of his 1911 *Theory of Harmony*, Schoenberg had suggested the possibility of creating successions of tone colors that possessed the same kind of musical logic that connected the pitches of a melody—a prospect he gave the name of *Klangfarbenmelodie* (tone-color melody). Such a technique, Schoenberg suggested, though perhaps merely a "futuristic fantasy," would prove capable of "heightening in an unprecedented manner the sensory, intellectual, and spiritual pleasures offered by art" and would "bring us closer to the illusory stuff of our dreams."[75] Schoenberg's idea followed logically from the well-established acoustic principle that timbre is largely a product of the frequency relations projected in the overtone spectrum of a given tone. Accordingly, Mager's shift in focus was not as radical a reorientation as it might first appear: from the subtle relations of pitch between tones, it was an intuitive transition to the microcosmic world of frequency ratios within a single musical sound—the "alchemy of tone" that creates what is perceived as timbre. The idea of the spectrum was simply extended from pitch to timbre, from tuning to tone color. This implication, too, lurked in Schoenberg's radical reinterpretation of the relationship between pitch and timbre: challenging the conventional notion that these were two independent parameters of musical sound, he suggested that tone color was the primary factor, of which pitch was simply "timbre measured in one direction."[76] Mager quoted this passage at length in *A New Epoch of Music through Radio.*

For Schoenberg, Klangfarbenmelodie had nothing to do with creating new timbres; rather, it was essentially a novel approach to orchestration.[77] In adopting the concept, which he gave the more general name *Klangfarbenmusik,* Mager thus joined two distinct ideas: the creation of original tone colors by means of electric tone generation and the manipulation of these timbres guided by an as yet inchoate compositional discipline. In light of such prospects, the inventor concluded, "Whoever has occupied himself even a little with electric sounds will be forced to the conclusion: there are yet things in music of which our musical book learning cannot dream."[78]

In his report from Donaueschingen, Herbert Weiskopf had portrayed the Spherophone as an advance on Helmholtz's tuning-fork synthesizer, arguing that while that device was of "merely physical significance," Mager's instrument represented a genuine solution to the problem of timbre composition.[79] Although this contrast is telling for the technological lineage it established, it was inaccurate in a technical sense: Mager's approach to shaping electric sound was entirely different from Helmholtz's.[80] Guided more by intuition and experiment than by scientific rigor, he used two distinct (but compatible) methods of controlling timbre on an empirical basis. The first technique was to affix plates of various shapes, sizes, and materials to loudspeaker drivers to obtain new tone colors. The resonant frequencies of these objects interacted with the harmonic spectrum of the electrically generated tones to create novel and unpredictable timbral effects. An account from the early 1930s describes the scene in Mager's electroacoustic studio:

> Instead of organ pipes, there is an odd collection of objects assembled behind a screen: large sheets of iron hanging from frames, square panes of glass, and wooden panels of the most varied provenance. These are the loudspeakers. [. . .] Earlier, Mager had used typical over-the-counter speakers. But with his increasing knowledge, he began to gather membranes of astoundingly varied sonic character, sought explicitly for his purposes. Glass sounds different than wood, hanging sheet metal different than an electrically excited gong.[81]

Mager's assistant Oskar Vierling reported that the inventor would even fasten loudspeaker drivers directly to the bodies of musical instruments such as violins in order to create an electric hybrid of the instrument's tone.[82] Mager explained his use of metal plates as resonators in a 1932 patent: the plates are shaped so as to resonate not only to the fundamental tone but also to the harmonics above that tone. This creates a subtle echo—what we might now call "reverb"—after the sound from the loudspeaker subsides, which confers upon the tone (in Mager's words) a "peculiar spatial effect."[83]

The second means of controlling timbre was to apply electric filters to sculpt a harmonically rich sound by blocking out frequencies above or below a designated level. This technique was pioneered by the engineer Karl Willy Wagner (1883–1953), whom Mager encountered at the Telegrafen-technischen Reichsamt (Reich Office for Telegraph Technology), where Wagner was president from 1923 to 1927. Wagner's experiments with electric filters represent some of the earliest applications of what would later be known as subtractive synthesis. He developed two kinds of filters, which attenuated frequencies above and below a designated cutoff point. Wagner noticed that if a low-pass filter is applied to a violin tone, the sound loses its characteristic timbre and resembles that of a flute. With high-pass filters, on the other hand, one can create timbres in which the lower partials are attenuated or cut out altogether. Because periodic tones typically have a greater accumulation of energy (volume) at the lower end of the frequency spectrum, a high-pass filter allows for the creation of timbres whose structure is in direct contradiction to the natural acoustic tendency of higher overtones to decrease in volume.

Sounding a familiar theme, Wagner was struck by the unearthly timbres that resulted from his electroacoustic manipulations: he noted the "odd musical charm" of sounds processed by the high-pass filter and remarked that "a melody played with these tones sounds peculiar, as if it came down to us from distant spheres."[84] For Wagner, as for many other listeners, electrically generated sounds evoked not technological images of spinning cogwheels or atomic particles but rather scenes of distant places, whether an exoticized Far East or other dimensions of space. Even those outside the charmed circle of electric music enthusiasts were susceptible to such reactions: in a 1927 article published in the generally conservative *Zeitschrift für Musik,* the author gushed over the instrument's "sound-clusters of immediately mystical effect" and declared that "with Mager's invention, the ancient oriental dream of a *music of the spheres* has become a reality, for entry to the tonal possibilities of the cosmos now stands open."[85] (The otherwordly resonances of electric sound can be traced at least back to Busoni, who called Cahill's Telharmonium a "transcendental tone generator"— when it is played, "the room is magically filled with sound, a scientifically perfect, never malfunctioning sound, invisible, effortless, and unremitting."[86])

While most of Mager's timbral experimentation involved modifying the harmonic spectra of stable periodic tones, he also delved into the domain of unpitched sounds and imitative effects. In one of his earliest patents, filed in 1925, Mager stated that the electrical components of the Spherophone could be configured to produce the "imitation of elementary sounds," such as birdsong, wind, and the splashing of water.[87] He claimed that the noises and sound effects created by his instruments were much sought after by producers of radio, film, and theater, and a reviewer likewise noted the instrument's aptitude for background noises *(Geräuschkulisse)* such as the clatter of dishes, footsteps, and engine and machine sounds, as well as its capacity for "comic noise symbolism," exemplified by vocal expressions such as yawns and snores.[88]

But Mager's use of noises wasn't limited to such straightforwardly mimetic effects. Hidden away in his later patents are techniques that straddle the boundary between the imitative reproduction of familiar sounds and sonic experimentation of a more speculative nature. In one of his patents from this period, Mager describes how tone color could be periodically altered by the filtration of high or low frequencies, creating an "entirely novel" pulsating contrast between bright and dark or sharp and dull. This procedure of enlivening timbre through controlled periodic motion helps clarify Mager's otherwise mystifying references to "timbre trills" and "timbre vibrato." What Mager meant by these terms is not entirely clear, but it seems likely that these involved the modulation of the filter cutoff frequency by a sine or square wave, in analogy to the functioning of a low-frequency oscillator (LFO) in later analog synthesizers.[89]

An even more radical technique is found in a 1932 patent in which Mager described an "apparatus for the generation not of music but of noise." In this configuration—which, like many of the innovations described in Mager's patents, was apparently never developed beyond an experimental stage—several electrically generated tones are modulated by an inaudible low-frequency oscillation. Because of the nonlinear nature of human hearing, adjusting the frequency of the modulating tone changes the frequencies of the four tones *and* their proportional relations to each other; for example, an increase of 200 hertz applied to all four tones will result in a different perceived intervallic shift for each. Mager describes a scenario in which four low tones in a very narrow frequency range create the sensation of rolling or rumbling through the beating of their vibrations. As the modulating frequency is increased, the sound changes from a rattling to a hissing. If the modulated tones lie in the middle range, the sense of definite pitch is lost; if they are very high in pitch, a slight alteration of the modulating tone creates a chirping sound, and a wider variation creates a sound like that of the howling of the wind. In his patent application for this technique, Mager declared, "Here lies the transition from sound to noise."[90] Such experiments went beyond the domain of Klangfarbenmusik to what Mager explicitly called "noise music" (*Geräuschmusik*), a phenomenon that he may have been the only one to hear.[91]

MAGER'S MAGIC ORGAN

At the time of Mager's 1927 demonstration in Frankfurt, his instrument was in a state of flux. In the exhibition's Spherophone Room, the inventor showed off no fewer than three distinct models: a Melody Type operated by a handle (corresponding to the original design), a Chord Type consisting of a panel with an array of buttons that sounded various harmonic intervals, and a Tone-Color Type, called the Kaleidophone, devoted to the manipulation of timbre and played from a conventional musical keyboard.[92] Mager's diverse musical interests had been parceled out into three distinct, highly specialized instruments. But of this trio, all but the last would soon be discarded: Mager's emerging focus on the electroacoustic manipulation of timbre—not to mention the difficulty of developing three instruments at once—led him to concentrate his attention on the new keyboard-operated model.

The outward form of the new instrument was strikingly conventional. While Mager's previous constructions could be mistaken for laboratory apparatus, the new model resembled the console of a pipe organ, with two keyboard manuals, a pedal board, and a bank of switches and knobs to control the tone color. Unlike the heterodyne-based beat-frequency oscillator of his earlier instrument, this new device generated audible tones through the feedback method earlier explored by radio engineers such as Armstrong and de Forest. Mager eventually dropped the name Kaleidophone in favor of *Klaviatur-Sphärophon* (Keyboard Spherophone), thus creating a nominal link with earlier models, in spite of the new design. The adoption of a conventional keyboard allowed him to redirect the player's attention from the instrument's interface to the shaping of electroacoustic tone color. This keyboard-centered design—which inspired talk of an "electric organ" in the press—would remain the basis of Mager's instruments from this time forward.

In spite of the instrument's new look, Mager had not abandoned his earlier microtonal ideals; rather, he had discovered a way of reconciling the production of microtones with the conventional keyboard interface.[93] This was a device he called the musical pantograph *(musikalischer Storchschnabel)*, a name borrowed from the v-shaped drafting device that connects a handheld pen to a second writing apparatus, allowing drawings to be duplicated automatically as the second pen copies the motions of the first. By adjusting the angle of the mechanical connection, the duplicated drawing can be made larger or smaller than the original. Analogously, the musical pantograph adjusted the capacitance of the sound-generating circuit so as to alter the musical intervals sounded by the instrument's keyboard. For example, if the interval of a tritone were "stretched" to span from one C to the next C above it, each adjacent key would sound a quartertone interval, instead of the usual semitone. Thus, the familiar gestures of keyboard technique could be mapped onto a new, electrically altered pitch space. The interval spanned by an octave on the keyboard could be made as small as a major second, so that each successive step on the keyboard represented an interval of a twelfth tone, resulting in a scale with 72 distinct pitches in each octave. In spite of the potentially radical compositional implications of this device, it was still a "fixed-tone" tuning, in contrast to the earlier *Kurbelsphärophon* and the Theremin. Mager had not given up on microtonality, but he had abandoned the free-floating glissando characteristic of the first generation of electric instruments.

Mager presented his new instrument in Darmstadt on October 6, 1928, at the yearly convention of the Reich Association of German

NOTENBEISPIELE
zu dem Aufsatz: NEUE ELEMENTE DER MUSIKERZEUGUNG
von Hans Kuznitzky in MELOS VI/4 (Aprilheft).

Notenſchrift für 72-Teilung der Oktave

Jörg Mager

Beiſpiel für „Nacheinander" von Viertel- und Halbtönen

FIGURE 12. Jörg Mager's notation system for the division of the octave into seventy-two equal intervals. Source: Hans Kuznitzky, "Neue Elemente der Musikerzeugung," *Melos* 6, no. 4 (1927): 230.

Musicians and Music Teachers (Reichsverband deutscher Tonkünstler und Musiklehrer), one of the oldest and largest professional organizations for musicians in Germany. He followed his "Demonstration of Electric Music" with a plea to the assembled musicians and professors, in which he depicted the dismal conditions of his makeshift studio in Berlin and stressed his need for more favorable working conditions. The fate of electric music, Mager declared, hinged on the emergence of patrons to support its development. His appeal apparently found a sympathetic audience: just months after his demonstration, he received an unprecedented offer of institutional backing. In order to further Mager's research, but also "to create for German genius, German perseverance, and German selflessness the role in the world that they deserve," a cadre of influential residents of Darmstadt joined forces to found the Society for Electroacoustic Music (Gesellschaft für elektro-akustische Musik) in January 1929.[94] Mager signed a three-year contract that required him to take up residence in the city and stressed the "industrial exploitation" of his inventions but otherwise accorded him broad creative liberties.[95] With the support of the Society, Mager was able for the first time to focus his energies exclusively on the development of his instruments. While he had previously cobbled together a living from intermittent school-teaching duties and stipends from a patchwork of government agencies, he was now guaranteed a generous yearly income. In addition, Mager was provided with an able staff of assistants and allowed to live and work in the Prinz-Emil-Schlößchen, a stately rococo manor constructed in the late eighteenth century. Here Mager would set up his "Electro-Music Laboratory," one of the first of its kind in the world.[96]

On August 25, 1930, Mager presented the first fruits of this new partnership to an audience of invited guests in Darmstadt. The latest model of his instrument was in essence an expanded version of the earlier Keyboard Spherophone, now equipped with three manuals and a pedal board for a total of four voices. Mager rechristened the instrument the *Partiturophon,* from the German *Partitur,* meaning "musical score": just as a score contained multiple parts, the instrument could play several independent lines, each with its own distinctive timbre. An account of Mager's demonstration—which featured arrangements of works by Bach, Beethoven, Wagner, and Mendelssohn—noted on the instrument's "overpowering" and "compelling" effect, which transported listeners to a "new, unsuspected, almost supernatural musical realm."[97] Among the audience members who witnessed the unveiling of the Partiturophone was the prominent conductor and champion of

FIGURE 13. Jörg Mager playing the three-manual Partiturophon, circa 1930. Note how his left hand is fingering keys on both the upper and the middle manual: this technique was required for polyphonic playing, as each manual could sound only one tone at a time. Source: Andy Mackay, *Electronic Music* (Minneapolis: Control Data Publishing, 1981), 19.

modern music Hermann Scherchen, who penned an extensive report on Mager's new instrument. Although noting shortcomings such as the lack of convincing brass and string timbres and a certain tonal monotony throughout its various registers, Scherchen offered a vigorous endorsement of the latest model. The instrument was far more welcoming than earlier versions: it could plug into any domestic electrical socket, and its keyboard interface would be familiar to most musicians. He also marveled at the Partiturophone's microtonal possibilities, its wide dynamic range, and its rich spectrum of "electro-tone timbres." In particular, Scherchen called attention to the instrument's potential for Klangfarbenmusik through the juxtaposition of four different tone colors, each of which can be varied continuously during the course of a passage. He declared Mager's instrument "entirely ready for artistic musical purposes."[98] Other press accounts concurred, judging the Partiturophon fit for mass production.[99]

The introduction of the Partiturophon in Darmstadt marked Mager's arrival as a musical celebrity. He was celebrated in the press as an eccentric genius and creator of a "magic organ." He received illustrious visitors in his Darmstadt laboratory, including the Grand Duke Ernst Ludwig of Hessen, who presented the inventor with a valuable silver plate to use as a loudspeaker membrane.[100] Mager's ascent into the heights of German musical culture was marked by two remarkable commissions in the early 1930s. First, he was asked by Winifred Wagner (Richard Wagner's daughter-in-law) to provide the sound of the "Grail bells" for the 1931 Bayreuth production of Wagner's last opera, *Parsifal*. The score calls for four low notes, which were traditionally played on huge bells or other metallophones. Because these couldn't fit in the orchestra pit, the ringing of the bells was typically coordinated by a team of performers using an elaborate system of cues. Mager's use of electrically excited metal plates, controlled from a keyboard by a single player, won widespread approval and sparked the interest of such luminaries as Arturo Toscanini and Oswald Spengler.[101] The following year, Mager was invited to provide electric music and sound effects for performances of Goethe's *Faust* in Frankfurt and Darmstadt as part of the nationwide festivities marking the centenary of the poet's death. As he describes it, Mager's musical contribution was not simply a naturalistic accompaniment to onstage action; instead, he sought to match the magical tenor of the play with the otherworldly sounds of his instrument: "In the prologue the sun intones in the old way with an ethereal, oscillating vibrato. The growling of the poodle is accompanied by microtones. For Walpurgis Night there is ghostly, demonic, eccentric music. The howling of the long-tailed monkey is created by powerfully vibrating metal membranes."[102]

At the start of the 1930s, Mager's career had reached a plateau hardly imaginable a few years earlier. But while his role as pioneer of electric music had been largely uncontested since his public debut in 1926, he soon found himself in the middle of a crowded field. Toward the end of the 1920s, a wave of new electric instruments began to appear not only in Germany but also in the United States, France, and the Soviet Union. Mager's most formidable domestic challenger would be the Trautonium of Friedrich Trautwein, which was unveiled just months before Mager's Partiturophone. The emergence of the Trautonium and the development of Mager's instruments during the 1930s will be examined in chapter 5.

Perhaps even more troubling than the growing field of competitors, however, was the absence of original compositions for the new instruments. Early in his career, Mager had acknowledged the necessity of music as a proof of concept: "How often have I already heard, 'Simply play something beautiful, [and] that would convince us more than pretty words and the most seductive *theory* of your music of the future!'"[103] But four years after the public debut of the Spherophone, Mager's instruments still lacked even the rudiments of an original repertoire. Early expressions of interest from composers such as Hindemith and Hába had come to nothing, and no others had stepped up in their place. In lieu of idiomatic original works, Mager presented a kind of electric music variety show: surviving accounts of his demonstrations give the impression of freewheeling, quasi-improvisatory displays of the instruments' technical capabilities, buttressed by set-piece arrangements of canonic classical works. (Beethoven's *Moonlight Sonata* seems to have been a favorite.)

The discrepancy between electric music's lofty promises and its modest results was widely recognized by both advocates and detractors. For the time being, however, awareness of this problem did little to dampen the zeal of the movement's supporters. Remarkably, even without original compositions, Mager was able to convince composers, journalists, and—most importantly—funders of his instruments' potential. Untroubled by questions of audience or repertoire, Mager focused his attention on his inventions, seemingly led by the assumption that practicalities would be resolved of their own accord once the instruments were perfected.

4

"Sonic Handwriting"

Media Instruments and Musical Inscription

Every sounding object employed by the composer is a musical instrument.[1]

—Hector Berlioz

By the end of the 1920s, two waves of technological activity had swept across the musical culture of the Weimar Republic. First, automatic instruments such as the Welte-Mignon mechanical piano offered composers a means of transmitting their work directly to a machine, bypassing the variability and physiological limitations of human performers. Second, electrophonic instruments such as Jörg Mager's Spherophone expanded the possibilities of musical expression through new, ultrasensitive playing interfaces and sound circuitry that enabled the discovery of hitherto unknown sonic phenomena. For the champions of the quest for new instruments, it was a small and self-evident step to seek the unification of these two ideals—an instrument that combined the unbounded potential of electric tone generation with the absolute authorial control of mechanical inscription. The technological basis for this "universal instrument" was to be found in an unexpected place: the sound recording media that had become all but ubiquitous in the first quarter of the twentieth century.

In the fall of 1926, a special issue of the modernist music journal *Musikblätter des Anbruch* appeared, bearing the title "Musik und Maschine." Alongside reports of the festival in Donaueschingen that featured original compositions for the Welte-Mignon mechanical piano, Hindemith and Schlemmer's *Triadic Ballet,* and Jörg Mager's demonstration of his Spherophone, there was a short article, "The Talking Film," under the byline of Dr. Guido Bagier, artistic director of the sound-film department of UFA, the premier film studio in Weimar Republic Germany.[2] Bagier's text introduced composers to the new technology of optical sound film, which allowed acoustic phenomena to be recorded on a tiny strip of film running parallel to the cinematic frames. Although the title of Bagier's article signalled that the primary appeal of sound film lay in the synchronization of sound and image in motion pictures, he touched on other possibilities that would endear the technology to modernist composers in search of new instruments. "In a word, we will have to abandon the concept of music based in *reality* and its *imitation* through the machine," Bagier wrote. "Rather, the machine will produce its *own* acoustic content in accordance with its nature."[3] Recording devices, Bagier realized, do not capture sounds themselves but only their traces, the grooves or patterns inscribed in the material medium. If these traces could be freely manipulated or even made by hand, a powerful new form of notation (and thus composing) could be born.

Inspired by this vision, a motley assortment of composers, musicians, artists, and intellectuals sought to refunction recording media as instruments for creative experimentation. Challenging the conventional relationship between musical production (composing) and reproduction (recording), they treated media not as a means of capturing performances but rather as a novel instrument capable of uniquely technogenic effects. The exploration of these "media instruments" underwent two technological iterations: at first, these efforts were focused on the gramophone record, and then from the late 1920s onward, composers turned to the new technology of optical sound film. The instrumentalization of recording media further encompassed two distinct compositional techniques—two ways of using the graphical representation of sound as musical material. In the first approach, recordings of natural and human noises, speech, and musical tones were manipulated and rearranged in a manner inspired by contemporary cinematic technique. In the second approach, the conventional recording function was bypassed altogether in favor of direct inscription onto the medium, creating entirely new sonic phenomena. In both cases, the purpose was not to capture a realistic approximation of an actual performance event but rather to construct a deliberately artificial work conceived on the basis of the technological medium and its formative potential.

Like automatic instruments such as the player piano, media instruments provided the composer with a means of notating music in a graphical form that could be realized precisely and repeatedly without human intervention. Writing in 1932, the critic Gerhard Lindner dubbed the new phenomenon "graphomusic" and compared composition for sound film to earlier experimental efforts with the player piano, arguing that sound film was "in principle nothing new, since it stands firmly in the intellectual lineage of the attempts of Hindemith and Toch to compose directly on the paper rolls of mechanical instruments." The aesthetic debates about mechanical music were, according to Lindner, in no need of revisiting:

> It is immediately clear that in the graphical production of tones there is no compulsion to imitate the traditional instruments. Further, one is not dependent on the potential of instruments (which are generally limited with regard to range), nor—most importantly—on the physiological capabilities of the instrumentalist. Perhaps this can be fully appreciated only by the *composer*, who need no longer be impaired by any attachment to old instruments or any consideration of physiological hindrances. It thus appears in all likelihood that sound film will someday become the most perfect musical instrument.[4]

At the same time, champions of these new instruments also echoed the rhetoric of electric music. In the same essay, Lindner noted that graphomusic offers not only unsurpassed precision but also the prospect of "new kinds of timbre" and "absolute mobility in tonal space." Like Mager's instruments, media instruments promised to transcend the pitch and timbre limitations of the nineteenth-century instrumentarium and furnish an expanded sonic palette that encompassed not only all manner of tones but also unheard synthetic timbres and noises previously considered unmusical. Media instruments seemed to offer the best of both worlds: the organic and the mechanical, fantasy and exactitude.[5] More than previous examples, however, the devices considered in this chapter resisted assimilation into familiar concepts of what an instrument is. Whatever their mysterious inner workings, both the player piano and electrophones at least bore outward resemblances to familiar instruments; recording media, however, had no such foothold in conventional models of instrumentality. Though based on the same underlying principles of musical inscription and electric tone generation, these devices lacked the visual and tangible characteristics of traditional musical tools. But the instrumental paradigm they represented—the encoding and manipulation of musical information in a symbolic language that could be "read" and reproduced only by machines—was as promising for some as it was disturbing for others. Indeed, if media instruments were among the most speculative and experimental manifestations of Weimar Republic sound technology, they were also arguably the most prescient of future developments.

PAINTING SOUND

To a greater degree than the devices surveyed in the preceding chapters, media instruments were products of the heady cross-pollination between the arts in 1920s Europe. Tracing their origins requires a historical excursus to the beginning of the decade. In June of 1921, the Italian futurist musician Luigi Russolo gave a series of performances in the Théâtre des Champs-Élysées in Paris. Amid attempts at disruption by Dada artists, Russolo presented a number of works composed for his specially built *intonarumori*, or noise instruments, with which he had been touring Europe since the publication of his manifesto *The Art of Noises* in 1913.[6] In the audience at one Russolo's Paris concerts was Piet Mondrian, a Dutch painter who had settled in the French capital in 1919. For several years, Mondrian had been developing the theory and practice of what he called "neoplasticism" *(Nieuwe Beelding)*, a rigorously geometrical approach to painting that was conceived as a means of achieving an extraindividual, universal kind of artistic expression. Mondrian pursued this ideal through a reduction of visual material to right angle lines and solid fields of color: in his mature style, his paintings consisted simply of black lines dividing the canvas into rectangles of various sizes, which were filled in with one of the three primary colors (red, yellow, and blue) or one of the three "noncolors" (white, black, and gray).

A few months after hearing Russolo's intonarumori, Mondrian turned his thoughts to music in an essay published in the Dutch art journal *De Stijl*.[7] Here Mondrian extended his neoplastic aesthetic on the basis of a sound-color correspondence, conceiving of music as an essentially *plastic* art: "Tone like color is free of volume," he wrote. "Thus music can immediately follow the lead of painting."[8] According to Mondrian, the fundamental duality of neoplastic music is the opposition of "tones" and "nontones" (or "determinate noises"), corresponding to the use of color and noncolor in painting.[9] Mondrian proposed dividing tones and nontones into three types, corresponding to the three primary colors and the three "noncolors." These tones and nontones are not timbres in the conventional sense but rather fully determinate sonic events, invariably fixed in duration, volume, and presumably, pitch.

The influence of Russolo's intonarumori on Mondrian's musical imaginings lay not in the instruments' noisy, abrasive timbres but in a more general idea of the technological control of sound. "If we are *to abstract* sound," he mused, "the instruments must first produce sounds *as constant as possible in wavelength and number of vibrations*. Then they must be so constructed that *all vibration will stop when the sound is suddenly broken off.*"[10] Mondrian rejected the aesthetics of subjective emotion and sought instead to express depersonalized, "universal" artistic values. Accordingly, pauses or rests have no place in neoplastic music, for silence constitutes "a void that is immediately filled by the individuality of the listener."[11] Likewise, he opposed the "rounded" timbres of traditional instruments to the "determinate, planar, and pure tones" of neoplastic music.[12] For Mondrian, the organic, natural, and "morphoplastic" voice was the expression of the "individual" as opposed to the universal. Conventional instruments, insofar as they were modeled on the voice, belonged to the same domain.[13] Organic sounds appeal to people as individuals, while rhythmic, material-mechanical sounds address them on the level of pure form. Mondrian foresaw a time when "man will no longer make use of the formal means of the past nor the human voice organ":

> Tones and noises that come from inanimate material will then be called for. The noise of a machine (as a timbre) will be more appealing to him than the songs of birds or men. This song will always touch him only as an individual, more or less according to the manner of its performance, while machine-generated, purely material rhythm exerts less of an effect on the individual. The sound of a pile driver (as a timbre) will be more familiar to him than the singing of psalms. Thus will the new man, through the force of things, arrive at the invention of truly "new" instruments. And this is absolutely necessary, because only new instruments will meet the demands of pure art.[14]

For Mondrian, only mechanical sound production could free music from the individualistic, "organic" mode of expression and allow it to attain universality. "*Mechanical intervention* will prove necessary," he declared, "for the human touch always involves the individual to some degree and prevents the *perfect determination of sound.*"[15] Years before H. H. Stuckenschmidt's first polemics on behalf of mechanical music, Mondrian had envisioned a radical new instrumental modality based on the automatic production of sound, which seemed to him the only means of achieving the sufficient degree of control for his rigidly geometrical conception of music. But Mondrian went no further in specifying the actual instruments that might make neoplastic music a reality.

He dismissed the futurists' intonarumori as too imitative and imprecise, without proposing an alternative of his own. "I am not able to work out my neoplastic music in full, as the instruments are not yet available," Mondrian wrote, striking a prophetic tone, "but I will set out the course it will take."[16]

However, Mondrian's imagined music prove influential. In July 1923, an article entitled "Neoplasticism in Music: Possibilities of the Gramophone" appeared in the German art journal *Der Sturm*.[17] The author was László Moholy-Nagy, a Hungarian artist who had immigrated to Berlin in 1920. A pioneer in experimental approaches to art informed by science and engineering, he had first written about technological extensions of music in an essay entitled "Production-Reproduction" published in *De Stijl* in July of 1922.[18] In this article he proposed using recording technologies in unconventional ways to bypass their merely "reproductive" function and turn them into experimental instruments. Instead of simply capturing reality, photographic film and gramophone records could be inscribed upon directly, thus creating new perceptual phenomena unique to the medium. Accordingly, Moholy-Nagy drew a distinction between "productive" and "reproductive" uses of technology: the latter simply duplicates what already exists, while the former creates aesthetic configurations without analogues in nature.

Like Mondrian and many other artists of the time, Moholy-Nagy sought new forms of production that bypassed the artist's personality in order to attain a more "objective" conceptual purity. In 1922, for example, he ordered five paintings in porcelain enamel on steel from a sign factory in Berlin. With a sheet of graph paper and the factory's color chart in front of him, Moholy-Nagy dictated the design of each painting to a worker over the telephone, thus demonstrating that the objective formal conception of the work, which could be conveyed at a distance, was more important than the "individual touch" of the artist's hand.[19] In these "telephone pictures," Moholy-Nagy severed the conception of the work from its execution, subordinating the artist's personality as expressed in his brushstrokes to the universal and anonymous formal dimensions of the work.

His article on neoplasticism in music was an elaboration of the ideas presented in Mondrian's essays, which had been published earlier that year in a German translation. Taking a typically interartistic perspective, Moholy-Nagy focused on three different recording media: the gramophone, the photograph, and cinematic film. In each case, he distinguished between conventional applications of the technology to record and reproduce, and unorthodox uses that allow for the creation of new artistic forms. He invoked the abstract visual projections of artists such as Walter Ruttmann, Thomas Wilfred, Viking Eggeling, and Hans Richter as models for nonmimetic approaches to the art of moving images. Likewise, Moholy-Nagy suggested, photographic film could be used in a "productive" way, "to receive and record various light phenomena which *we ourselves* will have *formed* by means of mirror or lens devices."[20] Such techniques had recently been employed by the American Man Ray, the German Christian Schad, and by Moholy-Nagy himself.

Moholy-Nagy's proposal for the productive use of the gramophone was a logical extension of these ideas to music. Instead of recording sound with microphones, he suggested, artists could make inscriptions directly onto the wax disc by hand. In this manner, they could "produce sound effects which would signify—without new instruments and without an orchestra—a fundamental innovation in sound production (of new, hitherto unknown sounds and tonal relations) both in composition and in musical performance."[21] Going further, Moholy-Nagy called for a methodical study of the correlations between inscriptions and their sonic effects in order to establish a "scratch-writing alphabet" encompassing all possible phenomena of sound, and so to create the "universal instrument" that would render all previous instruments superfluous.[22] he thus refined Mondrian's intimation of a fully automated form of musical production into the notion of direct inscription via media instruments. Over the course of the next decade, artists would pursue this technological gambit in two media: first, as already suggested by Moholy-Nagy, via the gramophone record, which in the early 1920s was the most advanced and widespread medium for sound recording; and at the end of the decade, in the new format of optical sound film, which offered a more transparent and malleable means of capturing, editing, and manipulating recorded sound.

GRAMOPHONE MUSIC

Moholy-Nagy's idea of using the gramophone as an experimental instrument was one of the formative influences on H.H. Stuckenschmidt's vision of "mechanical music," explored in chapter 2. In fact, Stuckenschmidt's eventual turn to the player piano represented something of an aesthetic compromise: compared with the relatively narrow sonic spectrum of the piano, the gramophone provided the composer with a virtually infinite tonal range and much finer pitch differentiation. In 1925, Stuckenschmidt made this assessment:

> The authentic gramophone has the great advantage over the mechanical piano, that it brings together all imaginable tone colors in an utterly small and simple apparatus. It will possess simply incalculable stimulations for the composer of the future. The number of tone colors is infinite. Every instrumental tone can be given whatever range. The differentiation of pitch is infinite. Quarter and eighth tones can be played with mathematical purity. The variety of sounds will leave the old orchestra in the dust.[23]

However, Stuckenschmidt acknowledged the technical challenges associated with such an approach. Above all, inscrutability of the gramophone grooves constituted a "seemingly insurmountable obstacle." In this respect, the notation of the piano roll was clearly superior, as it offered a transparent relationship between notation and acoustic result.[24] The fate of media instruments would hinge in large part on this question of what could be called *notational transparency*—the ability to establish an absolute and unambiguous relationship between the composer's "score" (reinterpreted as the recording medium) and the capabilities of the "performer" (reinterpreted as the reproducing apparatus). The unclear relationship between composers' inscriptions and the sounds they call forth would haunt all efforts to refunction recording devices as "universal instruments."

This problem had been highlighted during the mechanical music kerfuffle of the mid-1920s, when one of Stuckenschmidt's most vociferous critics, Heinz Pringsheim, questioned whether composers could attain any degree of artistic control over the gramophone disc. A gramophone recording, after all, contains the sum of all simultaneously sounding musical phenomena: the individual voices of the orchestra or ensemble are amalgamated into a single groove on the record. How could the composer begin to map the system of correspondences between these inscriptions and the sounds that they index? Pringsheim juxtaposed conventional notation, in which the clarity of the polyphonic structure is ensured by the "analytical" representation of the score, with the jumbled gramophonic "wave-script," where the entire sonic phenomenon is captured in a single, undifferentiated groove pattern. Conventional notation is far superior to the mechanical inscription of the gramophone record, Pringsheim argued, because it presents the instrumental lines in their independence. The score is not merely a practical necessity for the performance of a work; it is the logical representation of the musical processes that go into the act of composition. The gramophone groove, by contrast, represents complex, agglomerated systems of sound instead of interwoven lines of individual notes. Because the medium cannot isolate individual notes and motives, it forces the composer to think in terms of unwieldy sonic masses and timbral progressions *[Klangkomplexe-Fortschreitungen]*. By this reasoning, the very nature of gramophone inscription ruled out the discovery of a "sound alphabet" of audiovisual correspondences.[25]

In light of such critiques, early gramophone experimentalists adjusted their tactics. Rather than seeking a tabula rasa on which to construct a new musical language, they began by modifying existing recordings on a hands-on, empirical basis. Moholy-Nagy had made arrangements to begin working in record company laboratories in Berlin in early 1923. Stuckenschmidt and the American composer George Antheil lined up as collaborators, but before work got under way, Antheil left for Paris and Moholy-Nagy was summoned to teach at the Bauhaus in Weimar.[26] It was there, in the summer of 1923, that the first known efforts in modernist gramophone manipulation took place. Stuckenschmidt, who joined Moholy-Nagy in Weimar, later recounted: "We experimented together, playing records backward, which created surprising effects, especially with piano recordings. We drilled into the records in strange ways, so that they didn't play regularly, but wobbled and produced grotesque glissando tones. We even scratched into the grooves with tiny needles and so created rhythmic figures and noises that radically altered the sense of the music."[27] But from these rudimentary investigations, the two men quickly moved on to other projects. Stuckenschmidt turned his attention to the player piano, while Moholy-Nagy dismissed both player piano and gramophone as merely provisional stages in the inexorable technological evolution toward a truly universal instrument, "an apparatus that can be operated directly and produce all manner of tones in any number and quality, without an intervening medium."[28] For his part, Antheil would pursue his fascination with mechanical music in his infamous *Ballet méchanique,* originally intended to include sixteen player pianos.

The idea of using gramophone records as scores for machine-readable music would reemerge some years later. The only known performance of "gramophone music" took place at the New Music Berlin festival in 1930 and featured a set of short pieces by Paul Hindemith and Ernst Toch.[29] This event stood firmly in the lineage of the mechanical music phenomena of a few years earlier: both Hindemith and Toch had written pieces for the Welte-Mignon player piano in 1926 and 1927, and the Berlin concert was in fact part of the same festival (now relocated) that had hosted the earlier concerts in Donaueschingen and Baden-Baden. Hindemith's involvement was somewhat surprising, since he had rather firmly dismissed the possibility of "authentic composition" for the gramophone in an essay published in 1927.[30] His argument was similar to that made by Pringsheim: the sheer indecipherability of the tiny record grooves meant that even the simplest musical relationships would be virtually impossible to establish. But he and Toch found a way of working in the medium that sidestepped the problem of legibility. Their "original works for gramophone record" were made not by etching discs by hand but rather by using the gramophone to alter instrumental sounds. By adjusting the playback speed of recordings, they changed the pitch and tone quality of the originals; this modified output was in turn recorded on a separate gramophone machine.

Although the details of the 1930 *Grammophonmusik* performance remain fuzzy, the two surviving recordings (both by Hindemith) provide a glimpse into the composers' approach. A disc labeled "Song over Three Octaves" features a brief vocal melody, likely sung by Hindemith himself, which is heard in juxtaposition with two phonographically altered versions, one played at double the original speed (thus one octave higher), and another played at half the original speed (one octave lower). At the end of the one-minute piece all three voices sound together, creating a three-voice closing chord. The other recording, marked simply "Xylophone," is a roughly two-minute composition consisting of a two-voice xylophone part and two pizzicato string parts, likely Hindemith's viola played back at higher and lower speeds to sound like a violin and cello, respectively. Though fascinating in their own right, these recordings were apparently conceived as "sound material" for use in conjunction with live performance.[31] A witness to the concert describes how this took place: "The original music for gramophone record was produced through the cross fading of various recordings and live music, through the use of speed, pitch, and timbre that are impossible for live playing to attain. Thus emerged an original music that can only be rendered by the gramophone apparatus."[32] (The odd phenomenon of a performance of recorded music required the use of the phrase "actually played music" *[real gespielte Musik]* to distinguish what was performed "live" from what was merely played back.)

For Toch's three-movement work, entitled *Gesprochene Musik* (Spoken music), he recorded a chorus pronouncing precisely notated text passages and then modified the speed of playback on the gramophone record, changing the tempo and thus also the timbre, to create "a kind of instrumental music" in which the origins of the sounds were almost entirely obscured.[33] Toch described his intentions in terms that echo Moholy-Nagy's production-reproduction dichotomy: "The concept arose from the attempt to extend the function of the machine—which up to now has been intended for the most faithful possible reproduction of live music—by exploiting the peculiarities of its function and by analyzing its formerly unrealized possibilities (which are worthless for the machine's real purpose), thereby changing the machine's function and creating a characteristic music of its own."[34]

The works performed by Hindemith and Toch diverged significantly from the original conceptions of gramophone music. While Moholy-Nagy and Stuckenschmidt dreamed of coaxing from the disc sounds that had no acoustic correlate in the natural world, Hindemith and Toch exploited the playback mechanism of the gramophone to alter the sound of recordings made in the conventional way. But even if the 1930 concert of *Grammophonmusik* contained no purely synthetic sounds, the music was nonetheless estranged from the familiar world of acoustic phenomena. Georg Schünemann, head of the Radio Research Section in Berlin, where the pieces were produced, wrote of the "astounding effect" of Toch's pieces: "There was scarcely a musician there who could say where these unfamiliar sounds came from; no one knew whether musical instruments, voices, or even noises were being combined."[35] While composers and theorists made much of the distinction between synthetic sound and modified recordings, for listeners both forms could have a similarly otherworldly aesthetic effect.

SOUND FROM LIGHT: THE PHOTOELECTRIC CELL

The public debut of *Grammophonmusik* in 1930 turned out to be its swan song. But as it happened, the genre's demise coincided quite precisely with the appearance of its technological successor. Toward the end of the 1920s, a new recording medium emerged that promised once again to deliver the long-desired "universal instrument": optical sound film. Surprisingly, however, neither Hindemith, nor Toch, nor Stuckenschmidt would pursue the ideal of mechanical music into the new medium. Of the original cadre of gramophone experimentalists, Moholy-Nagy alone would champion sound film in the waning years of the Weimar Republic.[36]

The working of optical sound film is most readily understood in analogy to the more familiar technique of phonographic recording. In the latter process, acoustic vibrations cause a stylus to cut into a spinning cylinder or disc, thus encoding the sounds as a pattern of pits and grooves. Upon playback, another stylus "reads" the inscriptions in the record, thereby activating a diaphragm that produces acoustic vibrations that can be heard as a reproduction of the original sound. With optical sound film, by contrast, sounds are encoded as a two-dimensional graphical pattern on a spinning band of film. In the recording process, acoustic vibrations are picked up by a microphone diaphragm, as in phonographic recording or telephonic transmission. The vibrations are then converted to an electrical current, which in turn governs the intensity of a beam of light emitted by an electric lamp. The fluctuating rays of light are projected on the sound track of the moving band of film, where they are captured as a fixed graphical pattern. In playback, a beam of light is trained on a photoelectric cell. As the film is unspooled, it passes between the beam of light and the cell. The light falling upon the cell is thus modulated by the patterns inscribed in the film, and the sounds emitted by the cell in response to the light correspond to those captured on the film in the recording process.

Although sound film is usually thought of as part of the technological development of motion pictures, the underlying principle of "sound photography" has a much deeper history. As Thomas Levin has shown, optical sound film was a relatively late manifestation of the long-standing effort to establish nonarbitrary, scientifically grounded correlations between acoustic and visual phenomena. Until the late nineteenth century, these efforts resulted only in mute graphical traces: sound could be rendered as a visible pattern, but it could not be reproduced. With Edison's invention of the phonograph in 1877, however, this "soundwriting" became a form of *recording* in the sense in which we understand the term today, capable of capturing sound as an inscription and later reconstructing the acoustic phenomena by reversing the process by which it was encoded.[37]

The use of light in the process of sound recording had a lengthy history before the 1920s as well. Scientists had long realized that the quick, subtle vibrations of a beam of light were better suited to capturing the rapid oscillations of acoustic waves than the cumbrous mechanical apparatus of needles and wax cylinders.[38] The phonographic potential of light became apparent through the remarkable properties of the element selenium, which was discovered by the Swedish chemist Jakob Berzelius in 1817. Over the course of the nineteenth century, scientists found that the electrical resistance of certain allotropes of selenium varied in proportion to the element's exposure to light. Thus, a selenium cell could be used in electrical circuits to govern the flow of electricity. When it was dark, the cell's resistance was high enough that the circuit was effectively closed. When exposed to a fluctuating light source, however, the cell's resistance lowered, allowing electrical current to flow through the circuit.

The first practical attempt to connect sound and light using the photoelectric cell was the Photophone, invented in 1880 by Alexander Graham Bell and Charles Tainter. Essentially, this device replaced the electrical wire of the telephone with a beam of light. A thin, mirrored diaphragm functions as a "light microphone," vibrating in response to acoustic waves and modulating the light focused on it from an external source. The light beam, whose patterns of fluctuation correspond to the acoustic energy of the transmitted sound, travels some distance until it reaches the selenium cell, where it elicits analogous variations in electrical current. These, finally, are converted via a speaker diaphragm into acoustic vibrations that produce an approximation of the original sound.[39] At the root of this device is the phenomenon of transduction, through which different forms of energy can be transformed into each other and thereby encoded and transmitted. Similar to the functioning of the telephone, the underlying equivalence between the mechanical energy of sound waves and the electrical energy of the flowing current enables the transmission of sound over great distances.

Not long after the invention of the Photophone, the German inventor Maximilian Plessner sketched a prescient, if highly speculative, application of the photoelectric cell. He imagined a way to use light not to transmit sound but rather to encode it on a recording medium in a manner analogous to Edison's phonograph. This device, which Plessner envisioned but apparently did not construct, was dubbed the "optograph" to distinguish it from Edison's device.[40] The idea of using light to record rather than transmit sound was developed further in the Photographophone invented by the German Ernst Ruhmer around 1900.[41] In Ruhmer's contraption, the flame of an arc light (a gas lamp that could be made to flicker in response to acoustic vibrations) is focused on a lens positioned in front of a reel of photographic film. The fluctuations of light caused by the acoustic vibrations are thus captured on the film as fields of varying shades. After being developed, the film is played back at the same speed at which it was recorded, while a constant source

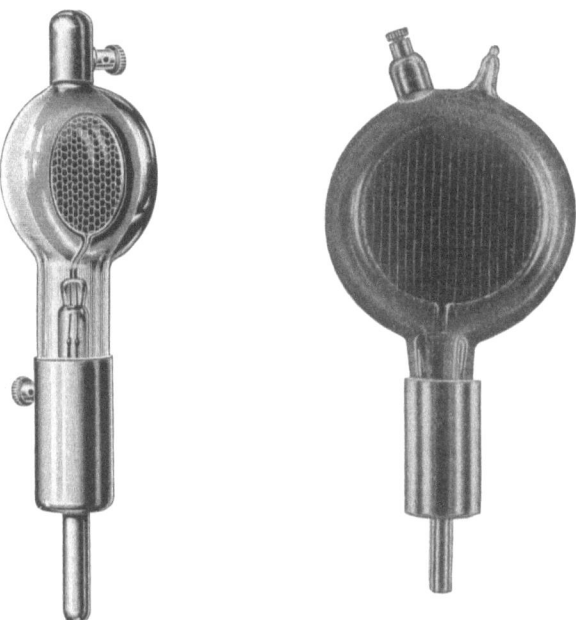

FIGURE 14. Photoelectric cells. These tiny devices transduce light into electricity; they were central to the development of optical sound film. Source: Heinrich Geffcken, Hans Richter, and Joachim Winckelmann, *Die lichtempfindliche Zelle als technisches Steuergerät* (Berlin: Deutsch-Literarisches Institut J. Schneider, 1933), 37.

of light is directed upon it. On the other side of the film from the light source is a selenium cell, which is connected to a battery and a telephone receiver, as in Bell's apparatus.[42] The patterns encoded on the film are thus transmuted into electrical fluctuations and again back into acoustic vibrations, re-creating the original sound. Ruhmer's Photographophone possessed the essential elements of later optical sound film recording systems, but its widespread adoption was hindered by the difficulty of recording and amplifying playback with the technology of the time. The sound film techniques of the 1920s picked up where he left off, making use of improved vacuum tube and loudspeaker technology.[43]

THE EMERGENCE OF SOUND FILM

The development of sound film in the 1920s was spurred above all by the burgeoning motion picture industry. The ability to synchronize

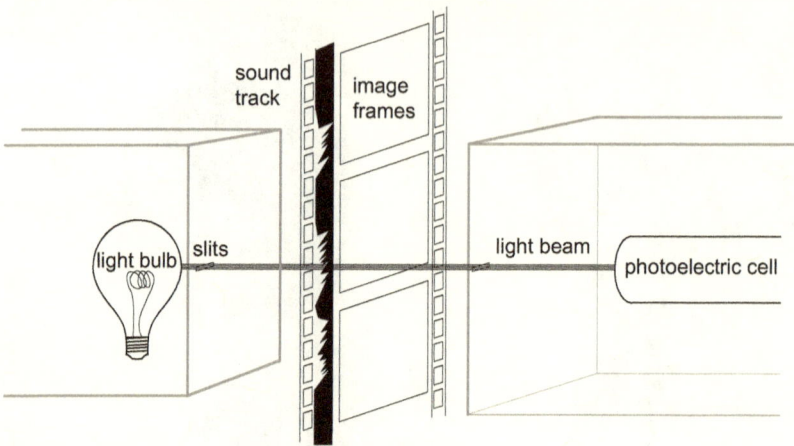

FIGURE 15. Diagrammatic representation of sound-film playback. Illustration by Wm. Stephen Scott.

the moving images of the film with a recorded sound track was widely hailed as a kind of cinematic holy grail, a breakthrough that would relieve motion pictures of their much-lamented muteness and create a new *Gesamtkunstwerk* for the twentieth century. But ironically, the advent of optical sound film toward the end of the decade provoked a decidedly negative reaction among some of the foremost directors in Europe. The French filmmaker René Clair, fearing that the synchronization of sound and image would lead to the dominance of spoken dialogue over visual interest, declared the new technology a "terrible monster, a creation against nature, courtesy of which the screen will become an impoverished theater."[44] Sergei Eisenstein and other Russian directors issued a statement declaring that sound film threatened "not only [to] hinder the development and perfection of the cinema as an art but also threaten to destroy all its present formal achievements."[45] But while many directors resented the aesthetic compromises augured by the arrival of sound film, some musicians welcomed the new technology as an instrument without precedent. Just as cinematic film had liberated the image from the shackles of sequential time and conventional narrative structure, sound film promised to free sound from the limitations imposed by notation and instrumental tone production. The techniques of the artistically advanced cinema—close-ups, slow motion, double exposure, and montage—could now be applied to the composition of music.

László Moholy-Nagy, champion of media instruments since the early 1920s, became the leading exponent of sound film as a vehicle for modernist experimentation. Echoing Ferruccio Busoni, who had called for a "protracted education of the ear" to orient musicians amid the musical possibilities of the twentieth century, Moholy-Nagy argued that the inherent "laziness of the ear" prevented composers from realizing the full potential of such new technologies as the gramophone, radio, and "ether instruments" (meaning the Theremin and other electrophones). In order to contribute to the progress of art, sound film "must go beyond the documentary function of recording and enrich our ears with previously unknown sonic properties."[46] Here Moholy-Nagy restated the basic argument of his earlier essays, in which he envisioned a creative, or "productive," role for technologies that had hitherto served merely naturalistic, or "reproductive," functions. The development of sound film as a vehicle for modernist art, according to Moholy-Nagy, hinged on the ability of musicians to conceive of the recording medium in a creative and nonnaturalistic way, just as avant-garde filmmakers had done in the visual domain.

Like the Russian authors of the "Statement on the Sound Film," Moholy-Nagy rejected the conventional uses of the new medium, such as reproducing dialogue and creating realistic sound effects to strengthen cinema's dramatic illusion. The proper function of sound film was instead analogous to the use of montage in silent film. Indeed, Moholy-Nagy essentially paraphrased the Russians' arguments about the need for an independent, "contrapuntal" relationship between sound and image in the modern film.[47] But before the goal of "opto-acoustic synthesis" could be attained, the musical potential of sound film must be dealt with on its own terms: "Sound film should thus pass through a provisional period of purely musical experiments," he wrote. "In other words, sound should at first be treated in isolation from the visual. In practical terms, this means separating the soundtrack of the film and experimentally combining individual compositions."[48] Moholy-Nagy believed that sound-film composition must go through a period of development equivalent to cinema's silent phase, an exploration of the inherent dynamics of the medium that was strictly limited to the acoustic dimension.

Drawing out a distinction implicit in his earlier theorization of "gramophone music," Moholy-Nagy differentiated between two basic methods of working with sound film. First, the composer could manipulate "real acoustic phenomena, as they present themselves in natural sounds, in the human voice, or in musical instruments." The possible techniques for such acoustic transmutation of recorded sound were drawn directly from contemporary cinematic methods:

> Just as the optical film possesses the possibility of capturing an object from different perspectives—from above and below, from the side and from the front, foreshortened—something similar must happen with sound. There must be different "angles of hearing" to correspond to the various "angles of view." To this can be added acoustic close-ups, slow motion, time lapse, distortion, washes—in short, all the means of a "tone montage."[49]

Second, Moholy-Nagy envisioned the creation of "optically notatable sound shapes, which are independent of actual objects, and which are photographically transferred to the sound track according to a precomposed plan and thereafter converted into actual tones." In this way, composers could circumvent the recording process altogether, imprinting patterns directly on the sound track to generate tones without correlates in acoustic nature.[50] Here sound film was treated not as a medium of recording in the strict sense but as a means of composition via the "opto-acoustic alphabet."

Both techniques had parallels in the cinema of the 1920s. The first tendency could be traced to surrealist-influenced films by filmmakers such as Clair and Germaine Dulac, in which cinematic devices such as montage, double exposure, and slow motion create a dreamlike simultaneity of images and undermine linear narrative flow. The second approach found precedent in the groundbreaking works of experimental animation of the early 1920s, in which various techniques were used to bypass the naturalistic function of the movie camera and construct a world of pure form and motion. (The German word for a cartoon, *Trickfilm,* highlights the medium's potential for legerdemain and illusion.) It was no coincidence that the three German pioneers in sound-film composition—Walter Ruttmann, Oskar Fischinger, and Rudolf Pfenninger—were all veterans of avant-garde cinematic production.

Another parallel to the groundbreaking efforts in optical sound film could be found in the experimental approaches to the new genre of the "radio play" *(Hörspiel)* that had been undertaken soon after the first national German radio broadcast in October 1923. A new breed of radio artists—sound engineers by training—such as Hans Flesch and Friedrich Bischoff created imaginative programs only loosely linked to literary or narrative models, guided instead by the seemingly limitless evocative potential of sound. (Flesch declared in 1929, "We need to fashion not only a new medium, but a new content as well: Our program cannot be created at a desk."[51]) The prospect of an "absolute radio art" also enticed classically trained composers such as Kurt Weill, who imagined a new form of music indigenous to radio, whose expanded repertoire of sonic material included "sounds from other spheres, calls of human and animal voices, the whirring of wind, water, and trees and a legion of new, unknown noises, which the microphone can generate artificially, when sound waves are raised or lowered, superimposed or interwoven, blown away and born again." Weill's projected radio-art featured two classes of sounds closely resembling Moholy-Nagy's categories: "nonmusical" noises derived from recognizable physical processes, and "abstract" tones with no purchase in known acoustic reality. Weill's thoughts on the matter were directly influenced by the experiments in absolute film, which he had experienced through a screening of films by Richter, Eggeling, Ruttmann, and Clair arranged by the November Group in Berlin in 1925. (A good leftist, Weill had joined the organization in 1922.) "Just as film has enriched the visual means of expression," he wrote, "so shall the acoustic means be multiplied to an unforeseeable degree through radiotelephony."[52] Like Mondrian, however, Weill belonged to those whose ability to imagine new forms of technological art outstripped their interest in exploring these new possibilities in their own work.

CINEMA FOR THE EAR: SOUND MONTAGE

Although the two techniques outlined by Moholy-Nagy—what might be called the *phonographic* (recording-based) and the *synthetic* (inscription-based)—were by no means incompatible, sound-film practitioners tended to focus on one or the other approach. The phonographic technique was the inspiration for Robert Beyer, who put forth an elaborate theory of experimental sound-film composition in a series of articles published between 1928 and 1930.[53] Beyer had an unusual background that combined experience in the film industry and classical musical training: after studying composition, conducting, and musicology at the Cologne Conservatory, he worked from 1928 to 1934 as a *Tonmeister* (sound engineer) for Tobis-Klangfilm, a company that consolidated the patents for Tri-Ergon and a number of other European sound-film systems.[54] Beyer's boosterism for sound-film experimentation resembled H. H. Stuckenschmidt's activism for "mechanical music" a few years earlier: like Stuckenschmidt, Beyer championed a musical movement in which he himself had no creative part. He envisaged a type of musical production possible only on the technological basis of optical sound film, "a new interpretation of the concept 'music' that is suitable to filmic form."[55] Just as cinema created a kind of visual representation distinct from traditional staged drama, Beyer argued, sound film would usher in a new music whose only link with previous forms was the shared medium of acoustic vibrations.

Beyer's vision of instrumentalized sound film began with the recording process itself. The first stage in the "composition of the audible" was the use of the microphone as an "acoustic camera." The microphone gave the composer complete control over the material of sound, freeing him from the inherent ephemerality of sound and opening up an unlimited space of creative possibility.[56] The centerpiece of Beyer's approach to sound recording was a technique he called *Raumton* (room tone), through which the recording process deliberately captures the ambient environment along with the intended sounds. When it is reproduced, the recording projects a sense of space separate from that inhabited by the listener. Because the sound is presented together with the spatial imprint of its environment at the time of recording, listeners are forced to confront it as what it in fact is: a technologically transfigured fragment of reality. This shattering of the illusion of immediacy—which calls to mind the famous "alienation effect" first theorized by Bertolt Brecht in 1935—fundamentally alters the listener's relationship to recorded sound.[57] Rather than bringing the sound into the room, Raumton projects the recording at a distance, so to speak. For Beyer, sound came into its own as an object of aesthetic perception only through this radical intervention of technology. Ironically, he explained the resultant "revolutionization of hearing" by means of visual metaphors: in confronting the "sound image" of the disembodied acoustic phenomenon, we become "auditors, or rather 'spectators,' in the truest sense of the word."[58] Extending the metaphor, he suggested that recordings are to "live" or "embodied" sound as the cinema is to the theatrical stage: a different medium with different rules.

Next, Beyer suggested that recording media such as optical sound film undermine the hallowed aesthetic distinction between musical and nonmusical sounds. The recording apparatus registers all phenomena indiscriminately; it knows no difference between tones and noises. In contrast to the holes on the piano roll, the blackened blotches on the film sound track relate ambiguously to the phenomena they encode. These markings, when read by the playback apparatus, *may* produce notes of definite pitch, but they also may not: the only thing that they *must* produce is sounds. Thus, Beyer declared, optical sound film makes it clear once and for all that *sound* and not *tone* is the irreducible element of music. The new medium ushers in the "wide-open orchestra, which secretly bears the sound of the world":

> One must naturally free oneself from the old notion of music if one wants to perceive the possibilities of sound-image photography. The concept 'music' must be more widely drawn so as to encompass the world of noises. [. . .] The inclusion of the endless multiplicity of the world of noises, which has become necessarily the primary function of music over against the soundless motion of the imagery, means something more than a linear expansion of its means and possibilities.[59]

Beyer was not alone in drawing a connection between the indiscriminate ear of the microphone and the musical viability of sounds hitherto dismissed as noise. Walter Gronostay, a Schoenberg pupil and a film composer, likewise suggested that sound film augured a new role for noise in music. Just as early silent film sensitized viewers to the visual "language" of reality, he argued, so too sound film must awaken our attention to the previously unheard world of noises. Gronostay proposed a taxonomy of noise as the foundation for the incorporation of these "nonmusical" sounds into contemporary composition. He distinguished between three types of "interesting noise": noises whose sources can be clearly determined, such as the siren of a fire engine; "unclassifiable" noises, whose sources cannot readily be ascertained; and noises with a salient perceptual contour, which Gronostay called "organized noises."[60] Across the Atlantic, the conductor Leopold Stokowski—at that time the conductor of the Philadelphia Orchestra—echoed this sentiment when he declared that "[sound] film is bringing into consciousness the idea that much in sound has aesthetical value that formerly we wouldn't call music at all. It evokes emotion, and if it evokes emotion, it is aesthetic, and if it is aesthetic, we must bring it into the field of music and not bar it and say that it is mere noise."[61] By taming and capturing the unpitched, ephemeral, and nameless acoustic phenomena previously dismissed as "nonmusical," sound film inspired musicians to reconsider the boundaries of their art form—just as, on a larger scale, magnetic tape would do some twenty years later.

Although the recording process alters the phenomenological status of sound by projecting it into a "virtual space" and expands the composer's material to include all acoustic phenomena that can be encoded on film, Beyer saw these effects as "only the smallest part of the creative process." The heart of the new compositional technique lay in the process of "sonic chemistry" through which the recorded material is transformed into acoustic figures, forms, and tropes—the syntactic units of the new musical language, comparable in function to the tones and themes of traditional compositional technique. The sound-film composer "atomizes" and "dynamizes" the recorded material, breaking it down to its component parts and reconstructing it into novel perceptual configurations.[62] These new figures are then assembled into larger compositional units via montage technique. Through this process, electric tone generation takes on a productive as opposed to reproductive meaning. Invoking Moholy-Nagy's distinction between productive and reproductive technologies, Beyer envisioned sound film as a means of not simply capturing and re-creating acoustic reality but of transfiguring recorded sound into a musical "second nature": "With these and other methods it will be possible to atomize sound, to construct from its basic elements new tone colors, to traverse a timbral domain of almost cosmic vastness, which far exceeds the known boundaries."[63]

All the techniques of experimental sound film are motivated by a common aesthetic objective: to allow the composer to work not with notes or other abstract entities but with the fabric of sound itself. "Ultimately," Beyer declares, "the desire to emancipate timbre as an independent element is the driving force that has fundamentally guided the musical development of the past decades."[64] Here the radical nature of Beyer's vision becomes clear. Arnold Schoenberg famously disliked the term *atonal* because of its absurd implication of music without tones.[65] But a music without tones—or in which tones and tonal connections are no longer the most important phenomena—is precisely what Beyer had in mind. His idea of *Klangfarbenmusik* involves not simply the incorporation of timbral logic into the existing compositional process but a complete transcendence of pitch relationships as the guiding structures of musical creation. In this respect, Beyer's defense of sound-film composition turns on its head earlier critiques of the medium's supposed intractability. Recall that Heinz Pringsheim had attacked the idea of composing directly onto recording media because the composer would be unable to isolate individual tones and forced instead to work with unwieldy "timbral complexes." From Beyer's perspective, this aspect of sound-film composition is precisely what constitutes the medium's aesthetic potential. Working with recorded sounds compels the composer to think in terms of "floating" timbral masses instead of the "point-like" tones of conventional music.[66] For Beyer, optical sound film heralded nothing less than an epochal transition from a tonal language of discrete pitches and timbres to a new musical order based upon the limitless nature of sound itself.

In his 1928 essay "The Problem of the 'Music to Come'", Beyer presented a poetic, almost incantatory description of what he called the "new tone":

> When we attempt to define more closely the materiality of the "new tone," which makes it possible for timbres to manifest in innumerable gliding transitions, we learn that we can produce only vague conceptions: we assign to it such predicates as floating, unbounded and open in its dying away, abruptly broken off; pendulous sound; uncertain in its origin, as if it came out of thin air; filling up space, resting and oscillating around a nucleus; it is the tone of the turning filmstrip and its potential, no longer to be grasped on the keyboard, nor devised by the measure of the human and its bodily dimensions, but a step beyond it, a new possibility in the empire of sound. One can approximate the impression of this "new tone" by striking a number of keys at random on the piano with the pedal raised and awaiting the sounds' decay, and then you will, as it were, begin to hear for the first time, when the tones flow into each other, and there emerges the shapeless buzzing of the sound mass. Similar sound images are produced by the whirring harmonies of jazz, the loudspeaker, the buzzing noise of machines, the metropolis, and the newest music. The "new tone" does not move according to the rules of vocal parts; it is beyond all attempts to give it form.[67]

The "new tone," then, is not a tone at all, in the traditional sense of a discrete acoustic phenomenon with determinate pitch, duration, and timbre. It is sound emancipated from the structures imposed upon it by conventional instruments and systems of notation—abstracted, objectified, and made malleable by the technology of sound film.

For Beyer, media instruments suggested nothing less than a new relationship between technology and the artistic imagination. Since Busoni's *Sketch of a New Aesthetic of Music*, advocates of new instruments had clung to the notion that technology had to be brought up to date with the needs of the contemporary composer. But by the early 1930s, this relationship appeared to be turned on its head. Now, it was the composer who must adapt himself to the exigencies of the new technology. Inverting Busoni's famous lament that "the progress of music is impeded by our instruments," Beyer asserted that the creative mind lagged behind the capabilities of its time. "The instrumental technology of sound film, and of music as such, surpasses our imagination," he declared.[68]

Without the proper creative energies to direct them, new technological forces are doomed to remain mere "dynamics, expansion in empty space." The apparatus awaits the animating spirit of artistic intelligence, Beyer argued, which alone can unleash from the machine the otherwise unfathomable lineaments of the "music to come." His remarks on sound film could be extrapolated to encompass the new and ever-expanding instrumentarium of the twentieth century:

> It can hardly be questioned that the progress of music—indeed, of art—goes through the machine. The problem is to switch art from manual to technological methods of production. [. . .] Today sound film is still in the periphery of music. Tomorrow the two will be organically united. Today sound film exists alongside music as an artistic genre with its own set of problems. Tomorrow these problems will no longer be its own but rather those of music as a whole.[69]

Not surprisingly, given the uncompromising nature of his vision, Beyer was dismissive of the contemporary technological experiments of which he was aware. Electric instruments, he claimed, in spite of their inventors' fantasies of unheard tone colors, were doomed by design to reproduce the circumscribed musical gestures of their performers. He singled out Paul Hindemith's compositions for the Trautonium, premiered at the Neue Musik Berlin festival in 1930, as evidence of the unwelcome persistence of contrapuntal, note-centered thinking. In these works, according to Beyer, the use of tone color is comparable to that of traditional orchestration technique; "the problem of transitions between timbres is not even glimpsed."[70] (The Trautonium will be discussed at length in chapter 5.) Theremin's "ether wave" instrument was likewise too closely tied to traditional models: in a strikingly contrarian argument, Beyer claimed that with the Theremin, "music returns to the primitive conditions that it had happily left behind it." The instrument is diametrically opposed to the spirit of the new music, "which strives precisely to overcome the 'handicraft' of tone generation and to eliminate the visual exhibition of the acoustic."[71] Though Beyer never mentioned Jörg Mager or his instruments, his critique of the Theremin would likely apply to other electrophones as well. In his view, all such devices hewed too closely to conventional models of instrumentality to do justice to the elusive and disembodied nature of "the new tone."

Beyer also dismissed contemporary efforts at "noise montage," such as the compositions of gramophone music by Hindemith and Toch and the sound track to Walter Ruttmann's film *Melodie der Welt*.[72] However, Beyer's writings on sound film predate the only surviving work of purely acoustic sound-film montage from the Weimar Republic: Ruttmann's eleven-minute composition entitled *Weekend*, which was first broadcast in June 1930. Based entirely on sounds recorded both in the studio and on the streets of Berlin, *Weekend* assembled this material into a "symphony of noises" comprising six programmatic movements: "The Jazz of Work," "Closing Time," "Journey into the Open," "Pastoral," and "Return to Work" (movements 5 and 6).[73]

By the time he created *Weekend*, Ruttmann had already established himself as one of the premier experimental filmmakers in Germany. His pioneering abstract films of the early 1920s (*Opus I–IV*, 1921–1925) employed a variety of advanced techniques, including photographing hand-shaped plasticine formations and painting directly onto the filmstrip. In the latter part of the decade, Ruttmann turned his attention to experimental documentary films, such as *Berlin: Die Sinfonie der Großstadt (Berlin: Symphony of a Metropolis)*, a cinematic ode to modern life without plot or characters, held together entirely by the uptempo juxtaposition of shots.

Ruttmann envisioned *Weekend* as a musical analogue to the cinema, both in technique and in effect: he called it a "study in tone montage" and a "blind film."[74] The purpose of the film was "to discover overarching rules governing the connection of sound elements and their combination into an aesthetic unity, as we have previously seen done with visual elements in silent film."[75] Like *Berlin*, to which it is closely related in terms of form, *Weekend* is a tour-de-force of montage technique and film editing. Ruttmann whittled 2,000 meters of film down to a mere 250 to create a composition consisting of 240 discrete "cuts." In Moholy-Nagy's terms, *Weekend* trafficked in the "real acoustic phenomena" of natural, human, and instrumental sounds. The focus is not on the development of sound-image correspondences or the discovery of new synthetic timbres but rather on the compositional organization of various recorded sounds, mostly of recognizable origin. These sounds, for the most part quotidian and referential, are rendered strange and artistically compelling through the rapid-fire contrasts and repetitions of montage technique.

Weekend was hailed as a groundbreaking success by many of Ruttmann's peers in the artistic vanguard. Hans Richter, like Ruttmann a pioneer of experimental film, wrote that "by not treating sound naturalistically as had become common in sound film—that means, when the mouth opens and moves, then words must come out—but instead treating sound creatively and musically, Ruttmann had in fact established the artistic domain for sound film. From isolated sonic impressions, he created new unities." According to Richter, Vsevolod Podovkin, one of the signatories of the "Statement on the Sound Film," likewise hailed *Weekend* as proof that sound could be handled in a dynamic and non-naturalistic way, rather than used to undermine the visual aspect of cinema, as many directors had feared.[76]

Given these plaudits, it is remarkable that *Weekend* was an artistic singleton, a work without parallel until the first experiments of musique concrète in the late 1940s. (Perhaps the closest counterpart was the groundbreaking 1931 documentary film *Enthusiasm: Symphony of the Donbass,* by the Russian filmmaker Dziga Vertov, who devised a plan for the sound track independently of the visual component of the work.)[77] One reason was the composer's own discontent with his work: Ruttmann judged the piece to be "difficult and incoherent," stating in an interview that the listener "gets lost in a sea of tones," grasping at associative threads while much goes by unnoticed.[78] Another factor may have been the "laziness of the ear" lamented by Moholy-Nagy: perhaps most listeners were simply not ready for a compositional genre based on the formal possibilities of sound film. Like so many other products of the Weimar period, Ruttmann's *Weekend* was of its time in being ahead of its time.

EXPERIMENTS IN SYNTHETIC SOUND

However visionary the notion of "sound montage" theorized by Beyer and put into practice by Ruttmann, there was another and arguably more radical way of subverting the intended use of optical sound film and turning it into a modernist instrument: synthetic sound. The fundamental realization behind this approach was that the same graphical patterns created by the recording process could also be made, so to speak, from scratch. In a sound-film recording of a speaking voice or a musical performance, acoustic phenomena are represented by inscriptions on the filmstrip. But if sounds could be captured and re-created in this manner, they could also be summoned up from nothing. In the words of media historian Dieter Daniels, "anything that was technologically reproducible could in principle be technically produced."[79] Rather than capturing sounds for later reproduction, the medium becomes the point of origin for the phenomenon it produces. Thus, in theory, all known sounds could be synthetically re-created by the careful etchings of the sound-film composer. Not only could any preexisting sound be reverse-engineered by hand-drawing its acoustic profile, but the technique of direct inscription could also create acoustic manifestations sui generis, phenomena with no correlate in natural or instrumental sound. Any imaginable combination of pitch, timbre, duration, and envelope had its corresponding graphical representation that could be codified and inscribed according to the composer's designs. Sound film could furnish the "universal instrument," allowing the composer complete control over the entirety of possible sound phenomena. Moholy-Nagy again led the charge:

> Sound film will have reached a genuine plateau of creative exploitation only once we have mastered the acoustic alphabet in the form of photographic projections. This means that—without actual acoustic events in the external world—we deliberately inscribe acoustic phenomena on the film strip, and, where necessary, synchronize them with the optical part. The sound-film composer can create a thought-out, but never before heard, indeed nonexistent play of sounds using only the opto-phonetic alphabet.[80]

As noted earlier, it was the painters Mondrian and Moholy-Nagy who first hatched the idea of media instruments, and the concept's later incubation was continually nourished by the interdisciplinary connections between music and the visual arts.[81] Eager to play up the parallels between the two, sound-film enthusiasts often described composition in the new medium as a kind of "painting with sound." But this metaphor obscured the fundamental opacity governing the relationship between input and output. To be sure, sound film was considered an advance on the gramophone record precisely on account of its greater legibility: composers could now actually see the visual designs that they made. But the next stage—the relationship between those markings and the sounds they produced upon playback—was trickier. Sound film was a different beast from the piano roll, the earlier pinned cylinder and, indeed, conventional musical notation, all of which function on the basis of clear relationships between inscriptions and the phenomena they represent. These earlier forms of notation transparently encode a virtual alphabet of compositional possibilities. With optical sound film, however, the relationship between the image on the filmstrip and the resulting sound turned out to be less straightforward than composers had hoped. Because the photoelectric cell reacts only to variations in light but not to particular patterns, different graphical traces could produce the same acoustic output.[82] These "homographs" gravely complicated the effort to establish a universal "sound alphabet": like verbal communication, this new musical language was beset by redundancies and breaks in the logic of the system.

In spite of these difficulties, by the early 1930s Europe was percolating with experiments in synthetic sound via optical film.[83] The leading exponents in Germany were Oskar Fischinger and Rudolf Pfenninger. Fischinger (1900–1967) was a visual artist whose ventures into experimental filmmaking were inspired by viewings of Ruttmann's abstract films in 1921. His most famous films were the series of *Studies,* in which he photographed thousands of hand-drawn shapes in charcoal on paper to create elegant sequences of abstract moving figures that "danced" to synchronized musical accompaniments. His first experiments with optical sound film likely took place around 1930. For Fischinger, sound film promised nothing less than the attainment of complete artistic self-sufficiency: "The composer of tomorrow will no longer write mere notes, which the composer himself can never realize definitively, but which rather must languish, abandoned to various capricious reproducers. Now control of every fine gradation and nuance is granted to the music-painting artist, who bases everything exclusively on the primary fundamental of music: namely, the wave vibrations or oscillation in and of itself."[84] In an essay entitled "Absolute Sound Film," published in January 1933, Fischinger argued that the value of sound film lay in its ability to free the composer from the onerous collective work processes that have traditionally diluted the creative energy of the individual artist: "Handmade film makes possible pure artistic creation." The product of this "authentic composition" is marked by the concentrated personality of the artist—the "writerly *[handschriftliche]*, irrational, and personal."[85] In stark contrast to figures such as Stuckenschmidt and Moholy-Nagy, who sought instruments that would purge these subjective qualities, Fischinger saw sound film as the consummation of the romantic aesthetic ideal of expressive immediacy.

Fischinger's compositional process involved drafting sequences of graphical patterns, transferring them to the sound track, and playing them back to determine correlations between image and sound. His work involved both reproductions of familiar timbres and "new musical sounds, pure tones with a precision of definition in their musical vibrations that could not be obtained formerly from the manipulation of traditional instruments."[86] He envisioned composers working with several film sound tracks in tandem in order to create polyphonic textures and orchestral layerings: "Each track would produce a different, well-defined sound, and planning them together, the composer could design and organize overlapping and intersecting wave patterns on the minutest level."[87] Contemporary accounts and photographs of Fischinger's work show a variety of graphical forms, including among others "diamonds, zig-zags, stair-step shapes, circles, stars, fish forms, sinuous lines, waves, curves, angles, saw-shaped edges."[88] Fischinger called these shapes "ornament tone" or "sounding ornaments" (*Ornament Ton, klingende Ornamente*).

According to his biographer William Moritz, Fischinger was struck by the ability of sounds to signal the objects from which they issued—a realization he had upon hearing a key hit the floor and recognizing the object instantaneously by its sound alone. But it wasn't just that things could sound like what they were. Fischinger surmised yet deeper bonds linking the visual and the acoustic. He found for example, that the ancient Egyptian symbol for a snake, when copied to the sound track, produced a distinct hissing sound.[89] Such hidden correspondences between different sensory codes resonated with the quest for a primal language connecting the outwardly unrelated phenomena of nature.[90] In fact, this aspect of Fischinger's work suggests a techno-aesthetic attitude quite at odds with his own avowals of absolute creative autonomy, according to which the instrument is treated as a subordinate means of realization for preformed artistic ideas. Arguably, his pursuit of sound correspondences signals his openness to the generative function of technological mediation and points to a new and overtly experimental conception of instrumentality.[91]

In spite of his predilection for suggestive audiovisual symbolism, Fischinger's goal in his *Ornament Ton* works was to establish systematic correspondences between sound and image: as one contemporary journalistic account stated, "he seeks above all the *elements* of a sound image, as it were the *characters* from which the sound writing is composed. Once these characters—which Fischinger sees as precise, ornamental figures—are found, he believes that the entire acoustic domain and the quality of any given sound can be captured in writing."[92] Fischinger made significant progress in wresting musical tones from their unruly medium: though he was apparently disturbed by the weird sounds created by the first test reels, a later account of a public demonstration emphasized that the films produced no "wild cacophony" but rather "tones, at times precisely defined, at times similar to this or that instrument."[93] In 1933, Fischinger's films were screened at the London Film Society and by Moholy-Nagy at the Bauhaus in Berlin, but soon thereafter he abandoned work in the medium of synthetic sound film.[94]

The work of Rudolf Pfenninger (1899–1976) presents both a parallel and a contrast to Fischinger's sound-film experiments. Pfenninger,

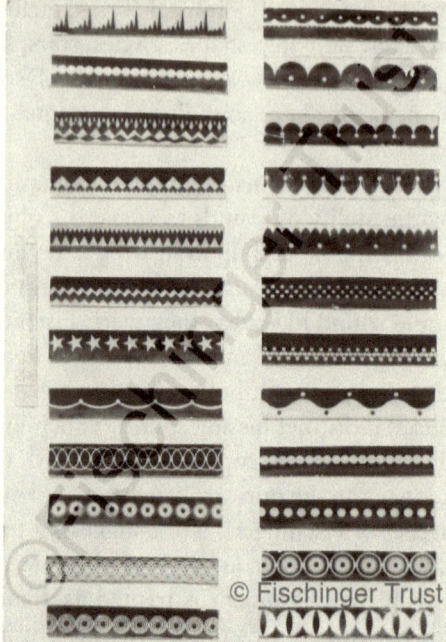

FIGURE 16. Oskar Fischinger, detail from *Ornamente Ton* (Ornament tone) display card (ca. 1932). Collection Center for Visual Music. © Fischinger Trust, courtesy of Center for Visual Music. All rights reserved.

who was trained as an animator and radio engineer, was driven to synthetic sound by economic necessity: unable to afford musicians or recording fees to produce musical accompaniment for his short animated films, in the late 1920s he began investigating the possibility of creating his own entirely artificial music. After drawing various patterns on paper and then photographically transferring them onto the sound track, Pfenninger was able to empirically determine how the different graphical patterns were interpreted as sound by the photoelectric cell. In this manner he could painstakingly create synthetic scores by arranging on the filmstrip the wave forms and timings corresponding to the tones and rhythmic values of a given composition. Invoking a metaphor of script, in contrast to Fischinger's ornament, Pfenninger called his approach to optical sound film *tönende Handschrift* (sonic handwriting).[95] Whereas Fischinger took ornamental visual forms as the starting point and asked how they sounded when "read" by the photoelectric cell, Pfenninger began with the repertoire of existing timbres and scales and systematically devised the graphical patterns required to summon them on command. He was unconcerned with formal analogies between sound and image, taking for granted an arbitrary

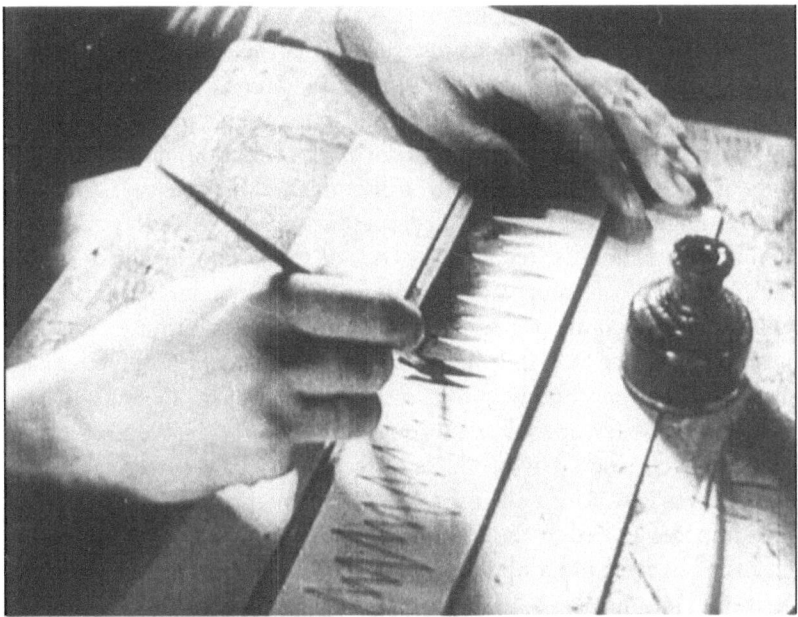

FIGURE 17. Rudolf Pfenninger at work on his "sonic handwriting." These hand-painted patterns would later be photographed and reproduced on the filmstrip on a much smaller scale. Source: *Animierte Avantgarde: Der künstlerische Animationsfilm der 20er und 30er Jahre*, curated by Ulrich Wegenast (Berlin: Absolut Medien, 2010), DVD.

relationship between the two, similar to that between words and their meanings in human language.

Pfenninger's surviving films highlight a striking discrepancy between the modernist tenor of sound-film theory and the decidedly childlike quality of the music.[96] *Pitsch und Patsch* (1932), for example, is an underwater fantasy that follows two fish as they encounter and evade a series of would-be predators. The seven-minute film calls to mind contemporaneous zoological animation such as Disney's famous *Silly Symphonies*. Pfenninger's music is simple and diatonic in terms of compositional structure, which is hardly surprising given the context. The timbre—bright, clipped, and unabashedly artificial—is largely consistent throughout, with a few minor variations for contrast and white noise bursts as an illustrative sound effect. Pfenninger was clearly uninterested in the exploration of tone color that entranced other sound-film enthusiasts such as Beyer and Fischinger – *Klangfarbenmusik* this is not! But in spite of the uniform timbre and the conventional, quality of the music, Pfenninger's sound track does occasionally astonish. Sudden flurries of notes create tonal blurs and dizzying auditory illusions. Indeed, these techniques recall similar effects in the compositions for the Welte-Mignon player piano discussed in chapter 2. In both cases, the monotony of unchanging tone color and metronomic pulse is enlivened by spasmodic bursts of activity, scalar runs of extrahuman speed, and tonal gestures that defy all sense of instrumental propriety.[97]

Pfenninger's mastery of the medium thus came at the cost of extreme simplification. In order to crack the code of sound film, he had to reduce the bandwidth of compositional information to a monophonic minimum: only one note at a time. His sound-film music thus exemplifies what philosopher Don Ihde has called the "amplification-reduction" effect of technology: the way that instruments narrow some aspects of work even as they open up new zones of freedom.[98] However, the simplifications arising as by-products of technological progress can themselves elicit new forms of inventiveness through the very constraints they impose. Forced to think monophonically, Pfenninger discovered a means of creating pseudopolyphonic textures with a single voice, and so arrived at a radically technogenic form of expression.

Reviews of Pfenninger's music called attention to the "mechanical" (or even "soulless") quality of the tones. Critics lamented the lack of subtle pitch variation (vibrato), unnaturally sharp attacks, and the bright, nasal timbre. One reviewer happily conceded the inventiveness of Pfenninger's technique but recoiled from the "abstract, skeletal music" it produced: "Our technological sense was fascinated, our imagination of the future provoked! [. . .] At the same time, I must admit that our music-loving ear did go on strike, and our lively artistic consciousness was troubled. Was this still music? [. . .] Rarely have we felt so clearly the inner difference between live art and technological construct."[99] Many critics harped on a similar discrepancy between the technological allure of the new instruments and the meager aesthetic quality of the works in which they were employed. In Pfenninger's case, however, this reaction was especially acute: technically the most accomplished exponent of synthetic sound film in Germany, he was at the same time aesthetically the most conservative.

At a presentation of experimental sound-film compositions in Frankfurt in late 1932, Moholy-Nagy hailed Pfenninger's work as the vindication of his own decade-long quest for synthetic sound: "Today, thanks to the excellent work of Rudolf Pfenninger, [these ideas] have been successfully applied to the medium of sound film. In Pfenninger's sound script, the theoretical prerequisites and the practical processes have achieved perfection."[100] Moholy-Nagy's acclaim is somewhat vexing in light of the conventional character of Pfenninger's music. In hailing Pfenninger's work, however, Moholy-Nagy was presumably addressing not the music itself but the means by which it was created and the further possibilities that it signalled. The work as an object of aesthetic contemplation was secondary to the demonstration of optical sound film as a viable medium for future artistic development.

In the same year, Moholy-Nagy offered his own contribution to the genre of synthetic sound film with a work entitled *Tönendes ABC (Sound ABC)*. The film "used all types of signs, symbols, even the letters of the alphabet, and [his] own fingerprints. Each visual pattern on the sound track produced a sound which had the character of whistling and other noises."[101] The optical track and the sound track of Moholy-Nagy's film were identical, allowing viewers to witness the graphical correlate of the sounds as they heard them. *Sound ABC* can thus be seen as the long-awaited fulfillment of modernist artists' synesthetic aspirations, bridging sound and image through the universal artistic medium of the electric current. This film, like so many of the period's most fascinating products, is considered lost.

5

"A New, Perfect Musical Instrument"

The Trautonium and Electric Music in the 1930s

This machine was so modern, so frightfully new,
no one knew quite exactly just what it would do.[1]
—Dr. Seuss

In 1933, the last year of the Weimar Republic, the German engineer and erstwhile instrument builder Peter Lertes published a book called *Elektrische Musik*. Bearing the elaborate subtitle "An accessible survey of its foundations, the present state of technology, and its possibilities for future development," Lertes's study was the first of its kind: a systematic overview of the new field of electric musical instruments, covering everything from the technical fundamentals of electroacoustics to a survey of the most important inventions of the time. Although the book was written for the most part in the sober and scientific tone of an engineering manual, Lertes allowed himself a brief commentary on the wider significance of his subject. In his foreword, he noted that "electric music" signified for most practicing musicians an "intrusion into a domain of culture and intellect in which there seems to be no place for technology." His book was meant to serve notice to those still living in denial of the new age of music to come:

> The time of music making on instruments that have been played by man for centuries must therefore necessarily be followed by an era of music that accommodates the present-day technical mindset of mankind, an era of music in which the most powerful force of nature, *electricity*—which has above all others contributed to the reshaping of our existence—imprints instrument

building with its own particular character, an era of music that is characterized by the shaping and capturing of the abundance of tone that virtually flows from nature itself. [. . .] Electric instruments would to a large extent fail to realize their purpose if they served merely to imitate mechanical instruments, or if they are employed only in the performance of traditional music. Thus there is a call for creative artists to conceive a new idiomatic compositional style for electric instruments, so that these instruments can become what they ultimately strive to be: instruments for *a new music of a new age*.[2]

The early 1930s were heady times for the burgeoning field of what was increasingly called, in a familiar abbreviated form, "electro-music." New instruments sprouted up like mushrooms on both sides of the Atlantic. Léon Theremin had settled in New York in late 1927 and continued to develop his eponymous device. In 1929, the Radio Corporation of America (RCA) unveiled a mass-produced model of the Theremin, the first such effort to make electric instruments available to consumers.[3] Theremin also devised new inventions such as the motion-controlled Terpsiton and, at the behest of the American composer Henry Cowell, a protosequencer known as the Rhythmicon, which allowed complex polyrhythms to be played via a photo-acoustic apparatus triggered by a conventional musical keyboard. Theremin's relocation to the United States did nothing to slow down the development of new instruments in the Soviet Union, where devices such as Sergei Rzhevkin's Cathodic Harmonium and Nikolai Ananiev's Sonar closely paralleled inventions in Western Europe.[4] In France, Maurice Martenot's Ondes Martenot made use of various speaker membranes reminiscent of Mager's instruments, and Armand Givelet and Edouard Coupleux built their Radiophonic Organ, a massive instrument with three keyboard manuals and over four hundred vacuum tubes.[5] But the center of the electro-music universe, at least in terms of sheer quantity of inventions, was Germany. By the time that Jörg Mager, widely recognized as the founder of the movement, unveiled his newest instrument, the Partiturophon, in 1930, the field was buzzing with activity, from the electromagnetic tone wheels of the Magnetophone (a predecessor of the Hammond organ) to Emmerich Spielmann's photoelectric proto-sampler, the Superpiano.

In addition to "pure" electric devices, inventors also developed a wide range of so-called electro-mechanical instruments, in which "acoustic" musical tones were electrically amplified and modified. Mager's former assistant Oskar Vierling designed an amplified piano called the

Elektrochord, whose tone could be treated by various electric filters, and also built a number of electrified string instruments along similar lines. Walther Nernst, working at Humboldt University in Berlin, led a design team that built the Neo-Bechstein grand piano, an innovation intended to revitalize the floundering German piano industry. Lacking a sounding board, it used thin strings and tiny hammers to generate barely audible tones that were amplified and modified by electromagnetic pickups. It also featured a built-in radio and gramophone player, making it an all-in-one musical solution that combined passive listening and active music making in a single device. A 1931 article in the *Journal of Instrument Building* captured the mood of the times: "There is currently a boom in the field of electroacoustic (ether-wave) music. More and more inventors are at work developing this new branch and opening new paths for music. [. . .] All these efforts have a single purpose: to conquer a new world of tones. Who can say if we already stand before this goal?"[6]

Among this swarm of new inventions, the most successful new instrument in Germany was the Trautonium, named after its creator, Friedrich Trautwein (1888–1956).[7] It came closer than any other invention of its kind to realizing the twin goals of electro-music: establishing an original, idiomatic repertoire and furnishing a universally accessible domestic instrument for the radio age. As this chapter chronicles, Trautwein's rise to prominence coincided broadly with Jörg Mager's decline: while Mager's career represented the early, idealist phase of electric music, Trautwein's ascent signaled the movement's attainment of a new degree of professionalization and public stature. Trautwein succeeded in part by co-opting his rival's rhetoric: like Mager, he portrayed electric music as a creative alternative to the dominance of reproductive sound technologies and gave voice to the hope of bringing artists and engineers together in common cause. In a 1930 interview coinciding with the unveiling of the Trautonium, Trautwein declared:

> While electroacoustics has occupied itself in the last few years primarily with the problems of reproduction, I would like to provide new expressive possibilities for the creative musician. Mechanical music has not enriched art as such, but only, for the most part, disseminated it. Above all, I hope through my work to serve creative art and thus to contribute to the reconciliation of the two falsely opposed branches of the human spirit: art and technology.[8]

Though both men's instruments would ultimately fall short of the lofty visions of the electro-music movement, this was as much due to political and economic circumstances as to the instruments' aesthetic and technical failings. Electric instruments, alone among the technological innovations of the 1920s, flourished in Germany during the following decade, even as many kindred artistic experiments were stamped out.

THE TRAUTONIUM

Like Mager and most other electro-music inventors of the time, Trautwein had a background in radio, and for him too the development of electric instruments stemmed directly from experiences with radio technology.[9] Although he had played organ as a child and studied music at the Heidelberg Conservatory, his later education focused on electrical engineering and acoustics. His first patents for electric tone generation were filed soon after he received his doctorate from Karlsruhe Technical University in 1921. He filed a number of patents during the 1920s, but—unlike Mager—he was cautious as an inventor and wary of unveiling his creations while they were still works in progress.[10]

In contrast to Mager's instruments, which underwent radical changes from year to year, the outward design of the Trautonium never significantly deviated from its first prototype. The playing interface was breathtakingly elegant, consisting of a single wire stretched over a parallel metal plate. When the player pressed down with his finger, the wire and plate made contact and an electrical circuit was closed. The point of contact on the left-right axis of the plate determined the circuit's resistance and thus the pitch of the generated tone.[11] A knob on the console allowed the player to adjust the pitch span of the manual in a fashion similar to Mager's "musical pantograph." In addition, there was a set of movable keys over the wire that the player could configure to create a scale of fixed pitch positions: instead of touching the wire directly, the player could press the key, which put the wire and the plate into contact at a determined point. Trautwein had bypassed the problem of tuning by allowing the player to choose between continuous and fixed division of the pitch spectrum.

The playing interface of the Trautonium thus represented a cunning solution to the question of continuous versus discrete pitch control: one observer described the interface as a hybrid between a violin string and a piano keyboard.[12] Trautwein highlighted this aspect of his instrument as an advantage over the Spherophone: while Mager merely "sought to expand the chromatic tuning by the insertion of quarter tones,"

FIGURE 18. Friedrich Trautwein with the first model of the Trautonium, circa 1930. Source: Leo Kestenberg, ed., *Kunst und Technik* (Berlin: Wegweiser-Verlag, 1930), 452.

Trautwein's instrument captured "continuous tonal space" and put it at the player's disposal.[13] (In practice, however, the Trautonium's fingerboard was most often used only for string-style vibrato and not for microtonal inflections.) Like Theremin and Mager, Trautwein wanted to simplify the process of learning and playing a musical instrument: "The player should be spared all unnecessary mechanical exertion; he does not need to generate the tone with his bodily energy [. . .] but rather he should create and form the tone in a purely artistic way."[14] The ideal was a "three-dimensional performance" that would give the player fluid and intuitive control over pitch, volume, and timbre.[15]

Instead of the vacuum tubes found in other electric instruments, the Trautonium's sound generating circuitry used tiny bulbs filled with neon gas. The bulb functioned as a relaxation oscillator, which gradually built up a charge and then suddenly released it, generating tones that resembled what would later be called sawtooth waves. In acoustic terms, these sounds have a spectrum of harmonic overtones gradually decreasing in amplitude as their frequency increases; their timbre is roughly akin to that of the violin or other bowed string instruments. But Trautwein found the unprocessed tone generated by the neon bulb to be somewhat raw and abrasive. Attempting to shape electric tones into musically viable timbres, he experimented with both additive and subtractive techniques, but ultimately found both unsatisfying. The superposition of overtones on a fundamental pitch led to the sensation of increased volume but not to a significant change in timbre. Trautwein found the technique of filtering harmonically rich waves more promising but judged the effect too far removed from the richness of "acoustic" instruments.[16] Seeking a new approach to the problem of electrically generated timbres, he developed a model based on the phenomenon of what he called *Hallformanten*—roughly, "formants generated by excitation."[17]

The acoustic phenomena known as formants were discovered by the German physiologist Ludimar Hermann (1838–1914), who coined the term to describe the frequency range emphasized by the oral cavity in the production of vowel sounds. They represented a crucial addendum to the overtone theory of timbre developed by Helmholtz.[18] While the harmonic spectrum of a given instrument is projected *relatively* to a fundamental pitch, formants are fixed, absolute zones of resonance shaping the timbre of an instrument over its entire range. To use an anachronistic comparison, formants resemble the bands of a stereo equalizer, which cut or boost certain frequencies across the spectrum. They are in large part responsible for the fact that instruments (including the human voice) have noticeably different registers—that is, various distinct tone colors particular to the low, medium, and high areas of their overall range. On the early models of the Trautonium, the frequency range of the formants could be adjusted continuously by means of rotary capacitors on the instrument's front panel. By moving the formants higher or lower, the player was able to shape the timbre of the electrically generated tone.[19] Trautwein's experiments showed that a low formant creates a dull tone resembling that of a bassoon; a mid-range formant results in a mellow, clarinet-like sound; and a high formant yields a sharp timbre similar to that of a trumpet.[20] One critic estimated that the adjustment of a single formant on the Trautonium could produce about fifty distinguishable timbres. As even the earliest models possessed several tunable formants, the number of potential tone colors reached into the thousands.[21] But according to Peter Lertes, just one formant allowed sufficient timbral variation for most musical needs. He judged the Trautonium's method of tone generation superior to that of all other electric instruments.[22]

In addition to stable timbres in which the formant remains in a single position, Trautwein described some more experimental effects attained by adjusting the formant while playing. If the player holds a tone while altering the formant's frequency range, the upper partials can be heard to shimmer, creating a kind of timbral glissando. If a tone is held while the formant is moved in a sudden, discontinuous way, the effect is of a rapid succession of discrete timbres. Finally, if a melody is played while the formant is modified, a unique phenomenon emerges: confronted with the simultaneous motion of both the fundamental tone and its overtone spectrum, the ear is "confused" and cannot decide which to follow. By the same means, human and animal vocal sounds could be imitated by moving both fundamental and formant continuously within a narrow range.[23] Trautwein suggested that such techniques may find use in the "music of the future."[24]

As this comment implies, Trautwein's relation to electro-music's futurist rhetoric was highly nuanced. In his writings and public remarks about his instrument, he often parroted the language that Mager had helped popularize, even as he subtly played up the contrast between his own professionalism and Mager's image as a quixotic amateur. In response to an interviewer's question whether the practicing musician might be overwhelmed by the unlimited supply of new timbres, Trautwein assented, drawing a distinction between the "infinite-beautiful" and the "limitless-banal." This was likely a jab at Mager and his effusive visions of Klangfarbenmusik. Likewise, even Trautwein's tribute to Mager as the "German pioneer of the idea of electric music" may have contained a backhanded attack: Mager had the dream, Trautwein suggested, while he himself delivered the reality.[25]

FROM LABORATORY TO CONCERT HALL

The late 1920s marked the arrival of what might be called an institutional approach to electric music, with large research teams, interdisciplinary collaboration, and substantial government funding replacing the more informal and ad hoc approach of earlier years. In May 1928, six months before the launch of the Society for Electroacoustic Music in Darmstadt, the Radio Research Section (Rundfunkversuchsstelle) was established at the Berlin Academy of Music with a broad mandate to research topics relating to the new acoustic technologies.[26] It was overseen by Georg Schünemann, the associate director of the Academy, a musicologist and administrator who sought to bring the utopian visions of Busoni's *Sketch of a New Aesthetic of Music* up to date with the technical possibilities of the 1920s. The goal was to elevate radio to a vehicle of culture *(Kulturträger)* and forge new channels of artistic experience fit for a mass society. Expressing the quasi-political hopes attached to the new medium, the scholar Arno Schirokauer declared in 1929 that with the advent of radio, "art has been socialized. From private ownership it has become everyone's possession."[27] Such claims mixed genuine sentiments of cultural populism with ignorance of the obstacles, from commercialization to government censorship, that stood in the way of a truly democratic mode of cultural production.[28]

Because it was housed in a major conservatory, the Radio Research Section could take advantage of the musical resources at its disposal: various choral, orchestral, and chamber music groups; a massive collection of musical instruments; and an archive of over ten thousand ethnomusicological recordings.[29] Its curriculum featured courses in *funkisches Sprechens* (speaking on radio) for would-be broadcasters, speech and gesture for film actors in training, sound-film recording techniques, and composition seminars geared toward writing for radio and motion pictures. The group's activities also touched on new pedagogical uses of radio technology: in 1932 it began broadcasting some of its classes via shortwave radio—a brief but prophetic experiment in "wireless education."[30]

Also in 1928, the Heinrich Hertz Institute for Oscillation Research was founded at the Berlin Institute of Technology (Technische Hochschule). Its director was Karl Willy Wagner, the engineer and acoustician whose research on electroacoustic filters had influenced both Mager and Trautwein. The broad remit of the HHI encompassed all vibratory phenomena, from acoustics to radio and telephony. Although it was more technically oriented than its counterpart at the Academy of Music, the two institutions were closely linked, and both were involved in the research and development of electric instruments. Fundamental to both was the goal of collapsing the distance between productive and reproductive technologies—instruments and media—through the close collaboration of artists and technologists.

Trautwein was appointed as a lecturer in acoustics at the Academy of Music in 1930 and immediately began working in the studio of the Radio Research Section.[31] There he found a valuable collaborator in Paul Hindemith, who had taught composition and film music at the Academy since 1927.[32] Hindemith, who had previously extolled Jörg Mager's instruments, was quickly won over to Trautwein's cause, and

FIGURE 19. The electroacoustic laboratories of the Radio Research Section (Rundfunkversuchsstelle), founded in Berlin in 1928. Source: Leo Kestenberg, ed., *Kunst und Technik* (Berlin: Wegweiser-Verlag, 1930), 449.

even had a hand in the Trautonium's design. Trautwein had originally intended to build a kind of electric organ, similar to Mager's Keyboard Spherophone. The instrument's string manual was seen as a provisional solution because it was cheaper than a full keyboard, but Trautwein eventually decided to keep the more unconventional interface, thanks in part to the encouragement of Hindemith, who, as a violist, found the metal wire appealingly familiar.[33] It was Hindemith, too, who introduced a third important player to the project. Shortly after Trautwein's arrival, Hindemith brought some of his students into the basement studio of the Radio Research Section to hear the experimental model of the Trautonium. Among the visitors was the nineteen-year-old Oskar Sala, a composition pupil of Hindemith's. With his dual interests in music and the natural sciences (he would later study physics at Humboldt University in Berlin), Sala was quick to perceive the instrument's potential, and he soon became involved in its development, serving as an intermediary between Trautwein's technical perspectives and Hindemith's musical concerns.[34]

Trautwein's first presentable prototype was a small, unimposing device comprising three elements: a manual consisting of a wire suspended over a metal track, a compartment containing the sound-generating circuitry, and a pedal used to control volume. This instrument was introduced to the public on June 20, 1930, as part of New Music Berlin, a relocated version of the Donaueschingen summer music festival that had presented original compositions for the Welte-Mignon reproducing piano, Jörg Mager's Spherophone, and various experiments with recording media such as sound film and gramophone. Just two days before his debut of the Trautonium, Hindemith and Ernst Toch had presented their original music for gramophone records (discussed in chapter 4). For the instrument's debut, Trautwein had pulled off nothing short of a publicity coup: a newly written work by one of Germany's most prominent composers. Paul Hindemith wrote a set of seven short pieces for three Trautoniums called *Des kleinen Elektromusikers Lieblinge* (The little electro-musician's favorites), which were performed by Hindemith, Sala, and the pianist Rudolf Schmidt. At first blush, these pieces were not particularly noteworthy. Featuring the mildly dissonant contrapuntal textures typical of Hindemith's compositions of the late 1920s, the music ranges from the lugubrious tone of the first movement, which includes a prominent quotation of the *Tristan* theme, to the spry rhythmic playfulness of the sixth movement, which ends with acrobatic cadenzas for each of the instruments in turn.

In spite of its generally light, innocuous character, Hindemith's music gave hints of what the new instrument was capable of. In the second piece, the score requires that the instrument's tones be projected from a distant speaker *(Fernwerk)*. In addition, Hindemith calls for two distinct tone colors, designated simply as I ("dull") and II ("sharp"). These are first juxtaposed in three separate phrases (I-II-I), the brusque changes of tone color suggesting contrasting stops on a pipe organ. In the final four measures, the two timbres are presented in gradual transition (again I-II-I) in conjunction with a dynamic swell from pianissimo to fortissimo and back again. The seventh and final movement likewise calls for both discrete and continuous contrasts between the two timbres and adds to the mix several alternations—including one mid-phrase—between the main and distant speakers. With these touches, Hindemith provided a modest but promising demonstration of the Trautonium's potential for new musical effects.[35]

Coinciding with the appearance of the Trautonium, Trautwein published a small book entitled *Elektrische Musik,* which doubled as a technical introduction to his instrument and an attempt to seize the reins of the young electro-music movement. The book was the first in

FIGURE 20. Paul Hindemith's sketch for the first movement of *Des kleinen Elektromusikers Lieblinge*. The handwriting at the bottom of the page reads: "Attempt at a composition for Dr. Trautwein's electric musical instrument." Source: Friedrich Trautwein, *Elektrische Musik* (Berlin: Weidmannsche Buchhandlung, 1930), 38.

a projected series of publications to appear under the imprimatur of the Radio Research Section. In his foreword, Schünemann trumpeted: "We are witnessing the realization of a dream long held by all musicians: we have an instrument that fulfills every musical wish, that can be used and altered in various ways, that combines the advantages of many musical instruments, that can be readily grasped and whose manner of playing is truly artistically executed."[36] The period of anticipation was over, Schünemann suggested; a new age of music had finally arrived.

ELECTRO-MUSIC FOR THE PEOPLE: THE VOLKSTRAUTONIUM

In the wake of its Berlin debut, the Trautonium quickly began to make the rounds of the emerging electro-music publicity circuit. In July 1931, Hindemith conducted his new *Concertino for Trautonium and String Orchestra,* with Sala as soloist, at the second Radio Music Convention in Munich. Trautwein's instrument also appeared at the 1932 Radio Exhibition (Funkaufstellung) in Berlin, where it was featured onstage as part of an "electric orchestra" that included Oskar Vierling's electric cello and violin, the Neo-Bechstein piano, and the Theremin. Notably, Jörg Mager's instruments were not represented. A few years into the new decade, it was clear that Trautwein had eclipsed Mager as the face of the electro-music movement. Georg Schünemann of the Radio Research Section, though hardly impartial, declared in 1931 that the Trautonium was "the only really musical instrument" among the new electrophones.[37]

Trautwein's instrument had an additional point of appeal beyond its sound: it was remarkably easy to produce. Using readily available electrical components, amateur do-it-yourselfers could build workable models at home. Indeed, just a year after the premiere in Berlin, an introduction to the Trautonium was published complete with a foldout blueprint to guide radio enthusiasts through the construction of their own copy of the instrument.[38] The idea of a homemade electric instrument was seized upon by the American publisher Hugo Gernsback, whose *Radio-Craft* magazine featured a cover story on how to build the Trautonium in March 1933. In a breathless editorial entitled simply "Electronic Music," Gernsback hailed the arrival of electric instruments, which, he declared, "will revolutionize the entire musical art [. . .] during the next decade."[39] More important for his readership of radio amateurs, though, was the fact that the construction of these instruments was, in Gernsback's words, "ridiculously simple." The feature article provided complete instructions and schematics for the construction of the original 1930 model of the Trautonium, slightly adjusted

FIGURE 21. "The Orchestra of the Future??" This photograph from the 1932 German Radio Exhibition shows a veritable who's who of the electro-music scene, with the exception of Jörg Mager. The sentence across the bottom of the photo reads: "And all these instruments produce their tones over loudspeakers, of which a great number are visible in the background." Source: *Funkschau* 52 (1932), frontispiece.

to account for the different components available to American radio enthusiasts. It described the Trautonium as "a simple musical instrument easily built at home by anyone [. . .] nothing elaborate, nothing expensive." What's more, in an echo of the dubious promises that accompanied earlier electric instruments such as the Theremin, the author assured readers that "one may learn to play it in a short time, even though one is not a musician."[40]

Hoping to seize on the simplicity of the instrument's design and the potential market for a mass-produced model, in 1931 Trautwein and Sala began to develop a new version with support from the radio and electronics firm Telefunken. Envisioned as an electric instrument perfectly suited for domestic music making (*Hausmusik*) and originally called the Telefunken-Trautonium, the instrument would soon become known as the Volkstrautonium. (Though later exploited by the Nazis, the *Volks*- prefix predated them and expressed a populist enthusiasm for affordable, mass-produced consumer goods.)[41] The manual and circuitry were consolidated into a single boxlike enclosure complete with a lid to protect the circuits from dust. Under the hood, the neon bulbs of the earlier model were replaced with a new kind of gas-filled tube called a thyratron, which helped to stabilize the instrument's pitch.[42] The Volkstrautonium also had several interface improvements to aid performers: an array of

FIGURE 22. The Trautonium in the USA. Source: Cover of *Radio-Craft* magazine, March 1933.

knobs and switches above the manual allowed for quick octave transpositions and timbral adjustments, while carbon resistors under the fingerboard enabled players to regulate dynamics by adjusting the weight of their touch. Finally, the instrument could be plugged directly into a radio receiver for amplification, meaning that it could be marketed as an add-on to that increasingly widespread domestic amenity.

FIGURE 23. The Telefunken-Trautonium, also known as the Volkstrautonium. Source: Peter Lertes, *Elektrische Musik* (Dresden: Theodor Steinkopff, 1933), 184.

Though motivated in part by sheer marketing savvy, the Volkstrautonium—and the broader goal of a mass-produced electric instrument—also reflected a widespread reexamination of the role of music in modern mass society. Many composers of the time decried the distance between artist and audience as a symptom of social alienation; they called for new forms of music that emphasized participation and engagement, rather than passive reception. This tendency found expression in the idea of *Gebrauchsmusik,* or "everyday music," one of the key concepts of Weimar Culture musical culture. Popularized by the musicologist Heinrich Besseler in the early 1920s and later associated above all with the music of Paul Hindemith, the notion of Gebrauchsmusik inspired a variety of efforts to establish new forms of contact between music and social life. Many composers abjured the pathos and complexity of late-romantic and expressionist music in exchange for a simpler and more direct idiom, often alluding to popular styles. Others turned their attention to "occasional" works meant to accompany social functions or wrote music intended for amateur performance. One of the most famous examples of these efforts to reconceive music's place in society was a 1929 collaboration between Hindemith and the playwright

Bertolt Brecht entitled *Lehrstück* (Didactic piece), in which the form of the music was freely adapted to the abilities and interests of the performers. The motto of the piece proclaimed: "Musik machen ist besser als Musik hören" ("It's better to make music than to listen to it").[43]

For some partisans of the movement, the Volkstrautonium appeared as the technological embodiment of the Gebrauchsmusik ideal. The instrument made possible the most radical interpretation of the concept yet: instead of writing music for amateurs, simply give them the means to make their own. In a provocative essay published in 1932, the composer and former Schoenberg pupil Walter Gronostay criticized the electro-music movement's disregard for the social ramifications of modern sound technology. The new instruments were not merely sources of novel timbres, he argued, but rather "presentiments of a new form of community." Gronostay, who taught a course on Gebrauchsmusik at the Radio Research Section, suggested that the true significance of electric instruments was not in "music for listening" but in "music for playing." In the midst of Germany's seemingly never-ending economic crisis, when learning an orchestral instrument had become a luxury for most citizens, electrophones offered a lifeline to the endangered practice of Hausmusik: "Electric musical instruments—and the Trautonium, in particular," wrote Gronostay, "offer the renewed opportunity for making one's own music. Virtually every home has a radio in it. The same source from which one receives music is equally capable of generating sounds itself."[44] From this vantage point, the Trautonium's viability as a concert instrument was a secondary matter; its true place was in the hands of nonprofessional musicians. Though hardly capable of standing alongside orchestral instruments, as an add-on to the home radio it could perform the more valuable function of "prompting the listener to noodle around, and thus drawing him out of his passivity."[45] With its affordability, ease of playing, and musical flexibility, the Trautonium could be to the twentieth century what the piano was to the nineteenth: the instrumental foundation of a culture of amateur musicianship.

The Volkstrautonium was presented to the public at the 1933 Radio Exhibition and appeared on the market in August of that year. A press report published in advance of the instrument's unveiling declared that the Volkstrautonium was ideal for domestic music making, where it promised to "replace virtually all other instruments."[46] Telefunken's marketing likewise pitched the device as a musical jack-of-all-trades: "There is no instrument better suited to making music in the home than the Trautonium. Its owner is no longer compelled to play only those pieces that are specially written for the instrument, and that he has mastered. Whoever plays the Trautonium can play any piece of music, no matter the instrument for which it was written, in a timbre appropriate to the original setting."[47] The marketing of the Volkstrautonium (like that of the RCA Theremin in the United States) was rooted in equal parts opportunistic hucksterism and the sincere belief in culture made universally accessible by modern technology.

In spite of the anticipation surrounding its appearance, the Volkstrautonium was, in Sala's memorable phrase, a "flop." The timing of the release could not have been worse. With unemployment hovering around 30 percent, the instrument's price of 400 reichsmark—equivalent to about two and a half months' wages for an average worker—was out of reach for most Germans.[48] Although it was intended to piggyback onto the increasingly ubiquitous radio receiver, the Volkstrautonium may in fact have been edged out of the market by the cheaper device. At the same 1933 Radio Exhibition where the new instrument was unveiled, the new People's Radio (Volksempfänger) was also introduced to the public. Priced at just 76 reichsmark, or about a fifth the cost of the Volkstrautonium, it sold some one hundred thousand units during the exhibition alone. Further dampening the Volkstrautonium's rollout were Telefunken's half-hearted marketing efforts: the company barely advertised it at all. (Even had the product sold well, Telefunken would not have turned a profit. They apparently saw electro-music as a growth industry in which it was worth a short-term financial sacrifice to establish an early foothold.) Of the two hundred units that were manufactured, only a handful were sold. Production was halted in 1937, and the remaining units were returned to Trautwein. Telefunken forwarded all future inquiries about the instrument directly to the inventor and forbade him from using the company's name in connection with the Trautonium.[49]

The Trautonium's troubled public reception stemmed in part from an instrumental identity crisis. Was its place in the home or on the stage? Not surprisingly, the instrument's marketers sought to have it both ways. A brochure entitled "A New, Perfect Musical Instrument" assured the reader that the Trautonium could produce both the new and the old—the ranges and timbres of all known instruments *and* "an overpowering abundance of new, dramatic timbres that are unique to the instrument."[50] The two prospects were almost always mentioned in tandem: on the one hand, any familiar timbre available at the turn of a dial; on the other, new tones never heard before. Although these two

FIGURE 24. One of the few known advertisements for the Volks-trautonium. The text reads: "Nearly unlimited richness of tone colors and potential for artistic expression, volume adjustable at will, a wide variety of special effects, simple and yet versatile playing technique—all this is offered by the Trautonium, the most versatile musical instrument for orchestras or solo playing." Source: Peter Lertes, *Elektrische Musik* (Dresden: Theodor Steinkopff, 1933), back matter.

uses of the instrument were by no means mutually exclusive, in reality there was a tension between the ideals of amateur music making, on the one hand, and modernist experimentation, on the other. If the sheer novelty of the technology had monopolized public and critical attention for the first few years of the electro-music phenomenon, by the early 1930s supporters of the movement were growing restless. As one observer noted in 1932, "The compositions for electric musical instruments have so far conveyed only the technical charm of the new and unfamiliar—not, however, new expressive possibilities for the stirring of emotions!"[51]

As long as the Trautonium was envisioned primarily as an instrument for domestic music making, the matter of original music could be set aside. But with the failure to conquer the mass market, the question of repertoire became suddenly acute. If it was to be a truly artistic instrument, its supporters reasoned, the Trautonium must have its own unique body of music. Even before the release of the Volkstrautonium, electro-music enthusiasts had sounded the warning bell. "We desperately need *new* music for electric instruments," declared Georg Schünemann of the Radio Research Section in an article published in January 1932. "There is certainly no shortage of technical solutions. [. . .] But the musicians, both composers and performers, follow too slowly. There are only a few who help tackle the technical challenges, but the technicians can make progress only by working hand in hand with musicians."[52] Schünemann voiced an idea that would be heard often in the new decade: no longer was technology the limiting reagent in the progress of music. The new instruments were there, but the artistic will to exploit them was lacking.

Over the course of the 1930s, the Trautonium became increasingly associated not with its namesake inventor but with its virtuoso performer, Oskar Sala. Lacking original compositions beyond Hindemith's few contributions, Sala was forced to rely on familiar showpieces of baroque, classical, and romantic music to demonstrate the Trautonium's musical capabilities. Reinforcing this gesture toward high-culture respectability, the prominent music publisher Schott published a book called *Trautonium School* in 1933, coinciding with the release of the Volkstrautonium. Edited by Trautwein, the book contained an overview of playing technique by Sala and compositional examples by Hindemith, including arrangements of Corelli and Mozart for two Trautoniums and piano.[53] But such uses of the instrument sometimes ran afoul of modernist partisans, who expected a new, idiomatic style of electro-music composition. "It bears repeating that the purpose of such a device is not to counterfeit existing instruments," wrote one critic. "Of course, with the Trautonium it is possible to create a violin or trumpet sound, or even to imitate the human voice. [. . .] But the goal of such a device can ultimately only be to create new sounds of great fullness and beauty, and in this way to enrich the music of our time."[54] Ironically, even Sala's grudging attempts to popularize the Trautonium by playing familiar tunes from the repertoire could backfire: traditionalists sometimes chafed against what they perceived as "experimenting with the classics."[55] In short, Trautwein and Sala caught flak from both sides: they were attacked for squandering the Trautonium's potential for genuinely new music and at the same time accused of irreverence toward canonic works and the instruments for which they were originally intended. "Thank you, Holy Cecilia, for giving us the violin, the clarinet, the cello, and the many other lovely instruments," jibed one critic. "For the Trautonium, you are not to blame."[56]

Two years after the release of the Volkstrautonium, yet another incarnation of the instrument appeared when the Reich Radio Society (Reichsrundfunkgesellschaft) commissioned Sala to build a new model that incorporated the many improvements he had made over the past couple years. The so-called Radio-Trautonium had a second fingerboard (allowing the performer to play two-part polyphony) and two pedals capable of modifying both volume and pitch. Its tone-generation circuitry was expanded to create "subharmonics" by means of a technique patented by Trautwein in 1934. In addition to a series of whole number multiples (2/1, 3/1, 4/1, etc.) above the fundamental tone, it could generate a chain of divisors (1/2, 1/3, 1/4, etc.) below the played note, and thus provide a new and distinctive timbral coloration. Hindemith noted the "strange possibilities" arising from the instrument's sonic wiring: each of the two voices could be doubled with an additional tone drawn from the subharmonic series, allowing for unexpected combinations.[57] He dutifully baptized the model with a new composition called "Langsames Stück und Rondo für Trautonium." It would be his last contribution to the instrument's repertoire.[58] Hindemith, like so many others, would soon become ensnared in the political webs of the Third Reich.

"THE INSTRUMENT OF STEEL ROMANTICISM": THE TRAUTONIUM IN THE THIRD REICH

While the protagonists of electric music enjoyed their fleeting heyday, the Weimar Republic was disintegrating around them. Beginning in 1930, parliamentary democracy was suspended and government conducted by means of constitutionally dubious emergency decrees. Unemployment soared as the aftermath of the U.S. stock market crash wracked the German economy, which was still recovering from the extreme instability of the early 1920s. The National Socialist Party, whose popular support peaked at 37 percent of the electorate in 1932, maneuvered its way into government alongside the traditional center-right parties, while on the left the Socialists and Communists were crippled by vicious internecine battles. Soon after Hitler was named chancellor in January 1933, the Nazis began their ruthless consolidation of power, and within months the already tottering government of the Weimar Republic lay in shambles.

The reprisals came quickly. Georg Schünemann, who had taken over from the composer Franz Schreker as director of the Berlin Academy of Music in 1932, was denounced as a Marxist and stripped of his office in April 1933. By order of Minister of Propaganda Joseph Goebbels, the Radio Research Section's budget was promptly cut; two years later the institution was shuttered.[59] The Heinrich Hertz Institute was targeted as well. Its director, Karl Willy Wagner, was ousted in 1936 after a lengthy persecution. Wagner's crime: he had resisted orders to dismiss Jewish members of the institute's staff. With typical thoroughness, the Nazis even removed Hertz's name from the institute's title on account of his Jewish ancestry.[60] In 1938, with the departure of Jörg Mager's erstwhile assistant Oskar Vierling, the institute's "electric music" research group was dissolved.[61] Another crucial site of artistic and technological experimentation, the Donaueschingen Festival, which had migrated from its original locale to Baden-Baden and thence to Berlin, also fell victim to the Nazis' cultural crusade. After 1930 it had been temporarily cancelled on account of the country's dire economic situation.[62] When it was resumed in 1934, the festival was a ghastly shadow of its former self. Once a cosmopolitan meeting place for contemporary musical currents from all over Europe, it now featured a purified cast of all-German composers. A typical program included marching music for the Hitler Youth and patriotic pablum with titles such as "Heimat, dir zu Ruhm und Ehr" (Glory and honor to thee, O homeland).[63]

Amid the shifts of power, electro-music inventors grappled desperately for political favor. In 1933, Mager, likely bitter about Hindemith having favoring the Trautonium over his own instruments, denounced the composer in a letter to Fritz Stein, the party loyalist who had replaced Schünemann as director of the Academy of Music.[64] Shortly after the closing of the Radio Research Section in 1935, Trautwein discovered a few scores of Communist fight songs composed by Mager among the archived documents. Apparently fearful of being implicated by association, he sent the scores to Stein along with an explanatory letter.[65] Two years later, Trautwein, who had joined the Nazi Party in 1933, was awarded a promotion to a professorship in acoustics at the academy.[66] His good standing also ensured that the apolitical Sala would be not only unmolested but substantially supported during the Nazis' twelve-year reign.

Trautwein's protection could not shield the Trautonium's foremost composer, however. Although Hindemith had moderated his bad-boy image since the 1920s, his indelible associations with the musical culture of the Weimar Republic made him an easy target for the Nazi culture police. Rumors of his emigration circulated as early as 1933.[67] The famed conductor Wilhelm Furtwängler publically intervened with a newspaper article defending the composer in November 1934, but when Goebbels denounced Hindemith as an "atonal noisemaker" in a speech to the Reich Chamber of Culture the following month, the writing was on the wall.[68] Hindemith resigned his post at the Academy of Music in 1937, and in the following year, he was pilloried alongside Mahler, Schoenberg, Webern, Krenek, and Weill as a "standard-bearer of musical decay" at the Degenerate Music *(Entartete Musik)* exhibit in Düsseldorf. He fled to Switzerland, and then, in 1940, to the United States.

In late 1933, a dispatch from Germany appeared in the American journal *Modern Music*. Bearing the title "Under the Swastika," it was from the pen of Hans Heinz Stuckenschmidt, who detailed the situation of contemporary music in the wake of Hitler's rise to power. While many Germans were convinced that the Nazis would be too busy managing the economic crisis to concern themselves with cultural matters, Stuckenschmidt astutely noted "the important part [that] art and culture play in the program of German fascism." With regard to the Nazis' attitude toward music, he distinguished between two camps: those who attacked "dissonant music" outright and those who had a more nuanced view that allowed for incorporating certain "modernist" elements into the artistic apparatus of the Third Reich.[69] It was the latter group that would hold more sway in shaping the Nazis' cultural policy. This flexibility was consistent with their broader tactic of *Gleichschaltung,* or forcible coordination, through which the Nazis insinuated themselves into all virtually aspects of German society by absorbing preexisting political, social, and cultural organizations and reconstituting them as compliant cogs in the totalitarian machine.

Even as they persecuted many of the movement's leading figures, the Nazis' policy toward electric music, like their reaction to Weimar culture in general, was characterized less by ideological consistency than by sheer opportunism.[70] In spite of their "blood and soil" rhetoric and their contempt for the rootless cosmopolitanism of modern life, the Nazis were no fusty reactionaries. They carefully positioned themselves between the irretrievable past of prewar Germany, on the one hand, and the despised "system" of the Weimar Republic, on the other. Their aesthetic ideology promised nothing less than an alternate modernity, one with all of the intoxicating energies but none of the troubling ambiguities. In his first public statement on the arts after being named chancellor in 1933, Adolf

Hitler condemned both modernism and traditionalism as equally foreign to the spirit of National Socialism.[71] In a similar vein, Goebbels pleaded, "We National Socialists are not unmodern; we are the carriers of a new modernity, not only in politics and in social matters, but also in art and intellectual matters. To be modern means to stand near the spirit of the present."[72] It was Goebbels who popularized the motto of Nazi aesthetics: "steel romanticism" *(stählerne Romantik)*, a concept that fused the soulful depths of the German artistic tradition with the tough and unsentimental attitude demanded by the challenges of modernity. Steel romanticism, explained Goebbels, was "harder and crueler" than earlier forms; it was "a romanticism that has the courage to confront problems and stare into their pitiless eyes without flinching."[73]

The Nazis' willingness to appropriate progressive tendencies in art was matched by their enthusiastic embrace of technology. The ground for this rapprochement had been prepared by the work of protofascist philosophers such as Paul Krannhals, whose writings attempted to reconcile the ostensibly opposed forces of *Technik* and *Kultur*. No different from liberal champions of modernity such as Ernst Cassirer or inventors such as Jörg Mager, Krannhals distinguished between wholesome, "organic" technologies that serve mankind's purposes and harmful, "mechanical" ones that subordinate ends to means. His magnum opus was tellingly titled *The Organic Worldview*.[74]

Electro-music thus fit perfectly into the Nazis' ideological program. Provided it was safely distanced from its unfavorable associations with the Weimar Republic and shown to benefit the new regime, the movement was allowed to live on in the Third Reich. The sincerity of the Nazis' interest in electric instruments was demonstrated by a remarkable meeting that took place in April 1935. At the Ministry of Propaganda, Trautwein and Sala presented the Trautonium to Goebbels and a specially invited audience of musicians, composers, and scholars. Accompanied by piano and cello, Sala demonstrated his mastery of the instrument by playing a Bach sonata, a Beethoven trio, and a sonata movement by Max Reger. Goebbels and Trautwein conversed at length about the Trautonium's prospects for composers and performers, but the minister made no secret of the fact that his primary concern was the instrument's ability to provide music for mass gatherings.[75]

While party officials such as Goebbels probed electro-music's propaganda value, the instruments' inventors rushed to make themselves useful to the new regime. They argued that their instruments were not mere technical novelties but sonic expressions of the emerging National Socialist Zeitgeist. Bruno Helberger, the coinventor of the electric instrument known as the Hellertion, argued that electric music was uniquely attuned to the world-historical destiny of the German nation. He appealed to the party faithful in an article published in the *Frankfurter Zeitung* in December 1936:

> It could well be claimed that our present worldview, with its commitment to the community of blood and labor, finds its commensurate instrumental expression neither in the dogmatically static sound-world of the organ nor in the military instruments such as drums and horns, nor again in the virtuosic instruments of our traditional art music. Instead we seek, in the organic connection of all things, a sound material that has grown out of the new practical possibilities of our technology and social organization and that is, so to speak, biologically connected to the present state of our culture and our worldview.[76]

If the country's leaders sought a musical form of expression that captured the energies of the historical moment, Helberger suggested, what better way than a new genre that combined the cultural prestige of "the most German of the arts" with the transfiguring power of modern technology?

Trautwein also took pains to justify electric music's existence in the new Germany. Here he battled on two rhetorical fronts: first, defending the artistic value of electric instruments to skeptical musicians, and second, framing the larger project of electro-music as a service to the German nation. Trautwein lamented that electric instruments still faced much of the same stubborn opposition that they had at the time of Mager's debut in the mid-1920s. "In many cases, the efforts of electro-music have been hindered not only by indifference but by open, sometimes acrimonious "resistance," he wrote. "The few pioneers of electro-music have found no sympathy for their ideas; unfortunately, then as now they were for the most part viewed as dreamers."[77] He insisted that electric instruments answered the profound necessity of artistic progress, which had been felt by great German musicians such as Bach, Mozart, Beethoven, Wagner, and—somewhat surprisingly, given his questionable Teutonic pedigree—Busoni. (Indeed, Trautwein's claim that "instrumental music is significantly constrained by the quality of musical instruments" was a paraphrase of Busoni's declaration that "the development of music is impeded by our instruments."[78]) Echoing sentiments expressed earlier by Mager and Theremin, Trautwein also

FIGURE 25. The three-voice Trautonium, circa 1936. To the original monophonic sound module (center), two additional modules have been added. Three playing manuals are located below the center module. The pedals on the right control volume; the one on the left allows for continuous modification of tone color. Source: Friedrich Trautwein, "Wesen und Ziele der Elektromusik," *Zeitschrift für Musik* 103, no. 6 (1936), unpaginated photo insert.

challenged the idea that electricity was incompatible with the direct, sensitive touch of true musical artistry and that the "mechanical," or technologically mediated, electric tone could not compare to the "organic" response of traditional instruments. Trautwein argued that it is not the source of the tone but its *shape* that determines artistic quality.

The constant, "automatic" flow of electricity provides merely the raw material to be cultivated into beautiful tones by the performer. Indeed, he suggested, the automation of tone production enables the performer to focus all the more intently on the nuances of technique.

Beyond vindicating his instrument on aesthetic and musical grounds, Trautwein faced the more ambitious task of reconciling his project with the ideological strictures of the Third Reich. He did this by inflecting the familiar tropes of electro-music rhetoric to make them conform to the Nazi worldview. Trautwein's invocation of the ancient unity of art and technology in the Greek concept of *technē* was nothing new, but such proclamations took on darker meanings in the Germany of the late 1930s, where the reconciliation of tensions was often used as a cover for political coercion.[79] Likewise, his claim that electro-music could rouse instrumental technology from the "hundred-year slumber" in which it had languished since the early nineteenth century has an ominous ring in light of Nazi slogans of national (and racial) awakening—"*Deutschland erwache!*" Most remarkable, however, was the way that Trautwein linked the travails of electro-music to the "individualistic capitalism" of the liberal bourgeois era.[80] He suggested that the new instruments had failed to become established in practice due to the shortsighted logic of the previous age, for which profitability was the sole measure of value. But now, in "the age of National Socialism [. . .] the economy is not the master but rather the servant of culture."[81] Technology, long reviled on account of its association with materialism and rootless modern rationalism, could now be embraced in clean conscience by German artists:

> Art now has the task of sustaining and deepening the spiritual exaltation of the people. To this end, the artist is dependent on the technological means of the modern age, and he shirks his task if he rejects these means in whole or in part on an unsound basis. Technology is no demon; it too is a product of our responsible countrymen, with whom the artist can and should work together as a comrade for the new Germany.[82]

Whether such statements expressed sincere ideological fervor or cynically curried favor with the new regime, they helped secure a place for electric instruments in fascist Germany. But electro-music inventors such as Helberger and Trautwein not only gave rhetorical support to the Nazi creed—they also lent their services to Hitler's high-tech propaganda apparatus. This was a mutually beneficial arrangement: the inventors won publicity and prestige for their instruments while the regime showcased the greatness of German technology and culture. The

1936 Olympic Games in Berlin presented the Nazis their first chance to shine on a global stage, and electro-music inventors featured prominently in the public spectacle. Trautwein offered his instrument to test the vast speaker system set up in the newly built Olympic Stadium and developed a variety of means to project sound for large audiences, and in dedicated towers. The Trautonium was also played three times in the official radio programming accompanying the games.[83] Bruno Helberger's Hellertion was used in the Nuremberg Rally the following month, where it was hailed in a press report as "the instrument that will bestow upon our age a new experience of music."[84] And of course, the same technology that emitted electric tones could also project human voices. For a 1938 celebration of the winter solstice in Nuremberg, Oskar Vierling devised an elaborate electroacoustic infrastructure, including a massive tower bedecked with loudspeakers capable of clearly projecting amplified speech some 600 meters.[85] Photographs from the period reveal a landscape dotted with inconspicuous bell-shaped loudspeakers affixed to poles like streetlights. Such images underline the ominous truth of Hitler's famous comment "Without the loudspeaker, we could not have conquered Germany."[86]

In exchange for their services to the regime, cooperative electro-music inventors enjoyed healthy, if selective, official support. One of the leading patrons was Strength through Joy (Kraft durch Freude), the government office tasked with fostering public contentment through administered leisure activities. The organization was a major funder of the KdF-Großtonorgel, an electric organ based on earlier models developed by Vierling. This instrument was used extensively during the 1936 Olympics, and was even played by Goebbels during a public demonstration.[87] The Trautonium, however, remained the flagship instrument of German electro-music, one that kept a high profile throughout the 1930s even as the inventions of Theremin, Mager, and others faded from public view.[88] Sala continued to concertize and developed a new, more portable version of the instrument specially suited for his travels: the Konzerttrautonium. From January 1938 until the outbreak of World War II in September 1939, Sala's performances were heard across the Reich thanks to a series of broadcasts on Radio Germany (Deutschlandsender), the state-run station that fell under the control of Goebbels's Ministry of Public Enlightenment and Propaganda. Called simply "Music on the Trautonium," this was a series of fifty-four broadcasts, each lasting 15–25 minutes.[89] Sala's performances continued even as World War II engulfed the European continent: from 1940 to 1944, he gave no fewer than forty-seven concerts and lecture-demonstrations throughout Germany, including performances of Harald Genzmer's Concerto for Trautonium and Orchestra with the Berlin Philharmonic in 1940 and 1942. The programs also featured music by Genzmer and arrangements of classical chestnuts by Paganini, Handel, Liszt, and others.[90] Many of these appearances were sponsored by Kraft durch Freude.

Genzmer, one of the most prominent younger composers active in Germany during the Third Reich, received numerous commissions and stipends from the National Socialist regime in the late 1930s and was honored with a bronze medal at the 1936 Olympics for his composition *Der Läufer* (The runner). In 1944 he was included on the list of the "God-graced" *(Gottbegnadeten)*, a select group of artists and cultural figures who were spared from military service by direct order of Hitler and Goebbels.[91] A former pupil of Hindemith at the Berlin Academy of Music, Genzmer eventually eclipsed his teacher as the foremost composer for the Trautonium. His concerto provided Nazi impresarios with a politically acceptable alternative to Hindemith's earlier works, filling the demand for original music and conferring a certain artistic legitimacy on the instrument by ensconcing it in the symphony orchestra. The style of the music was bracing but accessible. With energetic lines on the Trautonium and broad, dramatic gestures from the orchestra, the concerto conveyed a thrill of novelty while remaining safely within the bounds of late-romantic symphonic rhetoric. More than any other artifact of the time, Genzmer's concerto represented the consummation of the Nazi romance with electric music. Among the work's generally positive press, a 1942 review hailed the Trautonium as nothing less than "the instrument of steel romanticism."[92]

INTERLUDE: MUSIC FOR THE MASSES

The Nazis' use of electric sound to manipulate and amplify collective emotion was not so distantly related to Weimar-era efforts to bring music into the public sphere. In both cases, technology was thought to be capable of transcending the plane of aesthetics and altering the social dimensions of musical practice, "deprivatizing" musical experience in accordance with the collectivist impulses of political movements on both left and right. This was possible in large part thanks to an aspect of electrically generated sound that had been hitherto neglected: not pitch, tone, or timbre, but sheer volume.

In an essay addressing the problem of sound projection in outdoor settings, Trautwein lamented that the musical production values of the 1936 Nuremberg Rally had lagged far behind the stunning "cathedral of light" created by choreographed batteries of spotlights. For earlier forms of "open air" music, ensembles such as the brass band sufficed, but for the Nazis' huge gatherings of previously unimaginable size and scale, only electric instruments were up to the task. Trautwein claimed that a new genre of "mass rally music" *(Großkundgebungsmusik)* would be the sonic manifestation of the emerging culture of the "national community" *(Volksgemeinschaft)* equal in historical stature to the religious, courtly, and bourgeois cultures of past ages. (He also took pains to distance this form of musical spectacle from the politically tainted notion of Gebrauchsmusik, for which it might easily be mistaken.)[93]

But, as already suggested, the search for new forms of "music for the masses" was by no means a monopoly of the political right, and the interventions of Helberger and Trautwein had numerous precedents, many of which were of a more experimental character. In the early 1920s, the Russian composer, theorist, and arts administrator Arsenii Avraamov organized a number of massive open-air concerts of what he called the *Symphony of Sirens*.[94] The largest of these took place in the port city of Baku, Azerbaijan, in 1922, to mark the fifth anniversary of the October Revolution that brought the Soviets to power. In all likelihood the loudest and most ambitious musical event the world had ever seen, each performance of *Symphony of Sirens* marshaled the sonic resources of an elaborately orchestrated array of ships, artillery, infantry regiments, hydroplanes, steam locomotives, and factory sirens. The "Internationale," the de facto national anthem of the young Soviet Union, was played by a specially built ensemble of over twenty sirens. (In an almost Dadaesque touch, the tune of the "Marseillaise" was also sounded to the accompaniment of a "choir of automobiles.") Avraamov conducted this vast military-industrial orchestra by waving various colored flags from the top of a tower overlooking the arrayed participants. The *Symphony of Sirens* was intended to inaugurate a new genre of public, proletarian music, a festival of sound expressing the unified political will of the socialist state. Declared Avraamov, the music of industry will "oust the church bells of the old culture and replace them with the working roar of the sirens, the very timbre of which is so close to the proletarian heart."[95] (Not one to rest on his laurels, Avraamov later proposed a project of "topographical acoustics": "And if the sound of sirens is not powerful enough, what could we dream about? Clearly: about the devices of Theremin or Rzhevkin, installed on aeroplanes, flying above Moscow! An Aerosymphony!")[96]

This enthusiasm for masses—of sound and of people—was shared widely by modernist artists of the time. In his "Musico-Mechanico Manifesto" written in 1922 and published two years later, the American composer George Antheil (of *Ballet mécanique* fame) proclaimed a vision strikingly similar to that of Avraamov's industrial symphony. But while Avraamov's *Symphony of Sirens* was conceived as a spectacle celebrating the power of the state, Antheil imagined a technological transformation of humanity framed in metaphysical rather than political terms: "great music machines in every city, which give the life of the future world a new psychic vibration—a vibration that will have a different grasp of space, which will revolutionize the life of the man of the future."[97]

In his writings from the early 1920s, Jörg Mager, too, dreamed of his electric instruments taking part in ecstatic musical gatherings. At a time when his invention was hardly more than a laboratory prototype, Mager foresaw the possibility of a "twelve-horsepower fortissimo" that would dwarf the effects of even the most massive Mahlerian orchestra.[98] He envisioned a new form of open-air public music played by amplified electric instruments—communal concerts that would fuse the audience into a unified expressive organism through the power of sound:

> Today, when crowds of humanity are pressed densely together in great cities, *gigantic* constructions alone can meet their needs—also in artistic matters. Previously the *church* was the only organization that conveyed musical culture to the broad masses. Outside of the church, musical enjoyments were virtually unattainable, since the instruments of that time filled only small spaces. Thus the price had to be relatively high, in any event too high for the broad masses of the working population. Here the Spherophone will have revolutionary effects! With its ability to create hurricane-like swellings of tones, it will enable thousands of people at once to share a single musical experience. Thus will entirely new compositions come about by themselves; for whenever masses gather, there stirs a need for the musical expression of a powerful communal feeling, *human sentiment!*[99]

Explicitly posed as a modern alternative to both the superannuated rituals of the church and the elitist offerings of the bourgeois concert hall, Mager's techno-spectacle answered the musical demands of the new social order. Housed in a high tower and operated by trained musical engineers, the instrument channels into sound the collective passions of the assembled crowds: "Tone-color cascades spray over the thousands of people. [. . .] All the feelings evoked in the human soul by the miracle of spring—cheering and jubilation, tender intimacy, childlike zest—the Spherophone sounds them out into the distance, fuses them together, and raises them to a thundering ecstasy of springtime joy! A utopia—but for how much longer?"[100]

JÖRG MAGER'S LAST YEARS

Mager, like many others, rode the brief wave of electro-music euphoria in the early 1930s. This was the high point of his career, and it was not to last long. Following its introduction in 1930, the Trautonium quickly stole the spotlight from Mager and his instruments. With their formidable institutional and artistic alliances, Trautwein and Sala seemed poised to deliver what Mager had long been merely promising. But the Trautonium was just the beginning of Mager's woes—trouble was brewing among his supporters as well. His contract with the Society for Electroacoustic Music, though extremely favorable for the inventor, had come with strings attached. Mager had been promised substantial autonomy, but the society asserted an interest in the goal of "fostering and enabling the economic utilization" of his inventions. Practically speaking, this meant that the society's support ultimately hinged on the prospect of marketing an electric instrument. Prior to his contract with the society in 1929, Mager had developed his instruments without any apparent thought of mass production. Indeed, it seems likely that no one deemed such a thing possible until Theremin signed on with RCA in New York to begin the large-scale production of his instruments.[101]

The society's desire to get their hands on a saleable version of Mager's instrument became a source of continuous tension between the inventor and his benefactors. Although there was talk of mass-producing the Partiturophon in the wake of its 1930 debut, the instrument was still hampered by major technical shortcomings. The biggest limitation was that each keyboard manual was monophonic, meaning it could play only one tone at a time. Polyphony of more than two voices could be achieved only by playing two adjacent manuals with a single hand. Though the keys of the instrument were shortened somewhat in order to facilitate this technique, the monophonic manuals nonetheless imposed steep limits on the kind of music that could be performed, without—like Theremin's or Trautwein's instruments—introducing a novel playing technique. Another problem was that, the instrument's bulky loudspeaker membranes hardly lent themselves to domestic use.[102] Because Mager lacked the expertise to address these issues himself, the society brought in a number of technicians to assist him. But the inventor quickly drove them away with his stubbornness and suspicions about the security of his intellectual property.[103] The Society for Electroacoustic Music even considered the possibility of inviting Trautwein as a collaborator, but the distrustful Mager nixed the idea.[104]

Mager soon began to chafe under the society's pressure to adapt his instrument to the exigencies of the musical market. The friction between external demands and Mager's impractical idealism was exacerbated by the inventor's burgeoning friendship with the eccentric Estonian philosopher Count Hermann Keyserling (1880–1946). A Baltic German from an aristocratic family, Keyserling's wealth enabled him to live as an independent intellectual. He penned a number of influential writings that combined philosophical concepts with autobiographical reflections and attempted a synthesis of Eastern and Western intellectual traditions. His most popular book, *Travel Diary of a Philosopher*, written during travels to South and East Asia in 1911–12, sold some fifty thousand copies in the decade after its appearance. In 1920, Keyserling established an intellectual salon known as the School of Wisdom (Schule der Weisheit) in Darmstadt, whose gatherings attracted a number of the prominent intellectuals of the time, including Thomas Mann, Carl Jung, Hermann Hesse, and Rabindranath Tagore. Soon after meeting Mager in the late 1920s, Keyserling became an enthusiastic advocate for the inventor and his project. In an article published in November of 1930, he framed Mager's cause in the now-familiar language of mystical transcendence: "The musical creator of the future will possess a new means of expression that will open new and as yet unknown paths for their invention," Keyserling declared. "That which previously only the esoteric and sacred music of the East could achieve will become 'objectively' possible."[105] Keyserling also lashed out at the Society for Electroacoustic Music, whose members he portrayed as philistines intent on cashing in on Mager's invention by turning it into a cheap substitute for existing instruments. Emil Schenck, the chairman of the society, blamed Keyserling for encouraging Mager's impractical streak and fomenting discord between the inventor and his would-be supporters, but the count was more likely a mouthpiece for Mager's growing discontent with the society and its demands. The conflict between Mager and his backers came to a head in January of 1932, when the inventor allowed his contract with the Society for Electroacoustic Music to expire.[106] Mager soldiered on, entreating new supporters in an open letter published in the *Journal of Instrument Building*, where he trumpeted the still-untapped economic prospects of "electro-music."[107] But his career would never recover. In his 1933 book *Elektrische Musik*, Peter Lertes noted that "in spite of the years of labor Mager has put into the development of his instruments and the generous support that he has received in both financial and technical respects, [his] organ has not yet found entry into musical practice."[108]

The tensions between modernism and marketability that led to Mager's departure from the society also left their traces in his final instrument, the five-voice Partiturophon, developed between 1932 and 1934. Although Mager did not fundamentally deviate from the keyboard-based model after 1928, by the early '30s the Partiturophon had been outfitted with a number of new features. The instrument now had a pressure-sensitive keyboard that allowed players to apply vibrato to a held tone by rapidly altering their fingers' weight on the keys.[109] Even more remarkably, it now included an appendage known as the *Bauchschweller* (belly swell), which enabled the player to increase the volume of the tone by expanding and contracting his abdomen.[110] These additions highlight the extent to which Mager's instrument was conceived as an artificial extension of the body, a technological membrane that responded to the player's every nuance of performative gesture. But to Mager's critics, these modifications proved that he was more interested in gimmicks and novelties than in addressing the real shortcomings of his instrument.

Mager had still not solved the problem of the monophonic manuals, which he had acknowledged as his instruments' "Achilles' heel."[111] By the early 1930s, a number of other electric instruments were capable of polyphonic tone production. But instead of following this trend, Mager attempted to recast the Partiturophon's limitation as an advantage: "Precisely because each manual works only monophonically," he suggested, "one is forced to treat this monophonic line individually, so that—as in the polyphony of Bach, for example—each voice can be brought out as in a three-dimensional relief. In addition, each keyboard, being independent, can maintain its own appropriate timbre, which makes possible mixtures and contrasts of tone color of an almost orchestral quality."[112] Thus, Mager suggested, because each manual is timbrally independent, the Partiturophon could create the "illusion of chamber music" or even of a small orchestra. Further, the keyboard manuals could be pulled out

FIGURE 26. The five-voice Partiturophon, circa 1934. Both Mager's and Trautwein's instruments continued to grow during the 1930s, but both achieved polyphony only by multiplying monophonic manuals. Source: "Das 'Partiturophon'—Eine Hausmusik-Lösung," *Zeitschrift für Instrumentenbau* 54, no. 21 (1934): 329.

of the instrument's console like removable drawers, allowing a number of musicians to play a single instrument in consort. But these appeals to a potential market of amateur musicians were far-fetched, since the success of the Partiturophon as a home instrument was at least in part contingent on the existing repertoire of keyboard music being specially arranged for its monophonic manuals.

Whether oblivious to these difficulties or simply undeterred, Mager was now pitching the Partiturophon as an instrument of reproduction, as opposed to a tool of musical revolution. Instead of microtonality and Klangfarbenmusik, Bach fugues and the *Moonlight Sonata* served as examples of the instrument's capabilities. Nonetheless, Mager dusted off his old futurist proclamations of "radio music without transmission," now reconciled with the requirements of domestic music making:

> Electro-music is nothing other than the use of the elements of radio technology in the form of *direct*, not merely *reproductive* generation of oscillations. The Partiturophon Home-Organ is thus nothing other than a *broadcasting station,* which of course transmits not into the cosmos but only into the mu-

sic room. The miracle of electrical musical vibrations, used for *direct* music making without first having to play nonelectric instruments into the microphone, as in radio, [is] thus far more significant than the mere *reproduction of sound* through the radio.[113]

As Mager attempted to rebrand his instrument as an all-in-one device for amateur musicians, the press began to assimilate the Partiturophon to familiar organological models, calling it an "electric organ" or an "organ without pipes." The establishment of a stable and familiar design—a keyboard mechanism with multiple manuals, sustained tones whose timbre was controlled by banks of switches and buttons—made such labels intuitive. Not only Mager's Partiturophon, but also instruments such as the Welte Light-Tone Organ, the Magnetton, and the Coupleux-Givelet Radio-Tone Organ fit neatly into this model, although in each case the actual mechanics of tone production were different.[114] The shift in Mager's rhetoric thus corresponded to a process of organological consolidation in the development of electric instruments during the 1930s. Increasingly, due to both ease of construction and perceived prospects of mass marketing, electric instruments became synonymous with keyboard-operated "electric organs." Alternative interfaces such as those found on the Theremin and Trautonium were exceptions that proved the rule.

Another problem—and by now, a familiar one—was the lack of an original repertoire. Mager's instruments, to an even greater degree than Trautwein's, were plagued by a shortage of music written expressly for them. In lieu of idiomatic compositions, Mager had to make do with materials at hand: a 1936 account of one of his lecture-demonstrations reported him playing Bach, Beethoven, folk songs, and popular hits.[115] Remarkably, the one surviving piece of notated music for his electric instruments, published in 1935, was a composition by Mager himself for four-voice Spherophone entitled "Little Christmas Lullaby" ("Weihnachts-Wiegenliedchen"). Looking at the score of this tuneful piece in D minor, one is struck by the apparent blandness of the music. Was the radical potential of electric tone generation doomed to produce nothing more than exotic new colors with which to gild the late-romantic mausoleum? Despite its outward conventionality, however, the piece is of interest for the designations in italics underneath each of the four staves. The second and fourth staves are labeled with generic terms calling for a gong and sheet iron, respectively. The first and third feature brand names of German loudspeaker manufacturers, Seibt and Grawor.

For these voices, Mager likely used either prebuilt loudspeaker units or cobbled together his own speakers using components from these firms' models. Thus, the markings for each of the four staves specify loudspeaker plates or membranes used to color the tone of each of the four voices in Mager's composition: they are the equivalent of instrumental designations in a typical score. Seen from this perspective, and in light of the descriptions of Mager's experimental techniques in chapter 3, this piece of holiday kitsch becomes quite a bit stranger. With its juxtaposition of a nostalgic compositional language and unearthly metallic timbres, Mager's Christmas lullaby perfectly embodies the conflicts and paradoxes of the electro-music phenomenon.

Following the expiration of his contract with the Society for Electroacoustic Music, Mager was thrown back into economic uncertainty. Although he was politically a leftist and a pacifist, he attempted to ingratiate himself to the new government, going so far as to write a letter to Hitler arguing for the importance of his work to the German nation. (Mager's latent anti-Semitism, expressed in his contempt for Theremin's German representative Georg Julius Goldberg, who was Jewish, no doubt helped ease his approach to the Nazis.)[116] Whether his coziness with the regime was ultimately opportunistic or ideological, in the long run it hardly made a difference. Although Mager had powerful allies, including the journalist Fritz Stege, who wrote for the party-line *Zeitschrift für Musik,* and Peter Raabe, president of the State Music Bureau (Reichsmusikkammer), his continuing support was largely contingent on his instruments' dwindling propaganda value for the German government.

In 1935, the Prince Emil Manor in Darmstadt, where Mager had been allowed to stay following the dissolution of the Society for Electro-acoustic Music, was handed over to the Bund Deutscher Mädel, a branch of the Hitler Youth for adolescent girls. Mager left Darmstadt and never returned. For the next several years he led a precarious, seminomadic existence. He had long suffered from diabetes, and his poverty and frequent relocation exacerbated his illness. His last years offered some tantalizing glimmers of hope. A 1935 review of Mager's newest instrument spoke of his work in familiar tones of reverence and even featured a photograph of a bust of the inventor made by the sculptor Heinrich Jobst.[117] Mager appeared at the yearly gathering of the General German Music Association (Allgemeine Deutsche Musikverein) in Weimar in June 1936 alongside Trautwein, despite the latter's attempt to prevent him from attending.[118] (Trautwein by this time viewed Mager as an erratic amateur whose unprofessionalism harmed the cause of electric music.) The same year, Mager was invited to Berlin to contribute to the sound track for the UFA film *Stärker als Paragraphen*. (The resulting thirty-second clip of the Partiturophon is the only known recording of his instruments.) A press account from this period paints a melancholy picture of the indefatigable "sorcerer of sound" playing his instrument in a near-empty beer hall in Berlin.[119] In spite of his waning audiences, though, Mager was still able to cast a powerful spell on those who heard his demonstrations. The inventor's friend, the poet Julius Maria Becker, provided this exemplary effusion from the year 1936:

> Mager plays us a short, improvised piece, a truly intoxicating bacchanal of strangely mixed magical sounds, which gave one the impression that the door to another world had been thrown wide open. One doubts no longer the unique and unprecedented meaning of his work. The console, from which the closing of electrical contacts calls forth entire series of unexpected scales, entire floods of astounding harmony as if summoned from nothing, controls the gushing limitlessness of the sounding world. Mager stands on the threshold of something final and absolute, for no vibration, no wisp of tone color, no slightest trace of existing sound could resist the will of this magical organism. Everything must become sound, everything is subjected to the fate of tonal birth and must emerge into reality: from his console, Mager orchestrates the spheres themselves.[120]

Mager's last years paint a picture of seemingly inexorable decline. By the late 1930s, he was impoverished, sick, and desperate. In a letter from this period, the inventor referred to himself as a "music-futuristic Jesus" who had been "driven out of the temple of the holy Lady Musica by courtyard cattle-merchants and moneychangers."[121] A brief article from July 1938 reported that Mager had left the town of Bamberg, where he had set up a makeshift laboratory and enchanted the locals with a Christmas concert the previous year.[122] A final attempt to escape penury by selling his patents to international investors was nixed by Goebbels, who wanted to prevent Mager's instruments from falling into foreign hands but didn't care to purchase them for the German government either. Mager died the following year in a hospital in his hometown of Aschaffenburg. His obituary notice encapsulated the inventor's fate: "The perfection of his instruments, such as the Spherophone and the Partiturophon, was guided by the goal of creating the entire spectrum of instrumental timbres purely and independently from the ether waves, so to speak. A fitting exploitation of his gifts as an inventor

FIGURE 27. The inventor as hero. Bust of Jörg Mager by Heinrich Jobst. Source: Paul Zoll, "Jörg Magers 'Partiturophon': Eine umwälzende, elektro-akustische Erfindung," *Zeitschrift für Musik* 102, no. 12 (1935): 1332.

was unfortunately hindered by his inability to adjust to the practical demands of life."[123]

In the year of Mager's death, a brief notice appeared in the *Journal of Instrument Building* bearing the title "369 New Musical Instruments in Ten Years." The article recorded the effort of a Parisian publisher to catalog the hundreds of new devices created in the previous decade. However, the author noted that the majority of these inventions had disappeared almost as suddenly as they had sprung up. Just as few works of art survive the test of time, the author observed, most of the new instruments had failed to establish themselves in musical practice: "Scarcely more than a dozen were viable; the rest are played, if at all, by the inventors themselves."[124] This postmortem neatly sums up one of the most vexing aspects of the technological modernism of the 1920s and '30s: the discrepancy between the frenzy of inventive activity and the relative dearth of surviving artifacts, be they recordings, scores, or the instruments themselves. Mager's case is exemplary: not only were his inventions all destroyed or lost in the global conflagration that began in the year of his death, but virtually no trace of their music survives.

6

The Expanding Instrumentarium

Nothing that has ever happened should be regarded as lost for history.[1]

—Walter Benjamin

In the twenty-six years between Busoni's *Sketch of a New Aesthetic of Music* and the fall of the Weimar Republic, the technological situation of European music had undergone radical changes. The musty late-romantic orchestra lampooned by Busoni and Russolo now coexisted with a bewildering array of new instruments. There reigned a spirit of technological triumphalism. In 1932, after a decade that saw the emergence of such radical new currents as Gebrauchsmusik, neoclassicism, and the twelve-tone technique, the composer Walter Gronostay proclaimed that "the technification of musical sound sources is the one genuine novelty that has taken place in the last ten years of musical history."[2] Two years earlier, the former Busoni pupil Leo Kestenberg had edited an anthology of writings entitled *Kunst und Technik* (Art and technology), featuring contributions by a number of journalists, musicians, and intellectuals, including such luminaries as the philosopher Ernst Cassirer and the composer Ernst Krenek. The wide-ranging essays touched on themes from the philosophy of technology to the history of mechanical instruments and the sociological aspects of broadcasting and recording. In his introduction, Kestenberg called attention to the changing meaning of the word *Technik*. While previously, it referred to a musician's cultivated skill in performing or composing—that is, technique—increasingly the term was used to describe the material means of tone generation and transmission: technology. This new sense of *Technik,* argued Kestenberg, stands at the center of contemporary thought: not the discipline of the performer, but the capabilities of musical machines.[3]

Meanwhile, the valorization of science and technology inaugurated in the late nineteenth century had entered the mainstream, moving from the pages of engineers' trade journals to the essays of philosophers and cultural critics. Sounding the keynote, Cassirer, one of the leading intellectuals of the Weimar Republic, argued that technology, like philosophy itself, is concerned not simply with what is but with what could be—a quality it had in common with the "limitlessness of mental life." "[Technology] cannot be understood as a 'dead creation,'" he wrote, "but rather as a way of and orientation toward *creating*." Friedrich Dessauer, a physicist turned philosopher, likewise claimed in his 1927 book *Philosophy of Technology* that the essence of technology was not the mass production of commodities but the act of invention, which he portrayed as analogous to the process of artistic work.[4] In 1932, the German architect Fritz Schumacher issued a rebuke to the pessimistic attitude toward technology voiced in Oswald Spengler's book *Man and Technics*, which had appeared the year before. For Schumacher, the synthesis of humanity and technology was already a fait accompli: "It was not long ago that one was inclined to see technical and intellectual matters as opposed to each other," he wrote. "One saw only the mechanical *effects* unleashed by technology and overlooked the intellectual *forces* from which these effects issued. Only gradually has it been recognized that mind can be cast not only in the *dynamic* forms of the intellectual world but also in the *solid* forms of the technical world."[5] While Spengler characterized technology as humanity's war on nature, Schumacher proposed that it was an alliance forged between the two.[6]

Thinkers outside of Germany were likewise attempting to dismantle the traditional opposition between technology and culture. The French philosopher Henri Bergson attempted once and for all to cut the Gordian knot of "mechanics and mysticism" by arguing that the increase in physical power through modern technology calls forth a commensurate growth of humanity's spiritual resources. Instead of threatening each other with mutual annihilation, he suggested, spirit and material could expand reciprocally: "[Man] must use matter as a support if he wants to get away from matter. In other words, the mystical summons up the mechanical. [. . .But] we must add that the body, now larger, calls for a bigger soul, and that mechanism should mean mysticism."[7] Writing in 1934, the American historian Lewis Mumford portrayed the early twentieth century as a period of transition from "paleotechnics" to "neotechnics." According to Mumford, paleotechnics, which began with the scientific and mechanical advances of the Renaissance and reached its apex in the Industrial Revolution, was based on the maximization of force, authoritarian social systems, and an adversarial relationship between humanity and nature. Neotechnics, on the other hand, epitomized by electrical technologies of communication and expression, symbolized the promise of a human-built order in harmony with the collective needs of society and the finite resources of the natural world. These devices augured new human possibilities based on the principle of cultivation instead of conquest.[8] For a fleeting historical moment, *Geist* and *Technik* no longer appeared as irreconcilable forces, but as two aspects of an underlying unity.

But even as intellectuals and the general public both began to accord technology a new and central place in the culture of modern life, the position of music in this new order was thrown into doubt. Amid a general embrace of technology, the new instruments seemed suddenly in danger of being left behind. The causes of this shift were many and complex. First, and most obviously, there was the political situation: although some inventors and musicians, such as Trautwein and Sala, continued their careers largely unmolested after the Nazi seizure of power in 1933, the cultural pressures applied by the Nazis within Germany, in addition to the emigration of many figures, such as Hindemith, Fischinger, and Stuckenschmidt (who was barred from publishing in 1934 and fled to Prague three years later), exerted a decidedly chilling influence on the experimental arts of the time.

The political realignment of 1933, though drastic, was only one factor. Arguably, the movement for new instruments had become a victim of its own success. The sheer proliferation of inventions introduced unforeseen problems: though all these devices had some foundation in earlier technologies, the interface and sound-producing mechanics of each of them had to be mastered anew. Many of these artifacts challenged familiar notions of what an instrument was; some, like optical sound film, were all but unrecognizable *as* instruments. Further, the ever-accelerating pace of technological change meant that new inventions often outpaced the ability (or interest) of musicians to use them. By the time one technology had been brought to heel, another had already appeared to eclipse it. Champions of the new instruments could well have identified with the sorcerer's apprentice in Goethe's famous poem, unable to control the unruly spirits they had rashly summoned forth.

Perhaps the Achilles' heel of the movement, however, was the lack of original music. At the beginning of the twentieth century, it was assumed that the arrival of the new instruments would unleash a torrent of musical creativity. But by the early 1930s, the equation had been reversed: amid a technological glut, composers warily kept their distance. Modernist partisans considered the prospect that deeply entrenched artistic traditionalism could be just as formidable an obstacle to progress as outdated instruments. (The Chilean poet Vicente Huidobro put his finger on the problem when he noted, in conversation with Edgard Varèse, that "one can still make old songs with new sounds. The hand may be more important than the instrument."[9]) The dearth of new music is especially striking in light of the Weimar period's frenzy of writing, speculation, publicity, and invention—a disparity that confirmed the suspicions of those who saw the phenomenon as an elaborate exercise in technological puffery.

By the mid-1930s, it was clear that the heady futurism of the previous decade had given way to an impulse toward consolidation and stability. There was a backlash against the technological enthusiasm of the '20s, whose utopian visions increasingly appeared as distant, fevered delusions. Writing in 1931, the musicologist Boris de Schloezer declared that "all those splendid mechanisms, like Theremin's or Martenot's apparatus, which produce new timbres and open vast new horizons to music, are in a certain sense negligible, since they are not animated by the thought and will of man. Mechanical music is therefore only a myth."[10] The lasting influence of technology on music, de Schloezer argued, lay in the purely "reproductive" media of gramophone and radio. The American composer George Gershwin similarly circumscribed the new technologies' sphere of influence. As he saw it, the impact of the "machine age" extended only to the distribution of music, not to its production: "Composers must compose in the same way the old composers did," he stated. "No one has found a new method in which to write music."[11] Even more emphatically, the eminent musicologist Alfred Einstein proclaimed in 1935 that "there is not the slightest relationship between art and technology. [...They] are independent fields; they have nothing to do with each other."[12] Einstein was content to echo the verdict of Hans Pfitzner fifteen years earlier: art is timeless, technology ephemeral, and never the twain shall meet.

Nor were such dismissive appraisals unique to musical conservatives. Ernst Krenek, who counted among the more radical spirits of the Weimar period, joined the chorus of techno-skeptics, arguing that "all in all, we can scarcely speak of a direct influence or enrichment of the creative musician through contemporary technology."[13] Paul Bekker, the Viennese critic who had once battled alongside Busoni on behalf of the "new music," likewise registered his doubts in an essay published in 1934. Conceding the point that the mechanization of music in the twentieth century was the culmination of a macrohistorical trend, he drew from this premise an unexpected conclusion. A truly epochal turn in the history of music would be brought about not through the apotheosis of the machine but rather by a complete disavowal of technology: the "complete abandonment of the instrument as the vehicle of our musical thought and form." Only a renaissance of vocal music, whose first stirrings Bekker professed to hear, could dispel the machine once and for all.[14]

Perhaps the most devastating critique had been issued in 1930 by Curt Sachs, who just a few years earlier had observed the recent developments with guarded interest and written favorably of Jörg Mager's early inventions. Sachs now dismissed the new instruments wholesale, arguing that they were products not of any inherent musical need but of a perverse obsession with technical novelty:

> Whoever wants to take the dubious pleasure of perusing the musical patent applications of the last thirty years will receive a crushing image of the enormous sum of energy that has been squandered in the fundamentally misguided effort to bring together music and technology. [. . .] Nothing could more powerfully express our time's complete lack of instinct than the confusion that underlies this endeavor. We have developed electricity to such a point—why not electric musical instruments, then? Our technology allows us to amplify sounds—why not electrical amplifiers? Whether a musical need is answered thereby, this is not asked, and even less is it felt.[15]

In his 1940 *History of Musical Instruments,* Sachs elaborated on this judgment in a brief postscript on the twentieth century. While he conceded that the new instruments' fate was still unknown, he again attributed their appearance to the "experimentations of electroengineers" rather than the demands of performers and composers. More damningly still, he suggested that the rhetoric of electro-music, with its mania for ever greater volume and variety, was a vestige of the outdated aesthetics of late romanticism. For Sachs, the frenzy of instrumental innovation was not the augur of a new music to come, but an obstacle to the quest for "greater objectivity" that characterized modern music.[16] He wrote off the entire movement as a last gasp of artistic radicalism forestalling the international neoclassical consensus of the 1930s. Sachs likely spoke for many at the time in seeing the alliance of music and modern technology as a spent historical force.

AFTERMATH

But even in the late 1930s, as many observers were declaring the end of the movement for new instruments, its seeds were spreading on the wind. The same year Curt Sachs penned his denunciation of Weimar-era technological enthusiasm, the young American composer John Cage gave a talk in Seattle entitled "The Future of Music: Credo." In this brief statement, Cage foresaw electrical instruments that would "provide complete control of the overtone structure of tones [. . .] and make these tones available in any frequency, amplitude, and duration," and he called for the establishment of "centers for experimental music" where the new technological possibilities could be explored.[17] Though typically read as a bold vision of things to come, Cage's little manifesto appears in a new light when viewed in the context of the European experiments of the 1920s and '30s. As a reader of Henry Cowell's *Modern Music* magazine (where another of his pronouncements, "For More New Sounds," was published in 1942), Cage was well aware of happenings on the continent. In fact, he was an eyewitness: as an eighteen-year-old, he had been on an artistic pilgrimage in Europe when he stumbled upon the 1930 New Music Berlin festival where Hindemith and Toch presented their "Original Music for Gramophone Records."[18] This event likely had a formative influence on Cage's technological thinking that extended well beyond his later use of variable-speed turntables in works such as *Imaginary Landscape No. 1* (1939) and *No. 2* (1942).

Back in Los Angeles in 1937, Cage was introduced to Oskar Fischinger, who had fled Germany the year before. Fischinger invited Cage to his studio to lend a hand in the production of his animated film *An Optical Poem*. They worked together for several days, and Fischinger shared with Cage his ideas of secret correspondences between sounds and images. Cage's seemingly cryptic mention of "a portrait of Beethoven repeated fifty times per second" in the "Credo" is an allusion to optical sound film, and Cage's emerging sonic mysticism owed much to Fischinger's influence. Cage later honored the filmmaker with a mesostic that read in part, "When you said each inanimate object has a spirit that can take of the form of sound by being set into vibration, I became a musician."[19] Likewise, Cage's memorable attack on the Theremin was a veritable paraphrase of Moholy-Nagy's critique of reproductive technologies: he bemoaned that an instrument with "genuinely new possibilities" had been debased into a high-tech means of playing the same old tunes, its musical potential squandered for the sake of comfort and convention. "The Thereministes act as censors, giving the public those sounds they think the public will like," he lamented. "We are shielded from new sound experiences."[20] Whatever its prophetic elements, Cage's "Credo" belongs as much to the first half of the century as to the second, and extends a tradition of techno-musical speculation that reaches back to Busoni's *Sketch of a New Aesthetic of Music*, if not further.[21] Finally, it is important to note that just as the development of new technologies in the 1920s and '30s was driven by an explicitly experimental impetus, Cage's (and others') notion of experimental music was inextricably linked to the possibilities afforded by modern sound technologies. Only later did electronic and experimental music become differentiated as distinct, though historically related, artistic tendencies.[22]

As the example of Cage shows, in spite of the rupture of the 1930s and '40s, a broader historical perspective reveals a surprising degree of continuity between the first and second halves of the century. Even the global catastrophe of World War II could not slow what had been set in motion, and many of the key figures of the Weimar period reemerged in the 1950s to carry on the flame amid the ruins of postwar Germany. Hans Heinz Stuckenschmidt, pugilistic champion of "mechanical music," enjoyed a long and prestigious career as a journalist and professor at the Technical University of Berlin, where he taught from 1948 until his retirement in 1967, and he was involved in the electronic music studio founded there in 1953. Stuckenschmidt was keenly interested in the emerging technologies and contributed an essay for the first issue of *Die Reihe*, the house journal of the German serialist avant-garde.[23] Here he lauded the new "electronic music" (as it was now called) as the dawn of a "third stage" of the art, eclipsing the earlier vocal and instrumental epochs. For Stuckenschmidt, these works represented the realization of an ideal first envisioned a quarter century earlier: a form of music that "retains human participation in the compositional process, but excludes it from the means of realization."[24]

Oskar Sala resumed his hectic schedule as a one-man Trautonium evangelist, concertizing, publishing, broadcasting, and continuing to modify the instrument.[25] Sala's career in the 1950s witnessed some almost uncanny parallels with earlier history. In 1952, he unveiled a new version of the instrument, called the Mixturtrautonium, in conjunction with the premiere of Harald Genzmer's Second Concerto for Trautonium and Large Orchestra in Baden-Baden. The same year, Sala was asked to provide the sound of the Grail bells for the Bayreuth production of Wagner's *Parsifal,* just as Jörg Mager had twenty-one years earlier. He became best known for his music and sound effects for films, creating over three hundred sound tracks, including the famous avian screeching in Alfred Hitchcock's *The Birds* (1962).

Friedrich Trautwein, too, picked up more or less where he had left off after the war. His career seems to have been unscathed by the process of "denazification" through which the occupying powers attempted to purge German society of all influences of fascist ideology. This is all the more notable considering that Trautwein was an early and, to all appearances, enthusiastic member of the Nazi Party, and during the war he had done government-sponsored research on the long-distance guidance of missiles by electrical systems.[26] From 1950 until his death in 1956, Trautwein led a program in sound engineering at the Robert-Schumann-Conservatory in Düsseldorf. He was an active member of the postwar music scene in Germany, even publishing a number of articles in the journal *Gravesaner Blätter*, which—in another link to the Weimar years—was published by Hermann Scherchen, the conductor and champion of modernist music who had left Germany in protest soon after Hitler was named chancellor.

Trautwein and Sala's one-time collaborator Paul Hindemith, however, was conspicuous in his absence from the technological experiments of the 1950s. After immigrating to the United States in 1940, Hindemith became a vociferous opponent of what he saw as the ungrounded capriciousness of modernist tendencies in music, and his compositions moved toward a rapprochement with common-practice tonality. But he too was lastingly affected from his earlier experiences: Hindemith credited his work in electroacoustics with leading him to the neotonal theories laid out in his treatise *The Craft of Musical Composition*, written in the late 1930s.[27]

The biggest link between the earlier movement for new instruments and the postwar years was the Studio for Electronic Music of Northwest German Radio in Cologne, established in October 1951.[28] One of the founding members of the studio was none other than Robert Beyer, erstwhile theorist of experimental sound film. Remarkably, Beyer's writings from this period essentially restated his Weimar-era proclamations. Though the recording medium had changed from optical sound film to magnetic tape, the aesthetic vision was the same: Beyer imagined a new form of music in which the stifling constraints of traditional "embodied instruments" would be replaced with the "acoustic-chemical transformation[s]" of electric sound.[29] Further, the new technologies would enable the composer to "determine the acoustic form of his work down to the last detail."[30] Beyer saw the Cologne studio as the ideal setting for the realization of his long-held dream of electronic Klangfarbenmusik attained through the "conscious construction of tone colors."[31] In language redolent of the 1920s, he heralded this new form of music as the ultimate synthesis of *Kunst* and *Technik*: "Technology has indeed penetrated into art, but not art into technology," he wrote. "*The current challenge is to creatively connect material and spirit.*"[32]

Beyer was joined in the founding of the Cologne studio by the acoustician Werner Meyer-Eppler (1913–1960) and the composer-theorist Herbert Eimert (1897–1972). Eimert, like Beyer, had cut his teeth in the musical culture of the Weimar Republic. Though he was not actively involved in the technological experiments of the time, he had heard Jörg Mager's instruments in Frankfurt in 1927 and composed a piece of ballet music called *Der weisse Schwann* (The white swan) that called for custom-built mechanical instruments.[33] For Eimert, as for Beyer, electronic music meant the direct compositional manipulation of sound and its inscription in a recording medium—what their colleague Meyer-Eppler called "authentic music."[34] As it was fundamentally distinct from music produced by conventional instruments, Eimert reasoned, its principles could be derived "only from sound itself, which is its raw material."[35] He argued that electronic music—now strictly distinguished from the "electric music" of the 1920s—was made possible by the emergence of two technological prerequisites: the generation of tones by synthetic means and their storage and modification in a recording medium. Each of these by itself had previously served conventional purposes: the early electrophones of Mager, Trautwein, and others, despite their potential, had remained trapped within the limitations of traditional instruments, while recording had been used only for "documentary" (that is, reproductive) purposes. In conjunction, however, these two technologies provided the foundation for a "new sonic universe [. . .] in which the musical material appears for the first time as an infinite continuum of all imaginable sounds."[36]

In tone and particulars—down to his invocations of Busoni and Schoenberg—Eimert's position echoed that of Beyer twenty years earlier. In other respects, too, his writings and proclamations revisited the well-trodden ground of Weimar Republic techno-aesthetics: his refunctioning of magnetic tape as a "productive" instrument followed in the footsteps of Moholy-Nagy on gramophone records, Stuckenschmidt on the player piano, Mager on radio electronics, and Beyer on optical sound film. In an article portentously titled "What Is Electronic Music?" Eimert wrote:

In the ordinary way, the tape recorder provides the means of playing back tapes. But the new technique that is no longer satisfied with a mere playback is of the greatest significance here. The normal studio technique of broadcasting is transformed into a compositional means. Tape recorder and loudspeaker are no longer "passive" transmitters; they become active factors in the preparation of the tape. This is the essential secret of electro-musical technique. One might say that today we have perfected a "keyboard" of this elaborate and differentiated sphere of radio transmission; now we lack only the virtuosi to master it.[37]

Between 1951 and 1953, Beyer and Eimert collaborated on four pieces based on tape manipulations of sound fragments created on an electronic keyboard instrument called the Melochord.[38] These compositions—*Klang im unbegrentzen Raum* (Sound in infinite space), *Ostinate Figuren und Rhythmen,* and *Klangstudie I* and *II*—were presented to the public on May 26, 1953, along with examples of musique concrète by Pierre Schaeffer and lectures by Meyer-Eppler and studio technician Fritz Enkel.[39] With their lush, liquescent textures and unhurried sense of timbral exploration, these pieces can be heard as a displaced echo of the Weimar-era ideal of electro-music, complete with its weighty cosmic resonances. The music's aesthetic lineage was not lost on at least one listener: shortly after the broadcast, Eimert received an angry letter from Jörg Mager's son Siegfried, who accused him of "spiritual theft" for not properly acknowledging the late inventor's influence on the emerging school of electronic music.[40]

The collaboration between Eimert and Beyer was short-lived. Tensions had surfaced as early as 1951: during a radio broadcast entitled "Die Klangwelt der elektronischen Musik" (The sound world of electronic music), the two had sparred over the question of whether the apparatus of electronic tone generation was better suited to continuous timbral transformations or the intricate polyphonic weave of serial composition, whose complexities challenged even the most adventurous performers.[41] While Beyer held fast to his glittering visions of Klangfarbenmusik, Eimert inclined more and more to the serialist aesthetic that captivated the imaginations of many composers of the younger generation. (An early advocate of atonal music, he had penned one of the first books on twelve-tone composition in 1924.[42]) This tendency in Eimert's thinking coincided with the arrival of Karlheinz Stockhausen, who joined the studio at the older composer's invitation in early 1953. Whether through Stockhausen's influence or independently, Eimert's position soon came to approximate the serialist fundamentalism of the younger composer. Stockhausen and Eimert, like Beyer, were interested in the problem of timbre, but they took a very different approach to it. For them, tone color was not to be exalted as the focus of compositional effort but rather subordinated to the universal serial logic that penetrated into every dimension of the musical material. They eschewed the rich timbres of electric instruments in favor of basic sonic elements such as sine waves and bursts of white noise.[43] Eimert would later dismiss his collaborative compositions with Beyer by distinguishing them from the first "real works of electronic music," that is, the rigorously serial (and sonically austere) pieces presented the following year, which included Stockhausen's two *Studies*, which were of foundational for the subsequent development of *elektronische Musik*.[44] Eimert's electronic productions of the later 1950s, such as the *Fünf Stücke* (1955), demonstrate his continuing interest in the exploration of tone color refracted through the tightly controlled facture that characterized much of the studio's early output.

Shortly after the 1953 concert, with the dawn of the "Sine Era" looming on the horizon, Beyer left the studio. After his departure he attacked the serialist approach in terms that echoed or anticipated similar critiques by figures such as Theodor Adorno, Iannis Xenakis, and Pierre Schaeffer.[45] Serialism, Beyer suggested, represented a continuation of the trend toward "musical abstraction" inspired above all by the twelve-tone works of Anton Webern. But the younger composers—and here he likely had Stockhausen in mind—knew of Webern only through hearsay: by fixating on his compositional techniques, they lost sight of his music's expressive force. Case in point for Beyer was the application of serial techniques to the construction of electronic timbres, which he claimed ignored the empirical validation of ear. Dogmatically following Helmholtz's theory of overtones, the serialists disregarded such critical and less readily quantifiable acoustic factors as formants, attack transients, and the timbral fluctuation of sustained tones. "In the rigid sounds of serial electronic music there is no trace of a dynamic conception of acoustic phenomena," Beyer charged. "Time flows unarticulated through the static structure of the sine tone."[46] Serial composition, he claimed, dealt not with sound but with rows and formulas. The result is an "ascetic impoverishment of the sonic medium."[47] As the conflict between Beyer and Eimert makes plain, the search for new technological foundations for music remained fraught with ideological and aesthetic tensions.

The presence of figures such as Stuckenschmidt, Sala, Trautwein, and Beyer on the German scene helped sustain an historical awareness of the Weimar legacy in the years after World War II. Indeed, even the French exponents of musique concrète, in spite of the rivalry between the Paris and Cologne studios during the 1950s, acknowledged the influence of their German predecessors. Pierre Schaeffer's self-professed search for "the most general instrument possible" suggests he shared the technological idealism of Busoni, as does his paradoxical ideal of an instrumentally mediated immediacy—witness his statement, "I am seeking direct contact with sound material, without any electrons getting in the way."[48] The French were more forthright about one debt, in particular: Schaeffer counted Jörg Mager as an important influence, while his colleague Abraham Moles hailed the German inventor as "the true founder of electronic music."[49] But with the technological explosion in the decades after the war and the withdrawal or death of most veterans of the Weimar period, these figures quickly faded from memory. Their exclusion from historical accounts was also abetted by the leaders of the Cologne studio. For younger composers such as Stockhausen, the historical chasm created by the Nazi dictatorship and the Second World War helped to foster a mood of tabula rasa—the so-called Zero Hour—that militated against the thoughtful reckoning of historical forebears. In a 1970 essay, Stockhausen flatly stated that "electronic music began in Cologne in 1952–53," and made only passing mention of figures such as Beyer and Mager.[50] Eimert's record on this count is more ambivalent: though he singled out Mager as the one inventor of early electronic instruments who attempted to break free of conventional sounds, he suggested that early twentieth-century inventors were "led by commercial interests to imitate instrumental sounds" and consigned their work to the prehistory of electronic music.[51]

CONCLUSION: TECHNOVERTIGO

Such interpretations set the tone for music historians in decades to follow, laying the foundation for what, at the beginning of this book, I called the "myth of electronic music." Both academic and popular accounts have long treated the first half of the century as little more than a prelude to later developments, a pattern that seems to have been established in the very first histories of electronic music, written in the third quarter of the twentieth century.[52] This view has been echoed repeatedly since, in both specialist treatments of electronic music and general histories. The German musicologist Elena Ungeheuer, writing in 2008, argues that in the early part of the century "instrument builders did not wish to change the course of music history with new sounds and means of sonic manipulation, but rather to use electricity to imitate what was familiar and to optimize it from a pragmatic standpoint." She accordingly draws a distinction between the "imitative" instruments of the early twentieth century and the "innovative" sound machines of the post-1950 period.[53] In a similar vein, Richard Taruskin's *Oxford History of Western Music*, published in 2007, covers the technical innovations before 1950 in a seven-page "pre-history" to the chapter "Music and Electronic Media," whose focus lies squarely on the second half of the century.[54]

Ironically, while scholars such as Ungeheuer dismiss the new instruments of the early twentieth century on implicitly modernist grounds—that is, as insufficiently innovative or original—others have taken the opposite tack, arguing that these devices were too experimental and outré, too far outside the technological mainstream to be taken seriously by historians. Paul Théberge, in his 1997 study of sound technology in the late twentieth century, quotes approvingly Sachs's dismissive assessment of the earlier experiments and notes that, since circa 1900, "nearly half a century of technical experimentation had seen little, if any, production of lasting musical significance."[55] Likewise, in their history of the Moog synthesizer, Trevor Pinch and Frank Trocco write off early electronic instruments as mere "museum oddities," arguing that the importance of technologies should be measured by their enduring influence on musical practice, not the speculative intentions of their inventors.[56]

In short, there has been a general uncertainty about how to fit the technological experiments of the early twentieth century into the existing narrative of modern music. The problem is that historians have too often looked back hoping to find the beginnings of something—say, "electronic music" or the "synthesizer"—like mother hens waiting for an egg to hatch. But searching for origins is an inevitably circular endeavor: you have to know what you're looking for in order to find it. Philosophers of history have long warned against viewing the past in such goal-oriented terms, with certain events inexorably "leading to" later moments further down the timeline. Such a perspective neither illuminates the actions of historical actors, who were generally not thinking of themselves in this way, nor does it enrich the present, as it typically props up what we think we already know.[57] This teleological mindset is still pervasive, and perhaps nowhere so deeply rooted as in our thinking about both art and technology. Both these domains are often conceived as a lineage of influences, in which the meaning of a given phenomenon—an instrument, a composition—is defined in terms of what preceded and followed it in history, its place on the timeline.

But the influence of instruments, like that of all cultural phenomena, is often indirect and nonlinear: as historian David Edgerton has noted, some technologies are absorbed into culture long after their introduction, while others may disappear only to reemerge much later.[58] The last twenty or so years have provided ample evidence for this thesis in the domain of musical technology: take, for example, the resurgence of vinyl records as a listening medium, or the fact that analog synthesizers, long ago eclipsed by their putatively superior digital successors, are now enjoying an unexpected renaissance, with major manufacturers such as Korg even reissuing replicas of classic models from the 1970s. As a fitting symbol of this historicist turn in music technology, consider Berna, a piece of software created by Milan-based sound artist Giorgio Sancristoforo. On a single computer screen, the program digitally recreates the clunky assemblage of tape machines, tone generators, and filters that constituted the classic electronic music studio of the 1950s.[59] The reappearance of these once-antiquated technologies has called into question the familiar arc of twentieth-century music technology—from early electric instruments, to magnetic tape, to analog synthesizers, and finally to digital instruments and computer music. As these phenomena demonstrate, there is no simple criterion of "progress" governing the development of technology and cordoning it off from the teeming disorder of human society. There is only movement toward or away from particular ideals that are always culturally and historically contingent.[60]

To reject the teleological, timeline-oriented approach to sound technology does not mean a retreat to the foxholes of a purely "localized" historiography. It is, rather, a call for a more nuanced understanding of success and failure, influence and obsolescence. We have to discover new ways of finding through lines in the history of sound technology—diachronic as opposed to synchronic structures, to use a bit of historians' jargon. One approach to this challenge is, counterintuitively, to step back from the instruments themselves, to try to keep sight of the "metatechnological" problems that change more slowly than the apparatus itself. To take just one example, consider a comparison between the instruments of Jörg Mager and Friedrich Trautwein and the early analog synthesizers of the 1960s. In the newer devices, tiny transistors replaced bulky vacuum tubes, but the goal was largely the same: using electricity to convert the player's performative gestures into sonic expressions. The two best-known inventors of analog synthesizers in the 1960s, Robert

Moog and Don Buchla, differed primarily with regard to the question of playing interface: while Moog opted for a conventional keyboard, Buchla explored more experimental means of playing his instrument, such as a variety of touch-sensitive metal contacts that he called "kinesthetic input ports." In essence, Moog and Buchla grappled with the same problem faced by electro-music inventor Mager thirty years before: weighing the comfortable constraints of traditional playing mechanisms against the potentially alienating freedom of new interfaces.[61] Likewise, many techno-aesthetic debates of the later twentieth century can be traced to the conflict between what in the 1920s and '30s were known as "organic" and "mechanical" modes of instrumentality—that is, between conceptions of instruments as extensions of the human form and technological attempts to transcend the intolerable limitations of the body. Other connections, of course, are there for those who want to find them: between mechanical music of the 1920s and the emergence of computer music in the second half of the twentieth century; between the experimental sound generation described in Mager's patent papers and the post-1970 practices of noise music and circuit bending; and between the irrational and occult resonances of early electric sound and the later convergence of sound and psychedelia in the high-tech tribalism of electronic dance music.

More important than any particular technological lineage, then, are the deeper shifts in musical practices that have accompanied the instrumental upheavals of the last hundred years. Here, perhaps, lies the true legacy of the events chronicled in this book: not in an artifact but in an attitude of what might be called "open instrumentality." From Stuckenschmidt and Moholy-Nagy scratching phonograph records to the tape compositions of the 1950s, the evolution of the recording studio to the ever-expanding universe of computer music languages, instruments always leave room for that creative maneuvering that constitutes the ineradicable human essence of technology. "Around each product," writes the French philosopher Gilbert Simondon, "there exists a margin of liberty that allows it to be used for ends that were not foreseen."[62] The instruments of music, like those of science, do not simply proffer images of something already there: they construct worlds.

At the beginning of the twentieth century, modernists such as Busoni and Russolo lamented how existing instruments held back the tide of musical progress. By the century's end, however, musicians faced a different problem: how to build a coherent creative practice when the technological foundation was constantly shifting beneath their feet. Writing at the turn of the millennium, the American composer Ron Kuivila proposed three strategies for coping with the destabilizing ephemerality of musical technology: getting "under" it by working with basic acoustic principles, looming "over" it by devising works abstractly, or going "into" it by probing the latent potentials residing in familiar objects and ostensibly obsolete technologies.[63] For those who choose to operate outside of the increasingly embattled outposts of the European classical tradition, in particular, incessant technological change has become a fact of life, a basic working condition. The irony of this phenomenon is that technology, envisioned as a means of attaining mastery over the unruly material of sound, has itself become a source of instability—a state of affairs I call "technovertigo."[64] The deepening engagement with technology in twentieth-century music, born of a desire for control, has brought about a centrifugal expansion of the art (and indeed of all art), unleashing an almost incomprehensible multiplicity of sounds, techniques, politics, and practices. In place of the monolithic modernist vision of a technological promised land, a destination in history where the development of instruments would attain a state of perfection or at least provisional equilibrium, we are now faced with a state of chaotic oscillation or perennial flux, leading nowhere. Accordingly, the challenge for contemporary musicians is by no means a simple matter of remaining technologically "up to date"; instead, it is a question of navigating, at the deepest, cellular level of artistic practice, the unstable force fields spanning the gap between instruments and aesthetics, technology and technique.

Notes

Unless otherwise indicated, translations are the author's.

1. LISTENING TO INSTRUMENTS

1. Robert Donington, *Music and Its Instruments* (London: Methuen, 1982), 3.
2. Ferruccio Busoni, *Entwurf einer neuen Ästhetik der Tonkunst,* 2nd ed., ed. Martina Weindel (1916; Wilhelmshaven: F. Noetzel, 2001), 41.
3. Luigi Russolo, *The Art of Noises,* trans. Robert Filiou (1913; New York: Something Else Press, 1967), 6; and Edgard Varèse, *Écrits,* ed. Louise Hirbour (Paris: Christian Bourgois Éditeur, 1983), 23.
4. Joseph Schillinger, "The Electrification of Music," ca. 1918, JPB 86–8, box 9, fol. 16, New York Public Library.
5. John Redfield, *Music: A Science and an Art,* 2nd ed. (New York: Tudor, 1935), 119.
6. "Zum Inhalt," *Melos* 9, no. 3 (1930): 113.
7. There was a wealth of technological experimentation between 1900 and 1940 not only in Western Europe but also in the United States and Russia. Douglas Kahn's book *Noise Water Meat: A History of Sound in the Arts* (Cambridge, MA: MIT Press, 1999) and his collection *Wireless Imagination: Sound, Radio, and the Avant-Garde,* ed. Douglas Kahn and Gregory Whitehead (Cambridge, MA: MIT Press, 1992) are the best overviews of this field. For more focused studies, see Jean Laurendeau, *Maurice Martenot, luthier de l'électronique* (Montreal: Louise Courteau, 1990); Reynold Weidenaar, *Magic Music from the Telharmonium* (Metuchen, NJ: Scarecrow Press, 1995); Albert Glinsky, *Theremin: Ether Music and Espionage* (Chicago: University of Illinois Press, 2000); Luciano Chessa, *Luigi Russolo, Futurist: Noise, Visual Arts, and the Occult* (Berkeley: University of California Press, 2012); and Andrey Smirnov, *Sound*

in *Z: Experiments in Sound and Electronic Music in Early 20th-Century Russia* (London: Koenig Books/Sound and Music, 2013). For an overview of the influence of early twentieth-century technologies on compositional thought, see Hans-Joachim Braun, "Technik im Spiegel der Musik des frühen 20. Jahrhunderts," *Technikgeschichte* 59, no. 2 (1992): 109–31. The only two substantial precedents of this study of which I am aware are Erica Jill Scheinberg's "Music and the Technological Imagination in the Weimar Republic: Media, Machines, and the New Objectivity" (PhD diss., University of California at Los Angeles, 2007) and Peter Donhauser's *Elektrische Klangmaschinen: Die Pionierzeit in Deutschland und Österreich* (Vienna: Böhlau, 2007). Scheinberg's study, though covering some of the same ground as my book (particularly in chapter 2), differs in being primarily concerned with technology as an object of representation through music, rather than with instruments as such. Donhauser's book, though focused on electric instruments to the exclusion of the player piano and recording media, is of foundational importance for my work, and I draw from it extensively in chapters 3 and 5 of this book.

8. See Helga de la Motte-Haber, *Die Musik von Edgard Varèse* (Hofheim: Wolke Verlag, 1993), 30; and GloryLynn Foster Van Duren, "René Bertrand's Dynaphone; 'Roses de Metal' by Arthur Honegger" (thesis, California State University, Hayward, 1983).

9. Some of the most fascinating studies to emerge in recent years have focused on scientific and acoustic investigations of sound outside of the context of modernity that tends to dominate discussions of musical technology. See Penelope Gouk, *Music, Science, and Natural Magic in Seventeenth-Century England* (New Haven: Yale University Press, 1999); Myles W. Jackson, *Harmonious Triads: Physicists, Musicians, and Instrument Makers in Nineteenth-Century Germany* (Cambridge, MA: MIT Press, 2006); and Emily I. Dolan, *The Orchestral Revolution: Haydn and the Technologies of Timbre* (Cambridge, UK: Cambridge University Press, 2013).

10. Alfred Gell, "Technology and Magic," *Anthropology Today* 4, no. 2 (1988): 5–6.

11. On this point, see Emily Dolan's "Editorial," *Eighteenth-Century Music* 8, no. 2 (2011): 175–77.

12. "The opposition established between the cultural and the technical and between man and machine is wrong and has no foundation. What underlies it is mere ignorance or resentment. It uses a mask of facile humanism to blind us to a reality that is full of human striving and rich in natural forces. This reality is the world of technical objects, the mediators between man and nature." Gilbert Simondon, *On the Mode of Existence of Technical Objects,* trans. Ninian Mellamphy (London, ON: University of Western Ontario, 1980), 11. On instrumentality, see Peter Szendy, "Pour commencer . . . Suivi de: (Re)lire Bartók (Déjà, Encore)," in *Instruments,* ed. IRCAM–Centre Georges-Pompidou (Paris: Editions IRCAM, 1995), 10; and Philip Alperson, "The Instrumentality of Music," *The Journal of Aesthetics and Art Criticism* 66, no. 1 (2008): 37–51.

13. For a historical elaboration of this point, see Karin Bijsterveld, "A Servile Imitation: Disputes about Machines in Music, 1910–1930," in *Music and Tech-*

nology in the Twentieth Century, ed. Hans-Joachim Braun (Baltimore: Johns Hopkins University Press, 2002), 121–35.

14. Hans Mersmann, "Grenzwerte," *Melos* 6, no. 1 (1927): 30.

15. James Simon, "Musikalischer Expressionismus," *Musikblätter des Anbruch* 2 (1920): 408.

16. See Leo Marx, *The Machine in the Garden: Technology and the Pastoral Ideal in America* (Oxford: Oxford University Press, 1964).

17. Ernst Cassirer, "Form und Technik," in *Kunst und Technik,* ed. Leo Kestenberg (Berlin: Wegweiser-Verlag, 1930), 55. Many variants of this concept appear in the technological discourse of the early twentieth century. In 1923, the art critic Paul Westheim called out the "machine romanticism" of artists who sought to imitate the outward forms of modern technology. "Maschinenromantik," *Das Kunstblatt* 7, no. 2 (1923): 33–40. Another critic spoke of "machine enthusiasm" *(Maschinenschwärmerei),* invoking (in German) a key concept of romantic theory, *Schwärmerei,* or "emotional effusion." Erich Steinhard, "Maschinen," *Der Auftakt* 6, no. 8 (1926): 169. Such notions were not unique to German cultural circles: in his profile of Vladimir Lenin, H. G. Wells called the Soviet leader a "dreamer of technique." Quoted in René Fueloep-Miller, *The Mind and Face of Bolshevism: An Examination of Cultural Life in Soviet Russia* (New York: Harper & Row, 1965), 110.

18. Oskar Schlemmer, quoted in John Willett, *Art and Politics in the Weimar Period: The New Sobriety 1917–1933* (New York: Da Capo, 1996), 81.

19. Paul Klee, *Schriften, Rezensionen und Aufsätze,* ed. Christian Geelhaar (Cologne: DuMont Schauberg, 1976), 119.

20. László Moholy-Nagy, "Produktion-Reproduktion," *De Stijl* 7, no. 5 (1922): 98–100.

21. "Elektroakustische Hausorgel," *Zeitschrift für Instrumentenbau* 53, no. 2 (1932): 25.

22. This potential for unforeseen uses has been labeled *technological multistability* in analogy to the visual phenomenon in which a single graphical configuration can take on different spatial orientations. See Don Ihde, "Technologies—Musics—Embodiments," in *Embodied Technics* (n.p.: Automatic Press / VIP, 2010), 17–36.

23. Jonathan Sterne, "Media or Instruments? Yes," *Offscreen* 11, no. 8–9 (2007): 2–4.

24. See Benjamin Steege, *Helmholtz and the Modern Listener* (Cambridge, UK: Cambridge University Press, 2012), 16–42.

25. Hermann Helmholtz, *On the Sensations of Tone,* trans. Alexander Ellis (1885; repr., New York: Dover, 1954), 1; originally published as *Die Lehre von den Tonempfindungen als physiologische Grundlage für die Theorie der Musik* (Braunschweig: Friedrich Vieweg und Sohn, 1863).

26. Kapp hailed Helmholtz's work in experimental acoustics as the consummate synthesis of art and science: "Under the gaze of Helmholtz's scientific eye, the 'musical' instrument became as it were an 'instrument' in the highest sense, a tool for the delivery of insight into the organic substrate of mental operations. Music is turned into acoustics, science is explained and clarified by art." Ernst Kapp, *Grundlinien einer Philosophie der Technik* (Braunschweig:

Georg Westermann, 1877), 85. Kapp saw his theory vindicated by Helmholtz's research, which revealed keyboard instruments as technological externalizations of the organic bundle of resonating strings in the organ of Corti, and the pipe organ as a mechanized voice (88–98). On Kapp, see also Carl Mitcham, *Thinking through Technology: The Path between Engineering and Philosophy* (Chicago: University of Chicago Press, 1994), 20–24.

27. "Artists as Inventors and Invention as Art: A Paradigm Shift from 1840 to 1900," in *Artists as Inventors / Inventors as Artists,* ed. Dieter Daniels and Barbara U. Schmidt (Ostfildern, Ger.: Hatje Cantz, 2008), 39.

28. Max Eyth, *Lebendige Kräfte: Sieben Vorträge aus dem Gebiete der Technik* (Berlin: Julius Springer, 1905), 261–62.

29. Eberhard Zschimmer, *Philosophie der Technik* (Berlin: Ernst Siegfried Mittler und Sohn, 1917), 18.

30. Oswald Spengler, *Untergang des Abendlandes,* vol. 1 (Vienna: Braumüller, 1918) and vol. 2 (Munich: C.H. Beck, 1922). Abridged English version published as *Decline of the West,* trans. Charles Frances Atkinson (New York: Oxford University Press, 1991).

31. Max Weber, "Science as a Vocation," in *From Max Weber: Essays in Sociology,* ed. H.H. Gerth and C. Wright Mills (New York: Oxford University Press, 1958), 129–56. This essay was originally given as a speech entitled "Wissenschaft als Beruf" at Munich University in 1918.

32. For a classic study of *Lebensphilosophie* and its relationship to natural science in the early twentieth century, see Paul Forman's essay "Weimar Culture, Causality, and Quantum Theory, 1918–1927: Adaptation by German Physicists and Mathematicians to a Hostile Intellectual Environment," *Historical Studies in the Physical Sciences* 3 (1971): 1–115.

33. Peter Gay, *Weimar Culture: The Outsider as Insider* (New York: Harper and Row, 1968), 70–101.

34. Carl Dahlhaus, "Neo-Romanticism," *19th-Century Music* 3, no. 2 (1979): 97–105.

35. Curt Sachs, "Geist und Technik: Ein Blick in die Geschichte des Schaffens," *Die Musik* 20, no. 1 (1927): 30.

36. Ibid., 26.

37. Adolf Weissmann, *Music Come to Earth,* trans. Eric Blom (New York: E.P. Dutton, 1930), ix; originally published as *Die Entgötterung der Musik* (Stuttgart: Deutsche Verlags-Anstalt, 1928). I have slightly modified the translation of this passage. The word *Entgötterung,* which could be rendered as "desacralization," was used by the great German writer Friedrich Schiller in his 1788 poem "The Gods of Greece," where it appears in the phrase "entgötterte Natur." Thus, Weissman's image of a "godless" modern music resonates with a long intellectual tradition of concern with the side effects of the post-Enlightenment ascendancy of secularization, mass society, and techno-science.

38. Weissmann, *Music Come to Earth,* 6–7.

39. Ibid., 1; 9–10.

40. Busoni, *Entwurf einer neuen Ästhetik,* 42.

41. Ibid. Significantly, this passage was omitted from all English translations of *Entwurf einer neuen Ästhetik der Tonkunst* until the most recent one:

Ferruccio Busoni, *Sketch of a New Aesthetic of Music,* trans. Pamela Johnston (London: Precinct, 2012).

42. Busoni, *Entwurf einer neuen Ästhetik,* 52–53.

43. Hans Pfitzner, *Futuristengefahr: Bei Gelegenheit von Busonis Ästhetik* (Munich: Verlag der Süddeutschen Monatshefte, 1917).

44. Ibid., 4, 40.

45. Ibid., 5–7.

46. Ibid., 15.

47. Hans Pfitzner, *Die neue Aesthetik der musikalischen Impotenz: Ein Verwesungssymptom?* (Munich: Verlag der Süddeutschen Monatshefte, 1920), 56, 112.

48. Ferruccio Busoni, "Open Letter to Hans Pfitzner," in *The Essence of Music and Other Papers,* trans. Rosamond Ley (New York: Dover, 1965), 17–19.

49. Cassirer, "Form und Technik," 53.

50. Frank Warschauer, "Die Zukunft der Technisierung," in *Kunst und Technik,* ed. Leo Kestenberg (Berlin: Wegweiser-Verlag, 1930), 411–12.

51. In 1919 the Russian artist and philosopher Solomon Nikritin announced a movement he called "projectionism" and declared that "the artist is not a producer of consumer goods... but of PROJECTIONS of the METHOD—the organization of matter. The method, therefore, invented by the artist, becomes the purpose of the creative process." Quoted in Andrey Smirnov, *Sound in Z: Experiments in Sound and Electronic Music in Early 20th-Century Russia* (London: Koenig Books, 2013), 13. See also Andrey Smirnov, "Notation und visuelle Musik," in *Klangmaschinen zwischen Experiment und Medientechnik,* ed. Daniel Gethmann (Bielefeld: Transcript Verlag, 2010), 126. Renato Poggioli has called attention to this "anticipatory anachronism" as a central component of "the historical mythology of contemporary art." Renato Poggioli, *Theory of the Avant-Garde,* trans. Gerald Fitzgerald (New York: Icon, 1971), 70–71.

52. This notion of technology as trickster is borrowed from Erik Davis's book *TechGnosis: Myth, Magic, and Mysticism in the Age of Information* (London: Serpent's Tail, 1998).

2. "THE JOY OF PRECISION": MECHANICAL INSTRUMENTS AND THE AESTHETICS OF AUTOMATION

1. Jean-Jacques Rousseau, "Essai de l'origine des langues," in *Oeuvres de J. J. Rousseau,* vol. 9 (Paris: Deterville, 1817), 226. For an English version see Jean-Jacques Rousseau, "Essay on the Origin of Language," in *On the Origin of Language,* trans. John H. Moran and Alexander Gode (Chicago: University of Chicago Press, 1966), 62.

2. Erich Steinhard, "Donaueschingen: Mechanisches Musikfest," *Der Auftakt* 6, no. 8 (1926): 183.

3. Readers interested in a formal investigation of this music should refer to Francis Bowdery's "Music for Player Piano: A Study of Seventeen Selected Examples" (PhD diss., Loughborough University of Technology, 1995). Recordings of most of the pieces presented in Donaueschingen and Baden-Baden are

available as well: *Piano Music without Limits: Original Compositions of the 1920s,* Player Piano 4, MDG 645 1404-2, 2007, compact disc.

4. Paul Hindemith, "Zur mechanischen Musik," in *Aufsätze, Vorträge, Reden,* ed. Giselher Schubert (Zurich: Atlantis, 1994), 19.

5. Frank Trommler, "The Avant-Garde and Technology: Toward Technological Fundamentalism in Turn-of-the-Century Europe," *Science in Context* 8, no. 2 (1995): 398.

6. Le Corbusier, *Towards a New Architecture,* trans. Frederick Etchells (New York: Dover, 1986); Ludwig Kassák and László Moholy-Nagy, eds., *Buch neuer Künstler* (Baden: Verlag Lars Müller, 1991).

7. Quoted in John Willett, *Art and Politics in the Weimar Period: The New Sobriety 1917-1933* (New York: Da Capo, 1996), 117.

8. Martin Elste, "Hindemiths Versuche 'gramophonplatteneigener Stücke' im Kontext einer Ideengeschichte der Mechanischen Musik im 20. Jahrhundert," *Hindemith Jahrbuch* 25 (1996): 211. For the Stravinsky quote, see Erwin Felber, "Entwicklungsmöglichkeiten der mechanischen Musik," *Die Musik* 19, no. 2 (1926): 78.

9. Quoted in Henry Wong Doe, "Musician or Machine: The Player Piano and Composers of the Twentieth Century" (DMA diss., The Julliard School, 2006), 20-21.

10. Steinhard, "Donaueschingen," 183.

11. Wong Doe, "Musician or Machine," 6.

12. Quoted in Annette Richards, "Automatic Genius: Mozart and the Mechanical Sublime," *Music & Letters* 80, no. 3 (1999): 383. Quantz's remarks were inspired by his encounter with the famous flute-playing automaton of Jacques de Vaucanson.

13. Marie-Dominique-Joseph Engramelle, *Tonotechnie ou l'Art de noter les cylindres, et tout ce qui susceptible de notage dans les instruments de concerts méchaniques* (1775; repr., Paris: Hermann éditeurs des sciences et des arts, 1993).

14. The relevant works are Haydn's pieces for *Flötenuhr* (musical clock), Hob. XVIII, 1-32; Mozart's three compositions for mechanical organ, K. 594, 606, and 616; and Beethoven's *Wellingtons Sieg,* op. 91, which was originally composed for Johann Mälzel's Panharmonicon and later rewritten for orchestra.

15. For surveys of these instruments, see Arthur W. J. G. Ord-Hume, *Clockwork Music* (New York: Crown Publishers, 1973); and Alexander Buchner, *Mechanical Musical Instruments,* trans. Iris Urwin (London: Batchworth Press, 1959).

16. Quoted in Myles Jackson, *Harmonious Triads: Physicists, Musicians, and Instrument Makers in Nineteenth-Century Germany* (Cambridge, MA: MIT Press, 2006), 94.

17. Quoted in Elste, "Hindemiths Versuche," 200.

18. John Philip Sousa, "The Menace of Mechanical Music," *Appleton's Magazine* 8 (1906): 278-284.

19. Bowdery, "Music for Player Piano," 39-40.

20. See *Oxford Handbooks Online,* s.v. "Player Piano," by Thomas Patteson, November 2014, http://www.oxfordhandbooks.com/view/10.1093/oxfordhb/9780199935321.001.0001/oxfordhb-9780199935321-e-16.

21. See Werner König, "Über frühe Tonaufnahmen der Firma Welte und die Werke für das Welte-Mignon-Reproduktionsklavier," in *Jahrbuch des Staatlichen Instituts für Musikforschung Preußischer Kulturbesitz 1977* (Kassel: Verlag Merseburger Berlin, 1978), 31.

22. Jürgen Hocker, *Faszination Player Piano: Das Selbstspielende Klavier von den Anfängen bis zur Gegenwart* (Bergkirchen: Edition Bochinsky, 2009), 131–32.

23. Hocker, *Faszination Player Piano*, 132–36; König, "Über frühe Tonaufnahmen," 32.

24. Arnold Schoenberg, "Mechanical Musical Instruments" (1926), in *Style and Idea: Selected Writings of Arnold Schoenberg*, ed. Leonard Stein (Berkeley: University of California Press, 1984), 329. This argument turns up again and again in the writing of the time: see Hans Hensheimer, "Kontra und Pro," *Musikblätter des Anbruch* 8, no. 8–9 (1926): 355; and Arno Huth, "Mechanische Musik," reproduced in *Kunst der Zeit* 3, no. 1–3 (1928): 48.

25. Bowdery, "Music for Player Piano," 87; 94. Around the same time, Busoni prepared a Pianola arrangement of the overture to Mozart's *The Magic Flute*, a work replete with themes of mechanism and enchantment. See Carolyn Abbate, "Magic Flute, Nocturnal Sun," in *In Search of Opera* (Princeton: Princeton University Press, 2001), 55–106. Although the rolls containing this arrangement have not yet been recorded, a piano-roll recording of a 1927 performance of Busoni's later two-piano version of the piece survives. See Hocker, *Faszination Player Piano*, 211.

26. Edwin Evans, "The Foundations of Twentieth-Century Music," *The Musical Times* 58, no. 894 (1917): 351.

27. Ernest Newman, "Piano-Player Music of the Future," *The Musical Times* 58, no. 895 (1917): 391.

28. Ibid.

29. The piece originally included parts for other instruments as well, but Stravinsky removed them after receiving Evans's request. See Mark McFarland, "Stravinsky and the Pianola: A Relationship Reconsidered," *Revue de musicologie* 97, no. 1 (2011), 85–110.

30. Hocker, *Faszination Player Piano*, 214–16.

31. Bowdery, "Music for Player Piano," 83. The most famous example of mechanical music from the 1920s is George Antheil's *Ballet mécanique* (1923–1925), whose fascinating and complicated history is recounted in Hocker, *Faszination Player Piano*, 217–26.

32. The chronology of these publications is as follows: "Mechanisierung der Musik" (*Ma*, 1924), "Die Mechanisierung der Musik" (*Pult und Taktstock*, 1925), "Die Mechanisierung der Musik (*Das Kunstblatt*, 1925), "Mechanisierung" (*Musikblätter des Anbruch*, 1926), "Mechanische Musik" (*Der Auftakt*, 1926), "Mechanische Musik" (*Der Kreis*, 1926), "Mechanische Musik" (*Schallkiste*, 1926), and "Machines—A Vision of the Future" (*Modern Music*, 1927). For deeper background on Stuckenschmidt and his writings, see Erica Jill Scheinberg, "Music and the Technological Imagination in the Weimar Republic: Media, Machines, and the New Objectivity" (Ph.D. diss., University of California at Los Angeles, 2007), 25–72.

33. H. H. Stuckenschmidt, "Die Mechanisierung der Musik," *Pult und Taktstock* 2, no. 1 (1925): 4.

34. Hans Heinz Stuckenschmidt, "Mechanisierung der Musik," *Ma* 9, no. 8 (1924): unpaginated.

35. Andreas Maul, "Die Idee einer 'mechanischen Musik': Über Experimente von Hindemith und Toch mit dem Welte-Mignon-Klavier und der Welte-Philharmonie Orgel," *Neue Zeitschrift für Musik* 9 (1984): 6. It was likely that practices such as these inspired Schoenberg's jeremiad against false interpreters: "Were there among a thousand musicians just one with the will and the ability to discover from the score what is true and eternally constant, to present it and to make it fit the needs of a contemporary listener, then for the sake of this one man, the Sodom and Gomorrah of false interpreters, aiming only to glorify themselves at the music's expense, would deserve to be spared." Schoenberg, "Mechanical Musical Instruments," 328. See also Robert Hill, "Overcoming Romanticism: On the Modernization of Twentieth-Century Performance Practice," in Bryan Gilliam, ed., *Music and Performance during the Weimar Republic* (Cambridge: Cambridge University Press, 1994), 38–39.

36. Stuckenschmidt, "Die Mechanisierung der Musik," *Pult und Taktstock*, 6.

37. The essays in question are László Moholy-Nagy, "Produktion-Reproduktion," *De Stijl* 7 (1922): 97–101; and László Moholy-Nagy, "Neue Gestaltung in der Musik: Möglichkeiten des Grammophons," *Der Sturm* 14, no. 7 (1923): 102–6.

38. Stuckenschmidt, "Mechanisierung der Musik," n.p.

39. Heinz Pringsheim, "Die Mechanisierung der Musik," in *Allgemeine Musik Zeitung* (1925): 291. Anton Flettner (1885–1961) was an aviation engineer and inventor.

40. Ibid.

41. Heinrich Kaminski, "'Mechanisierung' der Musik?" *Pult und Taktstock* 2, no. 3 (1925): 36.

42. Heinz Tiessen, "Zur Mechanisierung der Musik," *Pult und Taktstock* 2, no. 4 (1925): 62.

43. Pringsheim, "Die Mechanisierung der Musik," 291. Although Pringsheim defends the inherent sociality of performed music, he implicitly rejects the idea that listening, too, could be a social act, arguing that it can as well be done in private: "With headphones in bed, in the bathtub, or even while smoking and reading the newspaper in a lounge chair, we could hear all that much more comfortably at home."

44. H. H. Stuckenschmidt, "Mechanisierung: Antwort an H. K.," *Pult und Taktstock* 2, no. 5 (1925): 82.

45. H. H. Stuckenschmidt, "Mechanische Musik," *Der Auftakt* 6, no. 8 (1926): 172.

46. Stuckenschmidt, "Mechanisierung: Antwort an H.K.", 83–84.

47. Rudolf Carnap, Hans Hahn, and Otto Neurath, "The Scientific Conception of the World: The Vienna Circle," in *Philosophy of Technology: The Technological Condition*, ed. Robert C. Scharff and Val Dusek (Oxford: Blackwell, 2003), 95.

48. Carnap, Hahn, and Neurath, "Scientific Conception of the World," 89.

49. Quoted in Peter Galison, "Aufbau/Bauhaus: Logical Positivism and Architectural Modernism," *Critical Inquiry* 16, no. 4 (1990): 720. As Galison points out, the Vienna Circle's central text, "The Scientific Conception of the World," reads more like an avant-garde manifesto than a typical philosophical paper.

50. Carnap, Hahn, and Neurath, "Scientific Conception of the World," 95.

51. The translation "New Objectivity" is potentially deceptive, as John Willett notes, since the German *Sache* at the root of the word *Sachlichkeit* could mean "affair" or "matter" as well as "object." Willett opted for the freer rendering of "New Sobriety" for the title of his book on the period, *Art and Politics in the Weimar Period: The New Sobriety 1917–1933* (New York: Da Capo, 1996).

52. Franz Roh, "Post-Expressionist Schema," quoted in Anton Kaes, Martin Jay, and Edward Dimendberg, eds., *The Weimar Republic Sourcebook* (Berkeley: University of California Press, 1994), 493.

53. Quoted in Elste, "Hindemiths Versuche," 208.

54. Curt Sachs, "Geist und Technik: Ein Blick in die Geschichte des Schaffens," *Die Musik* 20, no. 1 (1927): 30–31. Stuckenschmidt's attitude toward the New Sobriety was ambivalent: he identified with expressionism in the early 1920s and looked askance on the later anti-expressionist reaction, whose ban on strong emotions he compared to Caliban's rage at his mirrored image. See H.H. Stuckenschmidt, "Musik," *Die rote Erde* 1 (1920): 338–340, and "Neue Sachlichkeit in der Musik," *Der Auftakt* 8 (1928):3–4, both in H.H. Stuckenschmidt, *Musik eines halben Jahrhunderts* (Munich: Piper, 1976), 36–41. Stuckenschmidt's vaccilation supports Christopher Hailey's argument that the backlash against expressionism in the 1920s overshadowed the underlying continuity between the various artistic movements of the time. See Christopher Hailey, "Musical Expressionism: The Search for Autonomy," in *Expressionism Reassessed*, eds. Shulamith Behr, David Fanning, and Douglas Jarman (Manchester: Manchester University Press, 1993), 103–11.

55. Heinrich Strobel, "'Neue Sachlichkeit' in der Musik," *Musikblätter des Anbruch* 8, no. 6 (1926): 256.

56. Heinrich Strobel, *Paul Hindemith*, 3rd ed. (1928; Mainz: Schott, 1948), 8.

57. Paul Bekker, "Wesensformen der Musik," in *Organische und mechanische Musik* (Stuttgart: Deutsche Verlags-Anstalt, 1928), 42. Intriguingly, Bekker compares the mystique surrounding the act of composition to that accompanying the technological object: "The natural does not cease to be miraculous because I recognize its natural lawfulness. The distinction lies merely therein, that the miracle in the first case appears as the outcome of *magic*, in the second case as the manifestation of *natural forces*. The radio is as much a wonder for me as it is for the South Sea Islander, only I don't view it as magic, but rather am aware of the forces that achieve it." Thus the desire to explain does not, accordingly to Bekker, destroy wonder but merely undermines the "superstition and fetishism" that accompany it (46).

58. Bekker, "Wesensformen der Musik," 44, 47. On Bekker's role in articulating the aesthetic program of the "neue Musik," see Cristoph von Blumröder, *Der Begriff "neue Musik" im 20. Jahrhundert* (Munich: Musikverlag Emil Katzbilcher, 1981), 36–48. See also Brian Cherney, "The Bekker-Pfitzner

Controversy (1919–1920): Its Significance for German Music Criticism during the Weimar Republic (1919–1932)" (PhD diss., University of Toronto, 1974).

59. Paul Stefan, "Musik und Maschine," *Musikblätter des Anbruch* 8, no. 8–9 (1926): 343.

60. Paul Bekker, "Hanslick," *Musikblätter des Anbruch* 5, no. 10 (1923): 290.

61. Many of these ideas were channeled from the Soviet Union, which had close artistic ties with the German avant-garde throughout the 1920s. Moholy-Nagy's influential distinction between artistic "production" and "reproduction," for example, was adopted from Soviet constructivism, to which he was exposed through his friendship with the Russian artist El Lissitzky in Berlin in the early 1920s. The Soviet theorist Alexei Gan declared that "the fact that all so-called art is permeated with the most reactionary idealism is the product of extreme individualism. [. . .] Art is indissolubly linked with theology, metaphysics, and mysticism." Quoted in Stephen Bann, ed., *The Tradition of Constructivism* (New York: Da Capo, 1974), 35. See also Christina Lodder, *Russian Constructivism* (New Haven, CT: Yale University Press, 1983), 75.

62. Galison, "Aufbau/Bauhaus," 710–11.

63. Hannes Meyer, "The New World," in *Weimar Republic Sourcebook,* ed. Kaes, Jay, and Dimendberg, 448–49.

64. H.H. Stuckenschmidt, "Musik und Musiker in der Novembergruppe," *Kunst der Zeit* 3, no. 1–3 (1928): 97. The November Group also oversaw a series of publications that included Paul Bekker's lecture "Wesensformen der Musik" in 1925. See Paul Bekker, *Wesensformen der Musik* (Berlin: B. Lachmann, 1925).

65. Nils Grosch, *Die Musik der neuen Sachlichkeit* (Stuttgart: Metzler, 1999), 68–9. Reviews of this concert were reprinted in *Kunst der Zeit* 3, no. 1–3 (1928): 48, 82.

66. H.H. Stuckenschmidt, "Mechanisierung," *Musikblätter des Anbruch* 8, no. 8–9 (1926): 345.

67. H.H. Stuckenschmidt, "Machines—A Vision of the Future," *Modern Music* 4, no. 3 (1927): 8.

68. Stuckenschmidt, "Musik und Musiker in der Novembergruppe," 94. For a detailed study of the November Group with an emphasis on the visual arts, see Helga Kliemann, *Die Novembergruppe* (Berlin: Gebr. Mann Verlag, 1969).

69. Walter Benjamin, "The Work of Art in the Age of Mechanical Reproduction," in *Illuminations,* ed. Hannah Arendt (New York: Schocken, 1969), 217–51.

70. Dietrich van Strassburg, "Offener Brief an H.H. Stuckenschmidt," *Musikblätter des Anbruch* 8, no. 2 (1926): 81.

71. Hindemith, "Zur mechanischen Musik," 21–22.

72. Ernst Toch, "Musik für mechanische Instrumente," *Musikblätter des Anbruch* 8, no. 8–9 (1926): 346–47. Other critics voiced this argument as well. See for example Erwin Felber, "Entwicklungsmöglichkeiten der mechanischen Musik." *Die Musik* 19, no. 2 (1926): 77–83.

73. Paul Klee, "Schöpferische Konfession," in *Schriften, Rezensionen und Aufsätze,* ed. Christian Gelhaar (Cologne: DuMont, 1976), 118: "Kunst gibt

nicht das Sichtbare wieder, sondern macht sichtbar." Following a similar impulse, visual artists such as Man Ray and Christian Schad sought new applications of the photograph, using it as a means of not simply reproducing reality but creating innovative and often decidedly nonrealistic images. These connections will be explored further in chapter 4.

74. Toch, "Musik für mechanische Instrumente," 347–48.
75. Toch, "Musik für mechanische Instrumente," 348.
76. Ibid.
77. Erich Doflein, "Die neue Musik des Jahres," *Melos* 5, no. 12 (1926): 371.
78. See Dirk Scheper, *Oskar Schlemmer: Das Triadische Ballett und die Bauhausbühne* (Berlin: Akademie der Künste, 1988), 275–76.
79. Oskar Schlemmer, "Ausblicke auf Bühne und Tanz," *Melos* 6, no. 12 (1927): 520–24.
80. Quoted in Scheper, *Oskar Schlemmer*, 49.
81. Scheper, *Oskar Schlemmer*, 12.
82. Quoted in Scheper, *Oskar Schlemmer*, 34.
83. Scheper, *Oskar Schlemmer*, 29, 33, 55, 83, 85, 127–28, 131–32.
84. Hocker, *Faszination Player Piano*, 86–87.
85. Eberhard Preussner, "Musik und Technik in der Geschichte der Musik," in *Kunst und Technik*, ed. Leo Kestenberg (Berlin: Wegweiser-Verlag, 1930), 120.
86. Erich Katz, "Mechanische Orgel," *Die Musik* 21, no. 11 (1929): 817.
87. Quoted in Scheper, *Oskar Schlemmer*, 128–29.
88. Paul Hindemith, "Zu unserem Programm," in *Aufsätze, Vorträge, Reden*, 17. Although the original organ rolls containing Hindemith's music for the *Triadic Ballet* are lost, the composer excerpted parts of the score for a *Suite for Mechanical Organ*, which was recorded in 1931. Parts of this recording have survived and were released on CD in 1995. Paul Hindemith, *Organ Concertos / Suite for Mechanical Organ*, Koch Schwann CD 312022, 1995, compact disc.
89. Schlemmer, "Ausblicke auf Bühne und Tanz," 523.
90. Scheper, *Oskar Schlemmer*, 55.
91. Steinhard, "Donaueschingen," 184–85.
92. Oskar Schlemmer, "Theater (Bühne)," in *The Theater of the Bauhaus*, ed. Walter Gropius and trans. Arthur S. Wensinger (Middletown, CT: Wesleyan University Press, 1961), 88. This book is an English translation of *Die Bühne im Bauhaus* (Munich: Albert Langen Verlag, 1925).
93. Quoted in Scheper, *Oskar Schlemmer*, 49.
94. Schlemmer, "Man and Art Figure," in Gropius, *Theater of the Bauhaus*, 22. This notion was no doubt inspired by the passage in Kleist's marionette story in which the narrator ponders what would happen if even the motions of the puppeteer were "transferred entirely to the realm of mechanical forces." See Heinrich von Kleist, "On the Marionette Theatre," trans. Thomas G. Neumiller, *The Drama Review* 16, no. 3 (1972): 22–26.
95. "Nicht Jammer über Mechanisierung, sondern Freude über Präzision!" Quoted in Grosch, *Musik der neuen Sachlichkeit*, 57. Schlemmer goes on to declare that "artists are ready to convert the disadvantages and dangers of their mechanistic age into the advantages of exact metaphysics."

96. Schlemmer, "Man and Art Figure," 28–29.

97. Schlemmer, "Theater (Bühne)," 81. The convergence of opposites was a key tenet of Schlemmer's worldview. In this light, his invocations of such seemingly paradoxical notions as "mechanistic organisms" and "mystical objectivity" become comprehensible.

98. Kleist, "On the Marionette Theatre," 26.

99. See Grosch, *Musik der neuen Sachlichkeit,* 57–58.

100. An accomplished composer and concert pianist, Haass became director of recording for Welte in 1925. He recorded over three hundred rolls of popular and classical music and knew as well as anyone the capabilities and limitations of the machine.

101. Hans Haahs [sic], "Über das Wesen mechanischer Klaviermusik," *Musikblätter des Anbruch* 9, nos. 8–9 (1927): 351.

102. Haahs, "Über das Wesen," 352.

103. Hans Heinsheimer, "Kontra und Pro," *Musikblätter des Anbruch* 8, nos. 8–9 (1926): 355.

104. Bowdery, "Music for Player Piano," 184.

105. Hindemith, "Zur mechanischen Musik," 22.

106. Ibid., 24.

107. Stuckenschmidt had previously alluded to Thaddeus Cahill's Dynamophone as a more advanced example of a mechanical instrument. See Stuckenschmidt's essay "Mechanische Musik," *Der Kreis* 3, no. 11 (1926): 507.

108. Peter Lertes, *Elektrische Musik: Eine gemeinverständliche Darstellung ihrer Grundlagen, des heutigen Stand der Technik und ihrer Zukunftsmöglichkeiten* (Dresden and Leipzig: Theodor Steinkopff, 1933), 1.

109. Paul Bernhard, "Mechanik und Organik," *Der Auftakt* 10, no, 11 (1930): 239.

3. "THE ALCHEMY OF TONE": JÖRG MAGER AND ELECTRIC MUSIC

1. Oswald Spengler, *The Decline of the West,* trans. Charles Francis Atkinson (1918–1922; abr. ed. New York: Oxford University Press, 1991), 46.

2. Herbert Weiskopf, "Das Sphärophon," *Musikblätter des Anbruch* 8, nos. 8–9 (1926): 390.

3. Quoted in Peter Donhauser, *Elektrische Klangmaschinen: Die Pionierzeit in Deutschland und Österreich* (Vienna: Böhlau, 2007), 32–33, 245–46.

4. See John Willett, *Expressionism* (New York: McGraw-Hill, 1970); and John C. Crawford and Dorothy L. Crawford, *Expressionism in Twentieth-Century Music* (Bloomington: Indiana University Press, 1993).

5. See Erik Davis, *TechGnosis: Myth, Magic, and Mysticism in the Age of Information* (London: Serpent's Tail, 1999), 51.

6. Hans Kuznitzky, "Neue Elemente der Musikerzeugung, *Melos* 6, no. 4 (1927): 156. For Kuznitzky, electric instruments were the logical continuation of the quest for "elementary tone production" that had long allured Western music history. This striving, exemplified by such phenomena as the ancient hydraulos (water organ), the microtonal instruments of the Renaissance, and the

nineteenth-century revival of Pythagorean mysticism, finds its consummation in the technological breakthroughs of the early twentieth century: "The intellectual kernel forms itself again and again around the same point of energy, but the fructifying impulse is lacking—must be lacking—because the technical prerequisites [. . .] are not yet fulfilled. The age of radio-electricity provides this impulse!" Ibid., 157.

7. Hans Kuznitzky, "Betrachtungen zum Tänzerkongress in Magdeburg," *Melos* 6 (1927): 395.

8. Jörg Mager, *Vierteltonmusik* (Aschaffenburg: Franz Kuthal, n.d.), 3–4. Mager later stated that the text was written in 1915: see Jörg Mager, *Eine neue Epoche der Musik durch Radio*, (Berlin: Self-published, 1924), 2.

9. Quoted in Emil Schenck, *Jörg Mager: Dem deutschen Pionier der Elektro-Musikforschung zum Gedächtnis* (Darmstadt: Städtischen Kulturverwaltung, 1952), 6–7. This statement is something of an exaggeration, as Mager would later admit. In other writings, he acknowledged the previous work of Richard Stein, Georg Capellen, F.A. Geissler, and others.

10. Mager, *Vierteltonmusik*, 4.

11. Ibid. According to Willi Möllendorf, Mager applied for a patent for this instrument in 1912. Möllendorf, *Musik mit Vierteltönen* (Leipzig: F.E.C. Leuckart, 1917), 53; for an English translation, by Klaus Schmirler, see http://tonalsoft.com/monzo/moellendorf/book/contents.htm. Shortly after Mager built his quarter-tone harmonium, Möllendorf constructed a similar device, but with a novel design that featured brown keys between the existing black and white, with each successive step tuned a quarter tone apart.

12. Mager, *Vierteltonmusik*, 12.

13. Ibid., 7.

14. Herman von Helmholtz, *On the Sensations of Tone*, trans. Alexander Ellis (New York: Dover, 1954), 235. On Behrens-Senegalden, see "Klavier mit vierteltöniger Tonleiter," *Zeitschrift für Instrumentenbau* 13, no. 29 (1893): 685.

15. Arnold Schoenberg, *Theory of Harmony*, trans. Roy E. Carter (Berkeley: University of California Press, 1978), 25–26, 423–25. Peter Donhauser asserts that Schoenberg's passage on microtonality was a powerful impetus for Mager's work, although Mager does not refer to it in *Vierteltonmusik*. Donhauser, *Elektrische Klangmaschinen*, 31.

16. Max Weber, *The Rational and Social Foundations of Music*, trans. Don Martindale, Johannes Ridel, and Gertrude Neuwirth (Carbondale: Southern Illinois University Press, 1958). Weber's text was first published as *Die rationale und soziologische Grundlagen der Musik* (Munich: Drei Masken Verlag, 1921).

17. Ibid., 101–3. For an example of a triumphalist history of twelve-tone equal temperament, see Stuart Isacoff, *Temperament: The Idea That Solved Music's Greatest Riddle* (New York: Alfred A. Knopf, 2001). For an elaboration of Weber's theory of musical rationalization, see Daniel K.L. Chua, "On Disenchantment," in *Absolute Music and the Construction of Meaning* (Cambridge, UK: Cambridge University Press, 1999), 12–22.

18. See Max Weber, "Science as a Vocation," in *From Max Weber: Essays in Sociology*, ed. H.H. Gerth and C. Wright Mills, 129–56 (New York: Oxford

University Press, 1958). The essay was originally published as *Wissenschaft als Beruf* (Munich: Duncker und Humblot, 1919) and was based on a lecture Weber gave in 1917.

19. Julius Maria Becker, *Syrinx* (Leipzig: Breitkopf & Härtel, 1918), 126–27.

20. Ibid., 141.

21. Becker's book was written in 1914; a second edition appeared in 1918. On *Syrinx*'s relationship to Mager, see Schenck, *Jörg Mager*, 7–8; and Gerrit Walther, *Julius Maria Becker, 1887–1949: Ein Dichter zwischen den Weltkriegen* (Baden-Baden: Battert-Verlag, 1989).

22. Mager, *Vierteltonmusik*, 2.

23. Schenck, *Jörg Mager*, 8.

24. Donhauser, *Elektrische Klangmaschinen*, 26.

25. Hans Rudolf Zeller, "Ferruccio Busoni und die musikalische Avantgarde um 1920," in *Musik der anderen Tradition: Mikrotonale Tonwelten*, ed. Heinz-Klaus Metzger and Rainer Riehn (Munich: Edition Text + Kritik, 2003), 9–21.

26. Jörg Mager, *Eine neue Epoche*, 5. Mager states that this meeting took place in the winter of 1923, but Richard Stein's spring 1923 account has the date as the fall of 1922. Stein, "Vierteltonmusik," *Die Musik* 15, no. 7 (April 1923): 514. By this time, Mager had already built a prototype electric instrument: in a letter dated 3 November 1922, Hába hailed Mager's device as "suited to usher in an epochal development not only in instrument building, but in music itself." (Quoted in Mager, *Eine neue Epoche*, 13.)

27. Frederik Nebeker, *Dawn of the Electronic Age: Electrical Technologies in the Shaping of the Modern World, 1914 to 1945* (Hoboken, NJ: Wiley–IEEE Press, 2009).

28. Fleming called his device a *valve*, because of the one-way flow of electrons from cathode to anode; this term persists in British English. The equivalent U.S. English term is *vacuum tube*, referring to the lack of air inside the bulb.

29. Similar discoveries were made shortly thereafter by the American Irving Langmuir and the German Alexander Meissner.

30. On this history, see Lawrence Lessing, *Man of High Fidelity: Edwin Howard Armstrong* (Philadelphia: J. B. Lippincott, 1956), 53–69; Albert Glinsky, *Theremin: Ether Music and Espionage* (Chicago: University of Illinois Press, 2000), 20–22; and Frederik Nebeker, *Dawn of the Electronic Age: Electrical Technologies in the Shaping of the Modern World, 1914 to 1945* (Hoboken, NJ: Wiley–IEEE Press, 2009), 40–43. My thanks to Edward Jones-Imhotep for helping me navigate these technical shoals.

31. A. Lion, "Die technischen Grundlagen von Theremins Ätherwellenmusik," *Die Musik* 21, no. 5 (1929): 357–58.

32. Lee de Forest, "Audion Bulbs as Producers of Pure Musical Tones," *The Electrical Experimenter* (1915): 394–95.

33. Mager, *Eine neue Epoche*, 2.

34. Jörg Mager, "Eine Rundfunkprophezeiung," *Der deutsche Rundfunk* 2, no. 29 (1924): 2952.

35. Mager, *Eine neue Epoche*, 10.

36. The phrase "radio-music without transmission" comes from Richard Stein's article "Zukunftsmusik im Rundfunk," *Der deutsche Rundfunk* 3, no. 12

(1925): 733–36. The article was credited with making Mager's work known in the wider field of radio: see Donhauser, *Elektrische Klangmaschinen,* 27.

37. The date of Mager's first prototype, which is not clearly stated in the primary sources, is given as 1921 in Donhauser, *Elektrische Klangmaschinen,* 27.

38. The instrument was "simple," of course, only in comparison to its later forms. Even the humble hand crank has a deep history: for an enlightening overview, see Lynn White, Jr., "The Act of Invention," in *Machina ex Deo: Essays in the Dynamism of Western Culture* (Cambridge, MA: MIT Press, 1968), 116–19. White notes that the continuous rotary motion exemplified by the crank is "typical of inorganic matter, whereas reciprocating [back-and-forth] motion is the sole movement found in living things. [. . .] To use a crank, our tendons and muscles must relate themselves to the motion of galaxies and electrons. From this inhuman adventure our race long recoiled."

39. Mager, *Eine neue Epoche,* 5. Mager's mention of the *omnitonium* reveals his knowledge of the history of enharmonic and microtonal instruments, in which he had done considerable research. He discovered an 1890 article that mentioned a *Clavemusicum omnitonium,* a keyboard instrument built in 1606 with thirty-one keys to the octave, specially designed to allow for the playing of "enharmonic" (microtonal) intervals, including quarter tones: Shohé Tanaka, "Studien im Gebiete der reinen Stimmung," *Vierteljahrschrift für Musikwissenschaft* 6 (1890). Mager mentions this article by name in *Eine neue Epoche der Musik durch Radio,* without making explicit the provenance of the term *omnitonium.* Tanaka's reference to the instrument depends, in turn, on an article published two years earlier: "Die Musikausstellung zu Bologna," *Zeitschrift für Instrumentenbau* 9, no. 8 (1888): 122–23. This article describes an instrument built by a certain Gonzaga and modeled closely on Nicola Vicentino's better-known *arcicembalo.* Curt Sachs notes that Tanaka incorrectly gives the name as *Omnitonium,* instead of *Omnitonum,* an error inherited by Mager; Sachs also refers to the instrument as the only extant enharmonic harpsichord. See the entry "Clavemusicum omnitonum" in Curt Sachs, *Reallexikon der Musikinstrumente* (Berlin: Julius Bard, 1913), 88.

40. Richard Stein, "Vierteltonmusik," 516. Hába's letter is quoted in Mager, *Eine neue Epoche,* 3.

41. Mager, *Eine neue Epoche,* 15. The quoted passage appears in Helmholtz, *Sensations of Tone,* 371.

42. For a historical survey of the glissando in twentieth-century music, see Douglas Kahn, *Noise, Water, Meat: A History of Sound in the Arts* (Cambridge, MA: MIT Press, 1999), 83–91. See also Nikolai Kulbin, "Free Music," in *The Blaue Reiter Almanac,* ed. Wassily Kandinsky and Franz Marc and trans. Henning Falkenstein (Boston: MFA Publications, 2005), 141–46.

43. For more detail on the heterodyne technique, see Léon Theremin, "The Design of a Musical Instrument Based on Cathode Relays," *Leonardo Music Journal* 6 (1996): 49–50.

44. See Reynold Weidenaar, *Magic Music from the Telharmonium* (Metuchen, NJ: Scarecrow Press, 1995).

45. Ferruccio Busoni, *Entwurf einer neuen Ästhetik der Tonkunst,* 2nd ed., ed. Martina Weindel (1916; Wilhelmshaven: Noetzel, Heinrichshofen-Bücher,

2001), 52. The phrase *universal instrument* comes from Busoni's article "Futurismus der Tonkunst," in *Von der Einheit der Musik,* 184–86. Wolfgang Hagen suggests that Busoni's misunderstanding of the instrument's playing interface may have been influenced by his reading of the science fiction novels of Jules Verne, where one encounters machines replete with dials, meters, and other techno-scientific accoutrements. Hagen, "Busoni's Invention: Phantasmagoria and Errancies in Times of Medial Transition," in *Artists as Inventors / Inventors as Artists,* ed. Dieter Daniels and Barbara U. Schmidt (Ostfildern, Ger.: Hatje Cantz Verlag, 2008), 106–7. Curiously, Busoni elsewhere acknowledges that the instrument was played from a conventional keyboard. Busoni, *Entwurf einer neuen Ästhetik,* 64.

46. Mager, *Eine neue Epoche,* 16.

47. See Hagen, "Busoni's Invention, 86–107; and Wolfgang Hagen, "Busonis 'Erfindung': Thaddeus Cahills Telefon-Telharmonium von 1906," in *Klangmaschinen zwischen Experiment und Medientechnik,* ed. Daniel Gethmann (Bielefeld: Transcript Verlag, 2010), 53–71.

48. Significantly, Mager's use of this term predates by nearly two decades its general application in organology to refer to electric instruments. See *Oxford Music Online,* s.v. "Electrophone," by Hugh Davies, accessed 5 May, 2010, http://www.oxfordmusiconline.com.

49. Scheibler's allusion to "pure tuning" *(reine Stimmung)* is ironic considering that he pioneered a method of using specially manufactured tuning forks to tune keyboard instruments in equal temperament. The passage quoted by Mager can be found in Scheibler's *Schriften über musikalische und physikalische Tonmessung und Orgelstimmung* (Crefeld: Druck und Verlag von E.M. Schüller, 1838), 53. See also *Oxford Music Online,* s.v. "Scheibler, Johann Heinrich," by Kevin Mooney, accessed May 5, 2010, http://www.oxfordmusiconline.com. For deeper background on Scheibler, see Myles T. Jackson, "The Fetish of Precision I: Scheibler's Tonometer and Tuning Technique," in *Harmonious Triads: Physicists, Musicians, and Instrument Makers in Nineteenth-Century Germany* (Cambridge, MA: MIT Press, 2006), 151–81.

50. Jörg Mager, "Biographisches zum Sphärophon," *Musikblätter des Anbruch* 8, nos. 8–9 (1926): 391.

51. Quoted in Joseph Willimann, *Der Briefwechsel zwischen Ferruccio Busoni und Volkmar Andreae 1907–1923* (Zurich: Kommissionsverlag Hug, 1994), 162.

52. Donhauser, *Elektrische Klangmaschinen,* 32.

53. Quoted in Mager, *Vierteltonmusik,* 13.

54. Quoted in Donhauser, *Elektrische Klangmaschinen,* 245–46.

55. Weiskopf, "Das Sphärophon," 388.

56. Mager, *Eine neue Epoche,* 11.

57. Donhauser, *Elektrische Klangmaschinen,* 26; Glinsky, *Theremin,* 50.

58. Glinsky, *Theremin,* 51.

59. See Kuznitzky, "Neue Elemente der Musikerzeugung"; Siegfried Kallenberg, "Elektrische Musik," *Zeitschrift für Musik* 94, no. 10 (1927); Arno Huth, "Elektrische Tonerzeugung: Zu den Erfindungen von Jörg Mager und

Leo Theremin," *Die Musik* 21, no. 1 (1927): 42–45; and Max Eisler, "Elektrische Musik und Instrumente," *Zeitschrift für Instrumentenbau,* 52, no. 10 (1932): 192. See also Glinsky, *Theremin,* 53–56.

60. Otto Kappelmayer, "Klingende Elektrizität," *Die Musik* 24, no. 11 (1932): 817.

61. Quoted in Glinsky, *Theremin,* 68.

62. Mager, *Eine neue Epoche,* 14. Mager also put forward a curiously biomorphic argument for microtonality. Noting that acousticians had determined the ability to distinguish intervals much smaller than the tempered semitone and referring to Helmholtz's "place theory," according to which each nerve fiber in the cochlea of the inner ear responds to a tiny frequency band, Mager suggested that musicians were bound by a physiological imperative to exercise these fibers, lest they wither through disuse: "Doesn't the subtle apparatus of pitch differentiation in the ear, which encompasses the entire tonal spectrum, all but demand the use of finer tonal degrees in music? Doesn't the exclusivity of our semitone system leave valuable parts of the organ of Corti unused, uncultivated, and subject to atrophy?" Mager, *Eine Neue Epoche,* 6.

63. Heinrich Strobel, "Musik aus dem Äther: Professor Theremin im Berliner Beethoven-Saal," *Musikblätter des Anbruch* 9, no. 10 (1927): 435.

64. Note also, however, that he sees a way of partially transcending the "mechanism" of mechanical instruments by employing them for original composition. The categories "electric" and "mechanical" are thus implicitly mapped onto another key duality in Weimar techno-aesthetics, that of "production" and "reproduction."

65. Huth, "Elektrische Tonerzeugung," 45.

66. A. Lion, "Die technische Grundlagen von Theremins Ätherwellenmusik," *Die Musik* 21, no. 5 (1929): 358.

67. Richard Stein, "Zukunftsmusik im Rundfunk," 736.

68. Weiskopf, "Das Sphärophon," 389. Note that Weiskopf is using *mechanical* in the broad sense, referring simply to the products of modern technology.

69. Adolf Weissmann, *Music Come to Earth,* trans. Eric Blom (New York: E.P. Dutton, 1930), 125; originally published as *Die Entgötterung der Musik* (Stuttgart: Deutsche Verlags-Anstalt, 1928).

70. Mager, "Eine Rundfunkprophezeihung," *Der deutsche Rundfunk* 2, no. 29 (1924): 2954.

71. Mager, *Eine Neue Epoche,* 14.

72. Quoted in Paul Hindemith, "Zu unserem Programm," in *Aufsätze, Vorträge, Reden* (Zurich: Atlantis, 1994), 18.

73. Helmholtz, *Sensations of Tone,* 119ff. The use of the term *synthesizer* for Helmholtz's device, though anachronistic, is by now well established.

74. "Electricität und Musik," *Zeitschrift für Instrumentenbau* 8, no. 4 (1887): 48.

75. Schoenberg, *Theory of Harmony,* 421–22.

76. Ibid., 421.

77. See Carl Dahlhaus, "Schoenberg's Orchestral Piece Op. 16, No. 3 and the Concept of *Klangfarbenmelodie,*" in *Schoenberg and the New Music,* trans.

Derrick Puffett and Alfred Clayton (Cambridge: Cambridge University Press, 1987), 141–43; and Alfred Cramer, "Schoenberg's Klangfarbenmelodie: A Principle of Early Atonal Harmony," *Music Theory Spectrum* 24, no. 1 (2002): 1–34.

78. Mager, "Elektro-akustische Musikinstrumente," *Zeitschrift für Instrumentenbau* 51, no. 15 (1931): 419.

79. Weiskopf, "Das Sphärophon," 389.

80. In fact, replicating Helmholtz's technique of additive synthesis proved difficult with the electroacoustic technology of the time, because the relationship between electrical variables such as circuit capacitance and the resulting timbre was still too crudely understood to enable the precise shaping of the overtone spectrum. In any case, Helmholtz's artificial timbres were hardly musically viable, being stationary sounds that could not in any sense be "played." For this reason, Hindemith's idea of using an ensemble of Spherophones to create synthetic timbres also remained, to all appearances, unrealized. See Donhauser, *Elektrische Klangmaschinen*, 246.

81. "Elektroakustische Hausorgel," *Zeitschrift für Instrumentenbau* 53, no. 2 (1932): 25. The Ondes Martenot, which the French inventor Maurice Martenot patented in 1928, made similar use of resonant loudspeaker membranes.

82. Oskar Vierling, "Elektrische Musik," *Elektrotechnische Zeitschrift* 53, no. 7 (1932): 157–58.

83. Jörg Mager, "Schallstrahler für Musikinstrumente mit elektrischer Tonerzeugung in Form einer Platte," DE Patent 554,609, filed June 22, 1930 and issued June 23, 1932. This and more of Mager's patents can be found online at UbuWeb Electronic Music Resources, http://www.ubu.com/emr/patents/01individuals/mager.html (accessed March 20, 2013). Mager's experiments with electroacoustically driven resonance of metal plates can be compared to the later use of such techniques in the creation of artificial reverberation for studio recording; see Axel Volmar, "Auditiver Raum aus der Dose: Raumakustik, Tonstudiobau und Hallgeräte im 20. Jahrhundert," in *Klangmaschinen zwischen Experiment und Medientechnik*, ed. Daniel Gethmann, 153–74.

84. Karl Willy Wagner, "Die Frequenzbereich von Sprache und Musik," *Elektrotechnische Zeitschrift* 45, no. 9 (1924): 451–56.

85. Siegfried Kallenberg, "Elektrische Musik," 558.

86. Ferruccio Busoni, *Entwurf einer neuen Ästhetik*, 65.

87. Jörg Mager, "Electro-acoustic Musical Instrument," United States Patent 1,829,099, 3, filed October 27, 1931, UbuWeb Electronic Music Resources, http://www.ubu.com/emr/patents/_docs/patents/01individuals/mager/electroacoustic_instrument_mager.pdf (accessed March 20, 2013).

88. "Jörg Magers Elektroton-Orgel," *Zeitschrift für Instrumentenbau* 54, no. 2 (1933), 26.

89. Jörg Mager, "Einrichtung zur Erzeugung von Klangfarbeneffekten bei Musikinstrumenten mit elektrischer Tonerzeugung," DE Patent 572,173, filed on April 23, 1932 and issued on March 11, 1933, UbuWeb Electronic Music Resources, http://www.ubu.com/emr/patents/_docs/patents/01individuals/mager/DE572173C.pdf (accessed March 20, 2013).

90. Jörg Mager, "Verfahren zur elektrischen Erzeugung von Geräuschen," DE Patent 541,812, filed on August 1, 1929 and issued on December 24, 1931,

UbuWeb Electronic Music Resources, http://www.ubu.com/emr/patents/_docs/patents/01individuals/mager/DE541812C.pdf (accessed March 20, 2013).

91. Mager, "Einrichtung zur Erzeugung von Klangfarbeneffekten." It was likely such experimental sound research that Peter Lertes had in mind when he wrote that "through electrical musical instruments, 'noises' will be given artistic forms and occupy a larger space in composers' work than they have previously." Lertes, *Elektrische Musik*, 4. Mager's interest in *Seismophonie*, or the amplification and study of the movements of the earth's crust, also indicates the experimental applications of his instruments; see Donhauser, *Elektrische Klangmaschinen*, 210.

92. This summary of the admittedly bewildering state of Mager's instruments circa 1927 is based on Kuznitzky, "Neue Elemente der Musikerzeugung" and "Neues vom Sphärophon," *Melos* 6, no. 6 (June 1927): 282; Arno Huth, "Elektrische Tonerzeugung"; and Kathi Meyer, ed., *Katalog der Internationalen Ausstellung Musik im Leben der Völker* (Frankfurt: Hauserpresse, 1927), 319.

93. See Donhauser, *Elektrische Klangmaschinen*, 38–39; Schenck, *Jörg Mager*, 18–19; and Hermann Scherchen's detailed description quoted in "Jörg Magers Elektroton-Orgel," 26. Further evidence that Mager was still drawn to unconventional systems of tuning is found in a patent filed in 1930, in which he describes an instrument (apparently never built) consisting of many small electrical contacts that could be played in a rapid staccato by tiny mallets—a kind of microtonal electroxylophone. See Jörg Mager, "Musikinstrument mit Tonerzeugung auf rein elektrischem Wege," DE Patent 562,954, filed on December 25, 1930 and issued on October 13, 1932, UbuWeb Electronic Music Resources, http://www.ubu.com/emr/patents/_docs/patents/01individuals/mager/DE562954C.pdf (accessed March 20, 2013).

94. Donhauser, *Elektrische Klangmaschinen*, 40.

95. Schenck, *Jörg Mager*, 13.

96. The phrase "Elektro-Musik Laboratorium" appears in Jörg Mager, "Einführung der elektrischen Klangerzeugung," *Zeitschrift für Instrumentenbau* 52, no. 3 (1931): 45; it can also be seen on the letterhead of a document reproduced in Donhauser, *Elektrische Klangmaschinen*, 222.

97. Schenck, *Jörg Mager*, 16.

98. Scherchen, "Jörg Magers Elektro-ton Orgel," 26.

99. "Ein neues Instrument von Jörg Mager," *Zeitschrift für Instrumentenbau* 50, no. 24 (1930): 814.

100. Schenck, *Jörg Mager*, 17.

101. "Elektro-akustische Parsifalglocken," *Zeitschrift für Instrumentenbau* 51, no. 23 (1931): 598. See also Donhauser, *Elektrische Klangmaschinen*, 200–201. According to Hugo Leichtentritt, Mager's metal plates were actually gongs from a Javanese gamelan, whose "sound seemed to come from mysterious heights, far away." Leichtentritt, "Some New Mechanical Instruments," *Musical Times* 72, no. 1065 (1931): 1037.

102. Quoted in Donhauser, *Elektrische Klangmaschinen*, 204. The enigmatic phrase "eccentric music" reappears in a 1932 review of a demonstration of the Partiturophon, suggesting that such sounds were not used only to accom-

pany staged action. See "Elektroakustische Hausorgel," 25. Elsewhere Mager spoke of an "indirect music" to be created through the use of subtle background noises.

103. Mager, *Eine neue Epoche*, 15.

4. "SONIC HANDWRITING": MEDIA INSTRUMENTS AND MUSICAL INSCRIPTION

1. Hector Berlioz, *Berlioz's Orchestration Treatise: A Translation and Commentary*, trans. Hugh MacDonald (Cambridge: Cambridge University Press, 2004), 5.
2. Guido Bagier, "Der sprechende Film," in "Musik und Maschine," special issue, *Musikblätter des Anbruch* 8, nos. 8–9 (1926): 380–84. A year later, Bagier demonstrated the Tri-Ergon (the German trademark for optical sound film) recording procedure at the same festival, now relocated from Donaueschingen to Baden-Baden. Bagier is an intriguing figure about whom little information is available. Born in 1888, his writings include a book on the German composer Max Reger (1923), *Der kommende Film: Eine Abrechnung und eine Hoffnung* (1928), and an apparent work of fiction entitled *Das tönende Licht: Die Schilderung einiger seltsamer Begebenheiten seit der Erfindung der Kinematographie, unter Verwendung wichtiger und unbekannter Dokumente* (1943). He also worked as a producer on G.W. Pabst's 1931 film version of Brecht and Weill's *Die Dreigroschenoper*.
3. Bagier, "Der sprechende Film," 384.
4. Gerhard Lindner, "Graphomusik," *Die Musik* 24, no. 4 (1932): 265.
5. Another such instrument from around the same time was the radioelectric organ of the French inventors Givelet and Coupleux, which combined electric tone generation via vacuum tube oscillators with a paper-tape reader that allowed for automatic playback. See E. Weiss, "Nouveaux instruments de musique radioélectriques," *La Nature* 58 (1930): 258–67. Almost no information about this instrument is available in English.
6. On the *intonarumori*, see Barclay Brown, "The Noise Instruments of Luigi Russolo," *Perspectives of New Music* 20, no. 1–2 (1981–1982): 31–48.
7. Piet Mondrian, "De 'Bruiteurs Futuristes Italiens' en 'Het' nieuwe in de muziek," *De Stijl* 4, no. 8 (1921): 114–18, and 4, no. 9 (1921): 130–36. Mondrian later translated the essay into French, and it was published in 1922 as "La Manifestation du Néo-Plasticisme dans la musique et les bruiteurs italiens futuristes." See Mondrian, *The New Art—The New Life: The Collected Writings of Piet Mondrian*, ed. and trans. Harry Holtzman and Martin S. James (Boston: G.K. Hall, 1986), 148. Carel Blotkamp notes that Mondrian had begun thinking about neoplastic music as early as 1920. Blotkamp, *Mondrian: The Art of Destruction* (New York: Harry N. Abrams, 1995), 163.
8. Piet Mondrian, "Die neue Gestaltung in der Musik und die futuristischen italienischen Bruitisten," in *Neue Gestaltung* (Munich: Albert Langen Verlag, 1925), 33. However, Mondrian remained wary of analogies between the arts; see Blotkamp, *Mondrian*, 130.
9. Mondrian, "Die neue Gestaltung in der Musik," 30.
10. Piet Mondrian, "The Manifestation of Neo-Plasticism in Music and the Italian Futurists' *Bruiteurs*," in Mondrian, *The New Art—The New Life*, 153.

11. Mondrian, "Die neue Gestaltung in der Musik," 39. Mondrian was challenged in this assertion by Nelly van Moorsel, a pianist and the future wife of Mondrian's colleague, Theo van Doesburg. Van Moorsel argued, as would John Cage in the 1950s, that silence, not noise, was the negation of tone, as Mondrian suggested. See Blotkamp, *Mondrian*, 162.

12. Mondrian, "Die neue Gestaltung in der Musik," 26.

13. Ibid., 34.

14. Ibid., 37. Elsewhere Mondrian declared that "it is quite possible for music to become 'abstract' and cease to be dominated by the natural to the extent that its expressive means (sound) allow. [. . .] In music the expression of the art is becoming almost 'mineral.' [. . .] Nature, from mineral to animal, is expressed less and less abstractly, less and less purely." Mondrian, "Manifestation of Neo-Plasticism," 151–53. The mineral plane suggests here an undifferentiated physical primacy: mineral sounds are those that are entirely free of the aura of the individual that characterizes conventional vocal and instrumental timbres. This aesthetic materialism was a common theme among the avant-garde movements of the early twentieth century; in 1912, Marinetti, the spokesman of Italian futurism, declared the impulse "to substitute for human psychology, now exhausted, the lyric obsession with matter. [. . .] The warmth of a piece of iron or wood is in our opinion more impassioned than the smile or tears of a woman." Quoted in Daniel Albright, ed., *Modernism and Music: An Anthology of Sources* (Chicago: University of Chicago Press, 2004), 173.

15. Mondrian, "Manifestation of Neo-Plasticism," 153. Mondrian had given voice to the fantasy of a performerless music in an earlier text as well: "The more music becomes pure expression of equilibrated relationships, [. . .] the more it will find itself hampered by existing instruments. Other instruments will be sought—or mechanical means! [. . .] What effort a concert requires on the part of the musicians and the conductor, to avoid slackening the pace. Wouldn't it be fine, and far more reliable—if one could invent a machine to which the real artist, the composer, could entrust his work?" Piet Mondrian, *Natural Reality and Abstract Reality: An Essay in Trialogue Form*, trans. Martin S. James (New York: George Braziller, 1995), 98. This text was originally published in *De Stijl* in twelve installments from June 1919 to July 1920.

16. Quoted in Blotkamp, *Mondrian*, 162. Although Russolo's intonarumori provided the immediate inspiration for Mondrian's musings, this connection is something of a red herring. As Karin Bjisterveld has argued, Russolo and Mondrian were drawn to the sonic ideal of the machine for quite different reasons: Russolo placed emphasis on the continuous or "enharmonic" pitch spectrum of mechanical "noise-sounds," while Mondrian valued precise determination and clear-cut boundaries between sounds. Karin Bjisterveld, "A Servile Imitation: Disputes about Machines in Music, 1910–1930," in *Music and Technology in the Twentieth Century*, ed. Hans-Joachim Braun (Baltimore: Johns Hopkins University Press, 2002), 121–36. Further, Mondrian and others criticized the intonarumori for cleaving too closely to natural sounds. (See Mondrian, "Manifestation of Neo-Plasticism," 155.)

17. László Moholy-Nagy, "Neue Gestaltung in der Musik: Möglichkeiten des Grammophons," *Der Sturm* 14, no. 7 (1923): 102–6.

18. László Moholy-Nagy, "Produktion—Reproduktion," *De Stijl* 5, no. 7 (1922): 98–100. English translation by Mátyás Esterházy in Krisztina Passuth, ed., *Moholy-Nagy* (London: Thames and Hudson, 1985), 289–90. Moholy-Nagy would later help disseminate Mondrian's ideas: in 1925, German translations of five of Mondrian's essays were published as *Neue Gestaltung*, the fifth in a series of influential Bauhaus Books, edited by Moholy-Nagy and Walter Gropius.

19. See Richard Kostelanetz, ed., *Moholy-Nagy: An Anthology* (New York: Da Capo, 1970), 9–10.

20. Passuth, *Moholy-Nagy*, 289–90. See also Victor Margolin, *The Struggle for Utopia: Rodchenko, Lissitzky, Moholy-Nagy, 1917–1946* (Chicago: University of Chicago Press, 1997), 139, fn. 23.

21. Passuth, *Moholy-Nagy*, 289.

22. Moholy-Nagy, "Neue Gestaltung in der Musik," 104.

23. H. H. Stuckenschmidt, "Die Mechanisierung der Musik," *Pult und Taktstock* 2, no. 1 (1925): 8.

24. Ibid., 7.

25. Heinz Pringsheim, "Die 'Mechanisierung' der Musik," *Allgemeine Musik Zeitung* (1925): 289–93.

26. László Moholy-Nagy, "Musico-Mechanico, Mechanico-Optico: Geradlinigkeit des Geistes—Umwege der Technik," *Musikblätter des Anbruch* 8, nos. 8–9: 367.

27. Hans Heinz Stuckenschmidt, "Musik am Bauhaus," in *Vom Klang der Bilder*, ed. Karin von Maur (Munich: Prestel, 1985), 410.

28. Moholy-Nagy, "Musico-Mechanico, Mechanico-Optico," 367. Moholy-Nagy also considered the possibility of working on giant, blank gramophone discs that would allow the composer to easily see the groove patterns on which he worked. These oversized "production discs" could then be reproduced at regular size for playback purposes. This idea never came to fruition.

29. There are anecdotal accounts of other experiments in gramophone music. For example, Henry Cowell said that the Russian composer Nicolai Lopatnikoff "[planned] to make phonograph recordings of various factory and street noises, synchronizing and amplifying them as a percussion background for music written for keyboard recordings." Henry Cowell, "Music of and for the Records," *Modern Music* 7, no. 3 (1931): 32–34.

30. Paul Hindemith, "Zur mechanischen Musik," in *Aufsätze, Vorträge, Reden*, ed. Giselher Schubert (Zurich: Atlantis, 1994), 19–24.

31. Martin Elste, "Hindemiths Versuche 'grammophonplatteneigener Stücke' im Kontext einer Ideengeschichte der Mechanischen Musik im 20. Jahrhundert," in *Hindemith-Jahrbuch* 25 (1996), 220.

32. Heinrich Burkard, "Anmerkung zu den 'Lehrstücken' und zur Schallplattenmusik," *Melos* 9, nos. 5–6 (1930): 230.

33. Mark Katz, "The Rise and Fall of *Grammophonmusik*," in *Capturing Sound: How Technology Has Changed Music* (Berkeley: University of California Press, 2004), 102. As Katz aptly puts it, "These short, simple pieces may be thought of as etudes, but not in the traditional sense, for they explore the technical abilities not of the performer but of the instrument." For a meticulous

historical examination of these pieces, see Elste, "Hindemiths Versuche," 195–221. For more on Toch's pieces, see Carmel Raz, "From Trinidad to Cyberspace: Reconsidering Ernst Toch's 'Geographical Fugue,'" *Zeitschrift der Gesellschaft für Musiktheorie* 9, no. 2 (2012), http://www.gmth.de/zeitschrift/artikel/698.aspx; and "'Gesprochene Musik': The Lost Movements of Toch's 'Geographical Fugue,'" *Current Musicology* 97 (forthcoming).

34. Ernst Toch, "Über meine Kantate 'Das Wasser' und meine Grammophonemusik," *Melos* 9, no. 5–6 (1930): 221–22. Translated in Katz, "Rise and Fall of *Grammophonmusik*," 102.

35. Georg Schünemann, "Produktive Kräfte der mechanischen Musik," *Die Musik* 24, no. 4 (1932): 247.

36. As we have already seen, Moholy-Nagy laid out the principles of "optophonetics"—sound-image correspondence based in the technological equivalence of all phenomena—in the early 1920s, imagining the gramophone as the means of realization.

37. See Thomas Levin's essay "'Tones from out of Nowhere': Rudolf Pfenninger and the Archaeology of Synthetic Sound," in *New Media, Old Media: A History and Theory Reader,* ed. Thomas Keenan and Wendy Hui Kyong Chun (New York: Routledge, 2005), 45–81. Levin finds the earliest such relationship in the *Klangfiguren,* or "sound figures," of the acoustician E. F. F. Chladni, who discovered that sand dispersed on a metal plate formed patterns around nodal points when the plate was vibrated with a violin bow. As Levin notes, in an irony of media history the reproducibility of sound recording was won at the cost of its legibility: the traces read by the gramophone needle were inscrutable to the human eye.

38. On this topic, see Edward W. Kellogg, "History of Sound Motion Pictures," *Journal of the SMPTE* 64 (1955): 292.

39. See Alexander Graham Bell, "The Photophone," *Science* 1, no. 11 (1880): 130–34.

40. Maximilian Plessner, *Ein Blick auf die grossen Erfindungen des zwanzigsten Jahrhunderts: I. Die Zukunft des elektrischen Fernsehens* (Berlin: Ferd. Dämmlers Verlagsbuchhanndlung, 1892). Not having access to Plessner's rare pamphlet, I have relied on the commentary by Nils Klevjer Aas, available online at http://histv.free.fr/plessner/plessner.pdf.

41. See Ernst Ruhmer's 1901 article "The 'Photographophone'" *Scientific American* 85, no. 3 (1901), 36, available online at Machine-History.com, http://www.machine-history.com/Photographophone%201901 (accessed March 18, 2013).

42. Highlighting this technological lineage, Ruhmer's device was even referred to in the press as the "Film Photophone." See "The Film Photophone," *Science,* new series, 54, no. 1399 (1921): 373.

43. Edison spoke of sound film as early as 1899, but technical developments such as the photoelectric cell, the amplifier tube, and the loudspeaker were needed to make it possible. See F. Noack, "Die Technik des Tonfilms," *Anbruch* 11, no. 5 (1929): 174. The photoelectric cell found use in a number of playable electric instruments of the 1920s and '30s as well, including the Saraga-Generator, the Superpiano, and the Welte Lichtton-Orgel.

44. Quoted in Mervyn Cooke, *A History of Film Music* (Cambridge: Cambridge University Press, 2008), 62.

45. Sergei Eisenstein, Vsevolod Pudovkin, and G. V. Alexandrov, "Statement on the Sound Film," in Sergei Eisenstein, *Film Form* (New York: Harcourt Brace, 1949), 257–60.

46. László Moholy-Nagy, "Probleme des neuen Films," in *Künstlerschrifte der 20er Jahre*, ed. Uwe M. Schneede (Cologne: DuMont Buchverlag, 1986), 319. For an English version of this text, see "Problems of the Modern Film," in *Moholy-Nagy: An Anthology*, ed. Richard Kostelanetz (New York: Da Capo, 1970), 131–38.

47. Moholy-Nagy, "Probleme des neuen Films," 313–14.

48. Ibid., 319.

49. Ibid.

50. Ibid. Remarkably, Moholy-Nagy anticipated the opposition of what would become known in the 1950s as musique concrète and *elektronische Musik*. Ever the systematist, he also envisioned a third phase in which these two distinct forms would be used in conjunction.

51. Quoted in Mark E. Cory, "Soundplay: The Polyphonous Tradition of German Radio Art," in *Wireless Imagination*, ed. Douglas Kahn and Gregory Whitehead (Cambridge, MA: MIT Press, 1992), 339.

52. Kurt Weill, "Möglichkeiten absoluter Radiokunst," *Der deutsche Rundfunk* 3, no. 26 (1925):1625–28. Reprinted in Kurt Weill, *Musik und Theater: Gesammelte Schriften*, ed. Stephen Hinton and Jürgen Schebera (Berlin: Henschelverlag Kunst und Gesellschaft, 1990), 191–95. Significantly, Weill had studied composition with Busoni for nearly three years, from January 1921 until December 1923. Busoni's fascination with occult and otherworldly tones of modern technological provenance is echoed in Weill's catalog of strange new sounds.

53. Robert Beyer, "Musik und Film," *Die Musik* 21, no. 6 (1929): 447–49; Robert Beyer, "Tonfilm," *Die Musik* 21, no. 10 (1929): 747–50; and Robert Beyer, "Musik und Tonfilm," in *Kunst und Technik*, ed. Leo Kestenberg (Berlin: Wegweiser-Verlag, 1930), 365–94.

54. Marietta Morawska-Büngeler, *Schwingende Elektronen: Eine Dokumentation über das Studio für Elektronische Musik des Westdeutschen Rundfunks in Köln 1951–1986* (Cologne: P. J. Tonger, 1988), 7.

55. Beyer, "Musik und Tonfilm," 378.

56. Beyer, "Tonfilm," 748.

57. Beyer, "Musik und Tonfilm, 379. See Bertolt Brecht, "Alienation Effects in Chinese Acting," in *Brecht on Theater*, ed. John Willett (New York: Hill and Wang, 1964), 91–99. Brecht's notion of the *Verfremdungseffekt* was in turn influenced by the idea of *ostranenie*, or "defamiliarization," introduced by the Russian critic Viktor Shklovsky in his 1917 essay "Art as Technique."

58. Beyer, "Tonfilm," 749.

59. Beyer, "Musik und Film," 449.

60. Walter Gronostay, "Die Technik der Geräuschanwendung im Tonfilm," *Die Musik* 22, no. 1 (1929): 42–44.

61. Leopold Stokowski , "New Horizons in Music," *Journal of the Acoustical Society of America* 4, no. 1A (1932): 11.

62. Beyer, "Musik und Tonfilm, 390.
63. Ibid., 386.
64. Ibid., 388.
65. Arnold Schoenberg, *Theory of Harmony*, trans. Roy E. Carter (Berkeley: University of California Press, 1978), 432: "I am a musician and have nothing to do with things atonal. The word *atonal* could only signify something entirely inconsistent with the nature of tone."
66. Beyer, "Musik und Tonfilm," 391.
67. Robert Beyer, "Das Problem der 'kommenden Musik,'" *Die Musik* 20, no. 12 (1928): 864–65.
68. Beyer, "Musik und Tonfilm," 387.
69. Ibid., 376–77.
70. Ibid., 390.
71. Robert Beyer, "Zur Frage der elektrischen Tonerzeugung (nach Art der thereminschen Apparatur)," *Die Musik* 21, no. 5 (1929): 358–59.
72. Beyer, "Musik und Tonfilm," 392.
73. Original titles in German are "Jazz der Arbeit," "Feierabend," "Fahrt ins Freie," "Pastorale," and "Wiederbeginn der Arbeit." See Wolfgang Hagen, "Walter Ruttmanns Großstadt-Weekend: Zur Herkunft der Hörcollage aus der ungegenständlichen Malerei," http://www.whagen.de/vortraege/2003/RuttmannWeekend/ruttmann.pdf (accessed 24 October 2012), 3.
74. Hagen, "Walter Ruttmanns Großstadt-Weekend," 2. *Weekend* also had precedents in the experimental radio plays *(Hörspiele)* of the 1920s, such as Hans Flesch's *Zauberei auf dem Sender* (1924) and Friedrich Wilhelm Bischoff's *Hallo! Hier Welle Erdball* (1928). It is distinguished from these works, however, in being composed entirely via montage and in its almost complete lack of dialogue. See Daniel Gilfillan, *Pieces of Sound: German Experimental Radio* (Minneapolis: University of Minnesota Press, 2009), 67–86.
75. Quoted in Hagen, "Walter Ruttmanns Großstadt-Weekend," 3.
76. Hans Richter, *Köpfe und Hinterköpfe* (Zürich: Verlag der Arche, 1967), 156–57. Quoted in Jesse Shapins, "Walter Ruttmann's *Weekend*: Sound, Space and the Multiple Senses of an Urban Documentary Imagination," http://www.jesseshapins.net/writings/JShapins_RuttmannWeekend_Jan2008.pdf (accessed March 18, 2012), 13–14.
77. See Andrei Smirnov, *Sound in Z: Experiments in Sound and Electronic Music in Early 20th-Century Russia* (London: Koenig Books, 2013), 166–67; Lucy Fischer, "*Enthusiasm:* From Kino-Eye to Radio-Eye," in *Film Sound: Theory and Practice,* ed. Elisabeth Weis and John Belton (New York: Columbia University Press, 1985), 247–64.
78. Quoted in Hagen, "Walter Ruttmanns Großstadt-Weekend," 3.
79. Dieter Daniels, "Artists as Inventors and Inventions as Art: A Paradigm Shift from 1840 to 1900," in *Artists as Inventors / Inventors as Artists,* ed. Dieter Daniels and Barbara U. Schmidt (Ostfildern, Ger.: Hatje Cantz, 2008), 45.
80. Moholy-Nagy, "Probleme des neuen Films," 320.
81. In particular, theorists of synthetic sound drew inspiration from the pioneering works of "visual music" or "absolute film" created the early 1920s by filmmakers such as Walter Ruttmann, Oskar Fischinger, Hans Richter, and

Viking Eggeling. For an excellent anthology of texts stemming from this movement, see *Der Absolute Film: Dokumente der Medienavantgarde (1912–1936)*, ed. Christian Kiening and Heinrich Adolf (Zurich: Chronos Verlag, 2012). Ironically, "absolute film," which drew inspiration from the German romantic tradition in musical aesthetics, in turn exerted a decisive influence on the first experiments in optical sound film. The intertwined history of experimental film and music in the 1920s has scarcely been explored outside of German sources.

82. On this point see Volker Straebel, "How Light Is Changed into Sound: Eine kleine Geschichte der Photozelle in Musik und Klangkunst," *Neue Zeitschrift für Musik* 158 (1997): 5; http://www.straebel.de/praxis/index.html?/praxis/text/t-photozellen.htm (accessed March 18, 2013).

83. In addition to Germany, France and the Soviet Union were hot spots of sound film experimentation. See Andrei Smirnov, *Sound in Z*, 175–236; "Boris Yankovsky: Leben im Klangspektrum: Gezeichneter Klang und Klangsynthese in der Sowjetunion der 30er Jahre," in *Klangmaschinen zwischen Experiment und Medientechnik*, ed. Daniel Gethmann (Bielefeld: Transcript Verlag, 2010), 97–120; Richard S. James, "Avant-Garde Sound-on-Film Techniques and Their Relationship to Electro-Acoustic Music," *Musical Quarterly* 72, no. 1: 74–89; and Peter Manning, "The Influence of Recording Technologies on the Early Development of Electroacoustic Music," *Leonardo Music Journal* 13 (2003): 5–10.

84. Quoted in William Moritz, *Optical Poetry: The Life and Work of Oskar Fischinger* (Bloomington: University of Indiana Press, 2004), 179–80.

85. Oskar Fischinger, "Der absolute Tonfilm," *Deutsche Allgemeine Zeitung* (June 29, 1935), reprinted in Kiening and Adolf, *Der Absolute Film*, 314–16.

86. Quoted in Moritz, *Optical Poetry*, 180.

87. Ibid.

88. Albert Neuberger, "Schlanglinien singen: Noten im Zick-Zack," in Kiening and Adolf, *Der Absolute Film*, 310.

89. Emily D. Robertson, *"It Looks Like Sound! Drawing a History of Animated Music in the Early Twentieth Century,"* master's thesis, University of Maryland (2010), 32.

90. See Thomas Y. Levin, "For the Record: Adorno on Music in the Age of Its Technological Reproducibility," *October* 55 (1990): 41.

91. Here I differ with Levin, who claims that Fischinger's work is "fundamentally antitechnological." Levin, "'Tones from out of Nowhere'," 80.

92. Erich Lasswitz, "Gezeichnete Musik," in Kiening and Adolf, *Der absolute Film*, 312–13.

93. "Tönende Ornamente: Aus Oskar Fischingers neuer Arbeit," in Kiening and Adolf, *Der absolute Film*, 309; see also Moritz, *Optical Poetry*, 43.

94. Fischinger would revisit synthetic sound, albeit with a new technique, in 1948 and 1955: on the relevant films, see Moritz, *Optical Poetry*, 236–37. My thanks to Cindy Keefer of the Center for Visual Music for her comments on this section.

95. The only substantial source on Pfenninger in English is Thomas Levin's article "'Tones from out of Nowhere'."

96. Three films have been released in a commercial edition—*Serenade, Pitsch und Patsch*, and *Barcarole* (all created in 1932)—and can be found on *Animerte*

Avantgarde: Der künstlerische Animationsfilm der 20er und 30er Jahre, curated by Ulrich Wegenast, Absolute Medien, 2011, DVD.

97. These effects call to mind the techniques of early video game music, in which the limitations of the monophonic sound chips were circumvented by *trompe l'oreille* illusions of harmony created by the rapid arpeggiation of multiple tones.

98. Don Ihde, "A Phenomenology of Technics," in *Philosophy of Technology: The Technological Condition*, ed. Robert C. Scharff and Val Dusek (Oxford: Blackwell, 2003), 507–12.

99. R. Prévot, quoted in Levin, "'Tones from out of Nowhere,'" 65.

100. Quoted in Passuth, *Moholy-Nagy*, 322. Moholy-Nagy goes on to say that "it is said that Pfenninger is in a position today to write down every word and name; that is, he can read sound writing on sight!"

101. Levin, "'Tones from out of Nowhere,'" 81. Levin refers to Moholy-Nagy's approach as "surprisingly Fischingerian."

5. "A NEW, PERFECT MUSICAL INSTRUMENT": THE TRAUTONIUM AND ELECTRIC MUSIC IN THE 1930S

1. Dr. Seuss, *The Butter Battle Book* (New York: Random House, 1984), unpaginated.

2. Peter Lertes, *Elektrische Musik: Eine gemeinverständliche Darstellung ihrer Grundlagen, des heutigen Stand der Technik und ihrer Zukunftsmöglichkeiten* (Dresden and Leipzig: Theodor Steinkopff, 1933), 1, 5.

3. The RCA Theremin was a market failure—only about five hundred were produced at a time when the company was manufacturing about nine thousand radios per day. Although the cause of the instrument's failure has been attributed to the "Black Thursday" stock market crash, which took place just ten days after the RCA Theremin's public debut, price was surely a factor as well: the instrument cost over $3,000 in today's currency. See Andrew Baron and Mike Buffington, "The RCA Theremin," RCA Theremin.com, 2015, accessed August 21, 2015, http://rcatheremin.com; and Albert Glinsky, *Theremin: Ether Music and Espionage* (Chicago: University of Illinois Press, 2000), 92–128.

4. See Andrey Smirnov, *Sound in Z: Experiments in Sound and Electronic Music in Early 20th Century Russia* (London: Koenig Books, 2013), 94–98.

5. On the Ondes Martenot, see Albert Nodon, "La musique et les ondes musicales—L'appareil Martenot, *La Nature* 58 (1930): 489–92; and Jean Laurendeau, *Maurice Martenot, luthier de l'électronique* (Montreal: Louise Courteau Éditrice, 1990). On the Coupleux-Givelet instrument, see E. Weiss, "Nouveaux Instruments de musique radioélectriques," *La Nature* 58 (1930): 258–63; and L. Neuberger, "Die Erfahrungen mit der neuen radioelektrischen Orgel in Lausane," *Zeitschrift für Instrumentenbau* 55, no. 9 (1935): 126–27. Coupleux and Givelet's instrument appeared in multiple forms: Weiss describes devices that combine electric tone generation with automatic playback steered by piano rolls, while Neuberger, writing five years later, gives account of a more conventional "electric organ" meant to serve as a substitute for pipe organs.

6. "Elektro-akustische Musik," *Zeitschrift für Instrumentenbau* 51, no. 23 (1931): 598.

7. Lertes, *Elektrische Musik*, 162, 164.

8. Quoted in Hans Mersmann, "Dr. Trautweins elektrische Musik," *Melos* 9, no. 5-6 (1930): 229.

9. Peter Donhauser, *Elektrische Klangmaschinen: Die Pionierzeit in Deutschland und Österreich* (Vienna: Böhlau, 2007), 42-43.

10. Trautwein's patents date back to the early 1920s (1922 for DRP 462,980 and 1924 for DRP 469,775).

11. This design had been developed independently as early as 1927 by Peter Lertes and Bruno Helberger and implemented in their instrument called the Hellertion: see Donhauser, *Elektrische Klangmaschinen*, 68. The wire interface was apparently an example of independent invention: Nikolai Ananiev's Sonar (1926) was based on the same principle (see Smirnov, *Sound in Z*, 94-95), and Mager filed a patent for an instrument with a similar "electric string" playing interface around the time of the original Lertes-Helberger patent. See Jörg Mager, "Elektrisches Musikinstrument," DE Patent 578,477, filed on October 6, 1927 and issued on May 24, 1933, UbuWeb Electronic Music Resources, http://www.ubu.com/emr/patents/_docs/patents/01individuals/mager/DE578477C.pdf.

12. A. Lion, "Das elektrische Musikinstrument 'Trautonium,'" *Zeitschrift für Instrumentenbau* 53, no. 5 (1932): 80.

13. Mersmann, "Dr. Trautweins elektrische Musik," 229.

14. Ibid., 228.

15. Friedrich Trautwein, *Elektrische Musik* (Berlin: Weidmannsche Buchhandlung, 1930), 36.

16. In his discussion of filtering harmonically rich timbres, Trautwein cites the same paper by Karl Willy Wagner that Mager referred to in his own research—see Trautwein, *Elektrische Musik*, 8-10.

17. My thanks to Peter Donhauser for this suggested translation of the term.

18. Trautwein, *Elektrische Musik*, 12.

19. Ibid., 36.

20. Ibid., 17.

21. R. Raven-Hart, "Radio, and a New Theory of Tone Quality," *Musical Quarterly* 17, no. 3 (1931): 380-88.

22. Lertes, *Elektrische Musik*, 183.

23. Trautwein, *Elektrische Musik*, 22.

24. Raven-Hart, "Radio, and a New Theory," 388.

25. Trautwein, *Elektrische Musik*, 7.

26. See Dietmar Schenk, "Berliner Rundfunkversuchsstelle (1928-1935): Zur Geschichte und Rezeption einer Institution aus der Frühzeit von Rundfunk und Tonfilm," *Rundfunk und Geschichte* 23 (1997): 124-37; and Dietmar Schenk, "Die Rundfunkversuchsstelle," in *Die Hochschule für Musik zu Berlin* (Stuttgart: Franz Steiner Verlag, 2004), 257-72.

27. Arno Schirokauer, "Kunst-Politik in Rundfunk," *Die literarische Welt* 5, no. 35 (August 1929), 1. Translated in *The Weimar Republic Sourcebook*, ed. Anton Kaes, Martin Jay, and Edward Dimendberg (Berkeley: University of California Press, 1994), 609-10.

28. Detlev J.K. Peukert, *The Weimar Republic: The Crisis of Classical Modernity*, trans. Richard Deveson (New York: Hill & Wang, 1993), 170-71.

29. Schenk, "Die Rundfunkversuchsstelle," 260.
30. Ibid., 271–72.
31. Donhauser, *Elektrische Klangmaschinen,* 44.
32. Hindemith was friends with Oskar Fischinger, who suggested that the composer assign his students the task of writing a sound track for Fischinger's abstract animated film *Studie Nr. 6* (1930). Music by Hindemith, Harald Genzmer, and Oskar Sala was captured on gramophone discs, but the recordings are believed to have been destroyed in the Second World War. Whether the sound tracks made use of the Trautonium is unknown. See Schenk, "Die Rundfunkversuchsstelle," 268; and William Moritz, *Optical Poetry: The Life and Work of Oskar Fischinger* (Bloomington: University of Indiana Press, 2004), 29–30.
33. Dietmar Schenk, "Paul Hindemith und die Rundfunkversuchsstelle der Berliner Musikhochschule," *Hindemith-Jahrbuch* 25 (1996): 191.
34. Donhauser, *Elektrische Klangmaschinen,* 68–69; Schenk, "Die Rundfunkversuchsstelle," 263.
35. For a closer analytical look at Hindemith's compositions for the Trautonium, see Klaus Ebbeke, "Paul Hindemith und das Trautonium," *Hindemith Jahrbuch* 11 (1982): 77–113.
36. Trautwein, *Elektrische Musik,* 5. The later installments in the series did not in fact appear and were likely casualties of the deepening economic crisis that afflicted Germany in the early 1930s. Trautwein's book is not to be confused with Peter Lertes's volume of the same title, published in 1933.
37. Quoted in Schenk, "Die Rundfunkversuchsstelle," 264.
38. Joachim Winckelmann, *Das Trautonium—Ein neues Radio-Musikinstrument* (Berlin: Deutsch-literarisches Institut J. Schneider, 1931). See also Ebbeke, "Paul Hindemith und das Trautonium," 94–95.
39. Hugo Gernsback, "Electronic Music," *Radio-Craft* 4, no. 9 (1933): 521. Gernsback's use of the phrase *electronic* (rather than *electric*) *music* may be one of the earlier instances of the term in English; it is uncertain whether there is any intended semantic distinction between *electronic* and *electric*. Gernsback, best known for his work in popularizing the fledgling literary genre of science fiction, also had invented several electric instruments in the 1920s.
40. Clifford E. Denton, "The Trautonium: A New Musical Instrument," *Radio-Craft* 4, no. 9 (1933): 522. Certain aspects of Denton's article, such as his list of eight criteria for the success of a new instrument, suggest that he had read Winckelmann's book, which features a very similar list of six requirements. See Winckelmann, 3–4.
41. Donhauser, *Elektrische Klangmaschinen,* 132. See also Peter Donhauser, "KlarinettenBassgeigenTrompete im Holzkoffer," in *Zauberhafte Klangmaschine: Von der Sprechmaschine bis zur Soundkarte,* ed. Institut für Medienarchäologie (Mainz: Schott, 2008), 144–45.
42. Lertes, *Elektrische Musik,* 183.
43. See Stephen Hinton, "*Lehrstück:* An Aesthetics of Performance," in *Music and Performance in the Weimar Republic,* ed. Bryan Gilliam (Cambridge: Cambridge University Press, 1994), 59–73.
44. Walter Gronostay, "Die Klingende Elektrizität und der Komponist," *Die Musik* 24, no. 11 (1932): 809. Recall that H.H. Stuckenschmidt had argued

that the same economic factors would lead to performers being supplanted by mechanical instruments.

45. Frank Warschauer, "Was die Funkausstellung dem Musikfreunde brachte," *Melos* 11, nos. 8–9 (1932): 297.
46. Donhauser, *Elektrische Klangmaschinen*, 132.
47. Ibid.
48. Donhauser, "KlarinettenBassgeigenTrompete in Holzkoffer," 145.
49. Donhauser, *Elektrische Klangmaschinen*, 135–36.
50. Ibid., 133, image 4-4.
51. Otto Kappelmayer, "Klingende Elektrizität," *Die Musik* 24, no. 11 (1932): 821.
52. Georg Schünemann, "Produktive Kräfte der mechanischen Musik," *Die Musik* 24, no. 4 (1932): 248–49.
53. Friedrich Trautwein, *Trautonium Schule* (Mainz: Schott, 1933).
54. A. Lion, "Das Trautonium," *Die Musik* 24, no. 11 (1932): 833–34.
55. Donhauser, *Elektrische Klangmaschinen*, 132–33, 138–39.
56. Quoted in Donhauser, *Elektrische Klangmaschinen*, 189.
57. Journal entry from 1935, quoted in Ebbeke, "Paul Hindemith und das Trautonium," 96.
58. Donhauser, *Elektrische Klangmaschinen*, 141–43. The score for this piece was lost; in the 1980s Sala reconstructed and recorded a version based on an old gramophone recording of the original.
59. Schenk, "Paul Hindemith und die Rundfunkversuchsstelle," 185. Even after the closing of the Radio Research Section in 1935, the new director of the Berlin Academy of Music Fritz Stein maintained the laboratory in a limited capacity: see Schenk, "Die Rundfunkversuchsstelle," 272; and Donhauser, *Elektrische Klangmaschinen*, 128–29, 151.
60. See "History of the HHI," Frauenhofer Heinrich Hertz Institute, accessed August 8, 2015, http://www.hhi.fraunhofer.de/fraunhofer-hhi-the-institute/about-us/history-of-hhi.html.
61. Donhauser, *Elektrische Klangmaschinen*, 130.
62. Schenk, "Paul Hindemith und die Rundfunkversuchsstelle," 193.
63. Josef Häusler, *Spiegel der Neuen Musik: Donaueschingen* (Kassel: Bärenreiter, 1996), 431–32.
64. Fred K. Prieberg, *Handbuch deutsche Musiker 1933–1945* (PDF e-book, version 1.2–3, 2005), 2986.
65. Donhauser, *Elektrische Klangmaschinen*, 128–29.
66. Ibid., 68; Prieberg, *Handbuch deutsche Musiker 1933–1945*, 7233. Prieberg states that Trautwein's promotion took place in 1937, while Donhauser says simply "after the closing of the Radio Research Section in 1935," suggesting it may have been earlier than 1937.
67. Prieberg, *Handbuch deutsche Musiker 1933–1945*, 2985–86.
68. See Fondation Hindemith, "Biographie: Kampagne gegen Hindemith," http://www.hindemith.info/leben-werk/biographie/1933-1939/leben/der-fall-hindemith/ (accessed 30 July 2014).
69. See Peukert, *Weimar Republic,* 164. Indeed, the notion that the Nazis based their cultural favors according to sound stylistic or aesthetic distinctions

gives them too much credit. The inconsistency of their judgments stemmed in large part from the racial pseudoscience on which their ideology was based. Potentially "dangerous" art, such as twelve-tone music, was allowed if it was composed by those of good Aryan stock, while music that was steeped in the German tradition became suspect if its author was of Jewish heritage, as in the example of Mahler.

70. H.H. Stuckenschmidt, "Under the Swastika," *Modern Music* 11, no. 1 (1933): 49–50.

71. Quoted in Ehrhard Bahr, "Nazi Cultural Politics: Intentionalism vs. Functionalism," in *National Socialist Cultural Policy*, ed. Glenn R. Cuomo (New York: St. Martin's, 1995), 15.

72. Quoted in Peter Adam, *Art of the Third Reich* (New York: Harry N. Abrams, 1992), 56. Thomas Mann summed up the ideology of German fascism as "an affirmative stance toward progress combined with dreams of the past." Quoted in Jeffrey Herf, "The Engineer as Ideologue," *Journal of Contemporary History* 19, no. 4 (1984): 633. This paradoxical ideology is explored at greater length in Herf's classic study *Reactionary Modernism: Technology, Culture, and Politics in Weimar and the Third Reich* (Cambridge: Cambridge University Press, 1984).

73. Quoted in David B. Dennis, *Inhumanities: Nazi Interpretations of Western Culture* (Cambridge: Cambridge University Press, 2012), 177.

74. Paul Krannhals, *Der Weltsinn der Technik als Schlüssel zu ihrer Kulturbedeutung* (Munich: R. Oldenbourg, 1932), 43–44; and Paul Krannhals, *Das organische Weltbild: Grundlagen einer neuentstehenden deutschen Kultur* (Munich: Bruckmann, 1928).

75. *Zeitschrift für Musik* 102, no. 7 (1935): 830, provides a pithy account of this meeting. The lengthier article "Elektromusik im Propagandaministerium," from which I draw here, was mailed to Sala as a newspaper clipping in 1995; its original source is unknown. See "Biographie: 1933–1935," Oskar-Sala-Fonds am Deutschen Museum, accessed July 30, 2014, http://www.oskar-sala.de/oskar-sala-fonds/oskar-sala/biografie/1933–1935/grossansicht-2/.

76. Quoted in Donhauser, *Elektrische Klangmaschinen*, 147.

77. Friedrich Trautwein, "Über die Bedeutung technischer Forschung und die Zusammenarbeit von Musikern und Technikern für die Zukunft unserer Musikkultur," *Deutsche Musikkultur* 3, no. 6 (1938–39): 457–58.

78. Trautwein, "Über die Bedeutung," 456; and Ferrucio Busoni, *Entwurf einer neuen Ästhetik der Tonkunst*, 2nd ed. [1916] , ed. Martina Weindel (Wilhelmshaven: F. Noetzel, 2001), 41.

79. Trautwein, "Über die Bedeutung," 455.

80. Friedrich Trautwein, "Wesen und Ziele der Elektromusik," *Zeitschrift für Musik* 103, no. 6 (1936): 698–99.

81. Trautwein, "Über die Bedeutung," 458.

82. Trautwein, "Wesen und Ziele der Elektromusik," 698–99.

83. Donhauser, *Elektrische Klangmaschinen*, 155–57.

84. Ibid., 146, 148.

85. Ibid., 166.

86. The full quotation is "Ohne Kraftwagen, ohne Flugzeug, ohne Lautsprecher hätten wir Deutschland nicht erobert." Quoted in Heinz Pohle,

Der Rundfunk als Instrument der Politik (Hamburg: Verlag der Hans Bredow-Institut, 1955), 230.

87. Donhauser, *Elektrische Klangmaschinen*, 156–57.

88. Ibid., 184. The Theremin, played by Lucie Bigelow-Rosen, enjoyed one last tour through Germany in early 1936. According to Donhauser, this was allowed by the authorities only because the Nazis wanted to keep up appearances so as not to generate bad publicity in advance of the Berlin Olympics. Ibid., 153–54.

89. Ibid., 184.

90. Ibid., 187–93; 256–61.

91. Carsten Heinze, "Der Kunstwettbewerb Musik im Rahmen der Olympischen Spiele 1936," *Archiv für Musikwissenschaft* 62, no. 1 (2005): 32–51.

92. Donhauser, *Elektrische Klangmaschinen*, 189.

93. Friedrich Trautwein, "Dynamische Probleme der Musik bei Feiern unter freiem Himmel," *Deutsche Musik-Kultur* 2, no. 1 (1937–38): 35. See also Donhauser, *Elektrische Klangmaschinen*, 162–63.

94. Although this name has been adopted by historians, a more literal translation would be "symphony of steam whistles." See Miguel Molina Alarcón, liner notes to *Baku: Symphony of Sirens*, ReR Megacorp Compact Disc (2008): 71.

95. Ibid.

96. Quoted in Smirnov, *Sound in Z*, 152. In a 1928 article, the American writer Irving Weil noted that "magnitude of sound, like so many other things, goes back to the French Revolution," thus linking, in a roundabout way, the musical and political impetus of the modern mass spectacle. Apparently unaware of Avraamov's massive event in Baku in 1922, Weil invoked as historical precedent the *Fête of the Supreme Being*, for which the composer Étienne Méhul supposedly conducted a chorus of 300,000 voices, accompanied by the firing of amassed batteries of artillery. For his part, Weil envisioned the high-amplitude music of the future being provided by "little amplifying devils, minute in size but huge in magnifying sound; little inventions that, placed for example within the belly of a single violin, will give forth the tone of a thousand fiddles." Weil, "The Noise-Makers," *Modern Music* 5, no. 2 (1928): 24–28.

97. George Antheil, "Manifest der Musico-Mechanico," *De Stijl* 6, no. 8 (1924): 102.

98. Jörg Mager, "Eine Rundfunkprophezeihung," *Der deutsche Rundfunk* 2, no. 29 (1924): 2954.

99. Mager, *Eine neue Epoche der Musik durch Radio*, 15.

100. Ibid., 16. In yet another version of this trope, the composer Richard Stein extended the fantasy from a collective *listening* experience to a collective act of music making. According to Stein, the orchestra of players, each with his own instrument, was a relic of the "age of individualism"; the "age of collectivism," on the other hand, demanded the collaboration of many musicians working upon one massive instrument. Stein envisioned a huge ring-shaped organ played by some thirty to sixty musicians and surrounded by tens of thousands of listeners arrayed in concentric circles around the instrument. "An electric music organized in this way will *no longer* be a 'mechanical music'; it will express

the *collective will* of a multitude, whose artistic and and human instensity is immeasurably greater than that of the an individual conductor, however prominent he might be." The passage concludes, "Utopia? We will wait until Jörg Mager has come to an ultimate outcome of his years-long studies and practical work. Only then will one be able to discuss the problem of electric music in its full scope." Stein, "Elektrische Musik," *Die Musik* 22, no. 11 (1930): 862. Compare this to the language of Heinrich Besseler, the musicologist who helped coin the term *Gebrauchsmusik,* describing the social conditions of premodern musical performance: "Just as the familiar distance between music and listener seems to disappear, so to the otherwise strictly separated individuals are fused into a kind of vital rhythmic collective being, through which the music circulates as a connective fluid. [. . .] Here there can be no question of listening as one would in a concert." Besseler, "Grundfragen des musikalischen Hörens," *Jahrbuch der Musikbliblothek Peters* 32 (1926): 35–52; reprinted in *Aufsätze zur Musikästhetik und Musikgeschichte,* ed. Peter Gülke (Leipzig: Reclam, 1978), 29–53.

101. Glinsky, *Theremin,* 106.

102. Donhauser, *Elektrische Klangmaschinen,* 197–98. See also Jörg Mager, "Anordnung bei elektrischen Musikinstrumenten mit gleichzeitiger mehrstimmiger Tonerzeugung," DE Patent 542,376, filed on July 13, 1929 and issued on December 31, 1931, UbuWeb Electronic Music Resources, http://ubu.com/emr/patents/_docs/patents/01individuals/mager/DE542376C.pdf.

103. Ibid., 41–42.

104. Emil Schenck, *Jörg Mager: Dem deutschen Pionier der Elektro-Musikforschung zum Gedächtnis* (Darmstadt: Städtischen Kulturverwaltung, 1952), 15.

105. Hermann Keyserling, "Neue Möglichkeiten der Musik," *Zeitschrift für Instrumentenbau* 53, no. 8 (1933): 128–29.

106. Donhauser, *Elektrische Klangmaschinen,* 40–42, 196–200, 206–10.

107. Jörg Mager, "Einführung der elektrischen Klangerzeugung," *Zeitschrift für Instrumentenbau* 52, no. 3 (1931): 45.

108. Lertes, *Elektrische Musik,* 162, 164.

109. This expressive touch is comparable to the clavichord technique known as *Bebung.* Later, Mager adjusted the circuitry to automatically apply vibrato to each tone. See Jörg Mager, "Verfahren zur Erzeugung eines Vibratos bei Musikinstrumenten mit Tonerzeugung durch elektrische Schwingungskreise," DE Patent 562,955, filed on March 21, 1931 and issued on October 13, 1932, UbuWeb Electronic Music Resources, http://ubu.com/emr/patents/_docs/patents/01individuals/mager/DE562955C.pdf.

110. Schenck, *Jörg Mager,* 18. This apparatus is described in Jörg Mager, "Enrichtung zur Lautstärkenregelung von Tasten-Musikinstrumenten," DE Patent 535,317, filed on December 15, 1929 and issued on September 24, 1931, UbuWeb Electronic Music Resources, http://ubu.com/emr/patents/_docs/patents/01individuals/mager/DE535317C.pdf. A contemporary account read: "The player is provided with a number of ways to swell the tone, including one that is controlled back-and-forth movement of the stomach—a somewhat comical, but quite clever arrangement." See "Elektroakustische Hausorgel," *Zeitschrift für Instrumentenbau* 53, no. 2 (1932): 25.

111. Jörg Mager, "Das 'Partiturophon—Eine Hausmusik Lösung, *Zeitschrift für Instrumentenbau* 54, no. 21 (1934): 329.

112. Ibid.

113. Ibid.

114. "'Partiturophon,' ein neues elektro-akustische Musikinstrument," *Zeischrift für Instrumentenbau* 54, no. 15 (1934): 236; Hermann Matzke, "Ein Rundgang durch die Entwicklung der Elektromusik," *Zeitschrift für Instrumentenbau* 56, no. 11 (1936): 176; and L.E.C. Hughes, "Electronic Music," *Nature* 145 (February 1940), 172: "The dictionary definition of an organ must now be curtailed by the omission of any reference to pipes blown by air, for clearly an instrument which is played like an organ and sounds like an organ is certainly an organ, in spite of the purists."

115. O.S., "Jörg Mager und sein Partiturophon," *Deutsche Allgemeine Zeitung*, 15 May 1936, unpaginated.

116. Donhauser, *Elektrische Klangmaschinen*, 212. Trautwein claimed to have heard from a third party that Mager stated he had switched his allegiance from the Communists to the Nazis because the latter paid better.

117. Paul Zoll, "Jörg Magers 'Partiturophon': Eine umwälzende, elektroakustische Erfindung," *Zeitschrift für Musik* 102, no. 12 (1935): 1333–34.

118. Donhauser, *Elektrische Klangmaschinen*, 216–17. A contemporary account suggests the possibility that original music for the Partiturophon was performed at this event, but no scores or recordings survive. See "Elektromusikinstrumente auf dem Weimarer Tonkunstlerfest," *Zeitschrift für Instrumentenbau* 56, no. 19 (1936): 322.

119. Fritz Stege, "Jörg Mager in Berlin," *Zeitschrift für Musik* 103, no. 6 (1936): 728. Significantly, the *Zeitschrift für Musik* was by this time essentially a mouthpiece of the Third Reich, and Stege was a well-known partisan of the Nazi aesthetic in music. See Joel Sachs, "Some Aspects of Musical Politics in Pre-Nazi Germany," *Perspectives of New Music* 9, no. 1 (1970): 74–95.

120. "Das Lebenswerk Jörg Magers: Ein Besuch bei dem Erfinder der Sphärophon-Musik," *Münchner Neueste Nachrichten*, 14 February 1936. Quoted in Gerrit Walther, *Julius Maria Becker, 1887–1949: Ein Dichter zwischen den Weltkriegen*, 64.

121. Quoted in Schenck, *Jörg Mager*, 26.

122. Franz Berthold, "Verschiedenes," *Zeitschrift für Musik* 105, no. 7 (1938): 830–32.

123. "Jörg Mager †," *Zeitschrift für Instrumentenbau* 59, no. 14 (1939): 240. On Mager's last years, see also Donhauser, *Elektrische Klangmaschinen*, 215–21.

124. "369 neue Musikinstrumente in zehn Jahren," *Zeitschrift für Instrumentenbau* 59, no. 11 (1939): 173. The text of the article is at variance with the headline: it puts the figure at 396, not 369.

6. THE EXPANDING INSTRUMENTARIUM

1. Walter Benjamin, "Theses on the Philosophy of History," in *Illuminations*, trans. Harry Zohn (New York: Schocken, 1969), 254.

2. Walter Gronostay, "Die Klingende Elektrizität und der Komponist," *Die Musik* 24, no. 11 (1932): 809.

3. Leo Kestenberg, "Vorwort," in *Kunst und Technik*, ed. Leo Kestenberg (Berlin: Wegweiser-Verlag, 1930), 8.

4. Ernst Cassirer, "Form und Technik," in Kestenberg, *Kunst und Technik*, 24; and Friedrich Dessauer, "Technology in Its Proper Sphere," in *Philosophy and Technology: Readings in the Philosophical Problems of Technology*, eds. Carl Mitcham and Robert Mackey (New York: Free Press, 1972), 318. Dessauer's text was originally published as *Philosophie der Technik: Das Problem der Realisierung* (Bonn: Friedrich Cohen Verlag, 1927).

5. Fritz Schumacher, *Der 'Fluch' der Technik*, 2nd ed. (Hamburg: Verlag Boysen und Maasch, 1932), 5. See also Oswald Spengler, *Man and Technics: A Contribution to the Philosophy of Life*, trans. Charles Francis Atkinson (New York: Alfred A. Knopf, 1932), 87–88; originally published as *Der Mensch und die Technik: Beitrag zu einer Philosophie des Lebens* (Munich: C.H. Beck'sche Verlagsbuchhandlung, 1931).

6. Fritz Schumacher, *Schöpferwille und Mechanisierung* (Hamburg: Verlag Boysen und Maasch, 1933), 9.

7. Henri Bergson, *The Two Sources of Morality and Religion*, trans. R. Ashley Audra and Cloudesley Brereton (London: MacMillan, 1935); originally published as *Les deux sources de la morale et de la religion* (Paris: F. Alcan, 1932).

8. Lewis Mumford, *Technics and Civilization* (New York: Harcourt, Brace: 1934). More recently, Barry Brummett has traced an analogous division between "mechtech," corresponding to machine technology, with its gears, shafts, and noisily moving parts, and "electrotech," in which electrical power is the motive force, and the inner workings of the device become occluded and mystified. See his *Rhetoric of Machine Aesthetics* (Westport, CT: Praeger, 1999).

9. Quoted in Edgard Varèse, *Écrits*, ed. Louise Hirbour (Paris: Christian Bourgois Éditeur, 1983), 58–59.

10. Boris de Schloezer, "Man, Music, and the Machine," *Modern Music* 7, no. 3 (1931): 3.

11. George Gershwin, "The Composer in the Machine Age," in *Classic Essays on Twentieth-Century Music*, ed. Richard Kostelanetz and Joseph Darby (New York: Schirmer Books, 1996), 46.

12. Alfred Einstein, "Art and Technology," *Modern Music* 12, no. 2 (1935): 56.

13. Ernst Krenek, "Der schaffende Musiker und die Technik der Gegenwart," in Kestenberg, *Kunst und Technik*, 155.

14. Paul Bekker, "Dream at Twilight," *Modern Music* 12, no. 1 (1934): 8–11.

15. Curt Sachs, "Wandel des Klangideals," *Melos* 9, no. 3 (1930): 114.

16. Curt Sachs, *The History of Musical Instruments* (New York: W.W. Norton, 1940), 448–49.

17. John Cage, "The Future of Music," in *Silence* (Middleton, CT: Wesleyan University Press, 1961), 4, 6. This talk was given in 1940, though the reprint of this essay in the collection of Cage's writings published as *Silence* contains the incorrect date of 1937. See Leta E. Miller, "Cultural Intersections: John Cage in Seattle (1938–1940)," in *John Cage: Music, Philosophy, and Intention*, ed. David W. Patterson (New York: Routledge, 2002), 54–56.

18. Lawrence Weschler, "My Grandfather's Last Tale," *Atlantic*, December 1996, https://www.theatlantic.com/past/docs/issues/96dec/toch/weschler.htm (accessed July 29, 2014).

19. Quoted in William Moritz, *Optical Poetry: The Life and Work of Oskar Fischinger* (Bloomington: Indiana University Press, 2004), 77–78, 165–66. According to Cage, the two men's brief collaboration ended when he dumped a bucket of water on the older man to douse a fire that had started when Fischinger had fallen asleep and dropped his cigar during a particularly slow patch in their work together. Fischinger's wife, Elfriede, has questioned the plausibility of Cage's account: see "Oskar Fischinger. An Interview with Elfriede Fischinger," Fischinger Trust, http://www.oskarfischinger.org/EFZoetrope.htm (accessed May 3, 2015).

20. Cage, "The Future of Music," 4.

21. Take, for example, this remark by Jean-Jacques Nattiez: "Indeed, it is not impossible to see the foundation of IRCAM in 1974—along with a similar idea of Varèse, the studios in Cologne and Milan, and even the enterprises of Xenakis—as the final realization of Cage's vision." *The Boulez-Cage Correspondence*, ed. Jean-Jacques Nattiez (Cambridge: Cambridge University Press, 1993), 9.

22. See Cristoph von Blumröder, "Experiment, experimentelle Musik," in *Terminologie der Musik im 20. Jahrhundert*, ed. Hans Heinrich von Eggebrecht (Stuttgart: Franz Steiner Verlag, 1995), 118–40.

23. See Frank Gertich, Julia Gerlach, and Golo Föllmer, eds., *Musik . . . , verwandelt: Das Elektronische Studio der TU Berlin 1953–1995* (Berlin: Wolke, 1996).

24. H.H. Stuckenschmidt, "The Third Stage: Some Observations on the Aesthetics of Electronic Music," *Die Reihe* 1 (English version, 1955), 13.

25. The Trautonium became a virtual kitchen-sink operation, acquiring an electrically controlled percussion battery, a noise generator, an electric metronome, and a large plate reverb apparatus. This last addition, and the Rube Goldberg character of Sala's improvements, both call to mind Mager's capacity for endless tinkering. See "Oskar Sala: Biographie," Oskar-Sala-Fonds am Deutschen Museum, http://www.oskar-sala.de/oskar-sala-fonds/oskar-sala/biografie/ (accessed July 26, 2014).

26. Fred K. Prieberg, *Handbuch deutsche Musiker 1933–1945* (Kiel: self-published PDF e-book, version 1.2–3, 2005), 7233.

27. Paul Hindemith, *Unterweisung im Tonsatz I: Theoretischer Teil* (Mainz: Schott, 1940), 13.

28. For the history of the Cologne studio, see Marietta Morawska-Büngeler, *Schwingende Elektronen: Eine Dokumentation über das Studio für Elektronische Musik des Westdeutschen Rundfunks in Köln 1951–1986* (Cologne: P.J. Tonger, 1988); and M.J. Grant, *Serial Music, Serial Aesthetics: Compositional Theory in Post-War Europe* (Cambridge: Cambridge University Press, 2001), 39–71.

29. Robert Beyer, "Die Klangwelt der elektronischen Musik," *Zeitschrift für Musik* 113 (1952): 75.

30. Robert Beyer, "Musik und Technik," in *Darmstadt-Dokumente I*, Musik-Konzepte Sonderband, ed. Heinz-Klaus Metzger and Rainer Riehn (Munich: Edition Text + Kritik, 2007), 45–48.

31. Beyer, "Klangwelt der elektronischen Musik," 75–76. In this essay, Beyer restated his belief in the importance of *Raummusik*—the spatialized sound image captured by the microphone and projected by loudspeakers (discussed in chapter 4). He sought to draw out the implications of the fact that listeners to electronic music confront sound not in the shared space of the concert hall but rather in the distanced form of an electroacoustic projection. The resulting sonic image *(Klangbild)*, he suggested, is to "live" acoustic sound as the filmed scenes of cinema are to the staged theater. Beyer foresaw the development of new compositional principles such as "spatial counterpoint," a notion that was arguably put into practice in such works as Stockhausen's *Gesang der Jünglinge* and *Kontakte*. These themes are treated at great length in Gisela Nauck's *Musik im Raum, Raum in der Musik: Ein Beitrag zur Geschichte der seriellen Musik* (PhD diss., Technische Universität Berlin, 1995).

32. Beyer, "Klangwelt der elektronischen Musik," 79.

33. See Helmut Kirchmeyer, *Kleine Monographie über Herbert Eimert* (Leipzig: Verlag der Sächsichen Akademie der Wissenschaften zu Leipzig, 1998), 47.

34. See Herbert Eimert, "So begann die elektronische Musik," *Melos* 39 (1972): 42. Eimert referred to Meyer-Eppler's coinage as "unfortunate."

35. Herbert Eimert, "Electronic Music," trans. D.A. Sinclair, Technical Translation TT-601 (Ottawa: National Research Council of Canada, 1956), 1.

36. Herbert Eimert, "Elektronische Musik," in *Die Musik in Geschichte und Gegenwart* (Kassel: Bärenreiter, 1954), 1264.

37. Herbert Eimert, "What Is Electronic Music?" in *Die Reihe* 1 (English edition, 1955), 3.

38. Trautwein was also involved in providing sound machines for the Cologne Studio at this time: in 1952, he was commissioned to design an instrument called the Electric Monochord. (The title is significant, given the fundamentalist concern with the basic properties of sound among the composers of *elektronische Musik*.) This was essentially a stripped-down version of the Concert Trautonium with two monophonic manuals, lacking the subharmonic mixtures and the foot pedal controls for the switching of register. The instrument was built according to his design in 1953. See Friedrich Trautwein, "The Electronic Monochord," trans. H.A.G. Nathan, Technical Translation TT-606 (Ottawa: National Research Council of Canada, 1956), 1–12; and Eimert, "So begann die elektronische Musik," 42.

39. These pieces, with the exception of *Ostinate Figuren und Rhythmen*, can be heard on *Cologne—WDR: Early Electronic Music*, BV Haast Records 9106, 2005, compact disc.

40. Eimert, "So begann die elektronischen Musik," 42.

41. See Elena Ungeheuer, *Wie die elektronische Musik 'erfunden' wurde . . . Quellenstudie zu Werner Meyer-Epplers Entwurf zwischen 1949 and 1953* (Mainz: Schott, 1992), 123–27.

42. Herbert Eimert, *Atonale Musiklehre* (Leipzig: Breitkopf & Härtel, 1924).

43. See Marietta Morawska-Büngeler, *Schwingende Elektronen*, 33. Morawska-Büngeler quotes the composer Gottfried Michael Koenig recalling that the sine wave was "so ideologically important back then."

44. Eimert, "What Is Electronic Music?" 5.

45. Ironically, in his criticisms of the Cologne studio, Beyer also found himself in the same boat with Friedrich Trautwein, whose instrument he had harshly attacked in the early 1930s. See Friedrich Trautwein, "Das Klangfarben-Musikinstrument," *Musica* 7, nos. 7–8 (1953): 301–5.

46. Robert Beyer, "Zur Situation der elektronischen Musik," *Zeitschrift für Musik* 116 (1955): 455.

47. Ibid., 455.

48. Pierre Schaeffer, *In Search of a Concrete Music*, trans. Christine North and John Dack (Berkeley: University of California Press, 2012), 7.

49. See Évelyne Gayou, *Le Groupe de Recherches Musicales: Cinquante ans d'histoire* (Paris: Fayard, 2007), 24n1; and Abraham Moles, *Les musiques expérimentales: Revue d'une tendance importante de la musique contemporaine* (Paris: Éditions du cercle d'art contemporain, 1960), 26.

50. Karlheinz Stockhausen, "The Origins of Electronic Music," *The Musical Times* 112, no. 1541 (1971): 649–50.

51. Herbert Eimert, "So begann die elektronische Musik," 42. See also Eimert, "What Is Electronic Music," 2–3.

52. For examples by German, French, and American authors, see Eimert, "What is Electronic Music?", 1–10; Abraham Moles, *Les musiques expérimentales*, 21–28; and Herbert Russcol, *The Liberation of Sound: An Introduction to Electronic Music* (Englewood Cliffs, NJ: Prentice-Hall, 1972), 30–42. The works of Fred K. Prieberg are exceptions to this tendency. See Fred Prieberg, *Musik des technischen Zeitalters* (Zurich: Atlantis Verlag, 1956); and Fred Prieberg, *Musica ex machina: Über das Verhältnis von Musik und Technik* (Berlin: Verlag Ullstein, 1960). Prieberg's books are also among the earliest efforts to present a synoptic view of the subject.

53. Elena Ungeheuer, "Imitative Instrumente und innovative Maschinen? Musikästhetische Orientiertungen der elektrischen Klangerzeugung," in *Zauberhafte Klangmaschine: Von der Sprechmaschine bis zur Soundkarte*, ed. Institut für Medienarchäologie (Mainz: Schott, 2008), 49. Elsewhere, however, she offers a more balanced view: "Robert Beyer represents an unbroken tradition of electric tone generation whose origins can be traced to the beginning of the twentieth century. It is clear that a study of the reception of the idea of electronic music must be embedded in the context of the entire history of electric tone generation." Ungeheuer, *Wie die elektronische Musik*, 17.

54. Richard Taruskin, *Oxford History of Western Music*, vol. 6 (Oxford: Oxford University Press, 2004), 177–84. See Padmore, "Germany," in *Music in the Modern Age*, ed. F.W. Sternfeld (New York: Praeger, 1973), 95–133.

55. Paul Théberge, *Any Sound You Can Imagine: Making Music, Consuming Technology* (Hanover, NH: Wesleyan University Press, 1997), 17.

56. Trevor Pinch and Frank Trocco, *Analog Days: The Invention and Impact of the Moog Synthesizer* (Cambridge, MA: Harvard University Press, 2002), 7, 10.

57. See Herbert Butterfield's classic critique of triumphalist historiography, *The Whig Interpretation of History* (1931; repr., London: Penguin, 1973). Riffing on this notion, Bruce Sterling has called attention to the prevalence of the "Whig history of technology." See Bruce Sterling, "The Life and Death of Media," in *Sound Unbound: Sampling Digital Music and Culture,* ed. Paul D. Miller (Cambridge, MA: MIT Press, 2008), 75. In a different context Pinch himself has argued forcefully against using "success" as an arbiter of technological relevance, noting that "the success of an artefact is precisely what needs to be explained." See Trevor Pinch and Wiebe E. Bijker, "The Social Construction of Facts and Artefacts: Or How the Sociology of Science and the Sociology of Technology Might Benefit Each Other," *Social Studies of Science* 14, no. 3 (1984): 405–6.

58. David Edgerton, *The Shock of the Old* (Oxford: Oxford University Press, 2007). Art historian George Kubler's notion of "intermittent duration" is also relevant here: see his book *The Shape of Time: Remarks on the History of Things* (New Haven, CT: Yale University Press, 1962), 95–96.

59. The software is available at http://www.gleetchplug.com/gleetchplug/berna.html. Software such as Sancristoforo's seems to validate Marshall McLuhan's dictum that the content of new media is old media. See *Understanding Media: The Extensions of Man* (1964; Cambridge, MA: MIT Press, 1994), 8.

60. As José Ortega y Gasset reminds us, technology is the product of particular cultural desires rather than universal biological needs. It is, in his words, "supernatural." See José Ortega y Gasset, "Thoughts on Technology," in *Philosophy and Technology: Readings in the Philosophical Problems of Technology,* ed. Carl Mitcham and Robert Mackey (New York: Free Press, 1972), 290–313.

61. Pinch and Trocco, *Analog Days,* 44.

62. Gilbert Simondon, "On Techno-aesthetics," *Parrhesia* 14 (2012): 6.

63. "Composing with Shifting Sand: A Conversation between Ron Kuivila and David Behrman on Electronic Music and the Ephemerality of Technology," *Leonardo Music Journal* 8 (1998): 13.

64. This phenomenon is also discussed, though not by this name, in Théberge, *Any Sound You Can Imagine,* 255.

Bibliography

Adam, Peter. *Art of the Third Reich*. New York: Harry N. Abrams, 1992.
Adorno, Theodor. *Aesthetic Theory*. Translated by C. Lenhardt. London: Routledge & Kegan Paul, 1984.
Albright, Daniel, ed. *Modernism and Music: An Anthology of Sources*. Chicago: University of Chicago Press, 2004.
Alperson, Philip. "The Instrumentality of Music." *Journal of Aesthetics and Art Criticism* 66, no. 1 (2008): 37–51.
Animerte Avantgarde: Der künstlerische Animationsfilm der 20er und 30er Jahre. DVD. Curated by Ulrich Wegenast. Absolute Medien, 2011.
Antheil, George. "Abstraktion und Zeit in der Musik." *De Stijl* 6, no. 10–11 (1925): 152–56.
———. "Manifest der Musico-Mechanico." *De Stijl* 6, no. 8 (1924): 99–102.
———. "My Ballet Mécanique." *De Stijl* 6, no. 12 (1925): 141–44.
Attali, Jacques. *Noise: The Political Economy of Music*. Translated by Brian Massumi. Minneapolis: University of Minnesota Press, 1985.
Bagier, Guido. "Der akustische Film." *Melos* 7, no. 4 (1928): 163–66.
———. "Der sprechende Film." In "Musik und Maschine," special issue, *Musikblätter des Anbruch* 8, nos. 8–9 (1926): 380–84.
Bahr, Ehrhard. "Nazi Cultural Politics: Intentionalism vs. Functionalism." In *National Socialist Cultural Policy*, edited by Glenn R. Cuomo, 5–22. New York: St. Martin's, 1995.
Bailey, Lee Worth. *The Enchantments of Technology*. Urbana and Chicago: University of Illinois Press, 2005.
Baker, Ray Stannard. "New Music for an Old World." *McClure's Magazine* 27, no. 3 (1906): 291–301.
Bann, Stephen, ed. *The Tradition of Constructivism*. New York: Da Capo, 1974.

Basalla, George. *The Evolution of Technology.* Cambridge, UK: Cambridge University Press, 1988.
Baron, Andrew, and Mike Buffington. "The RCA Theremin." RCA Theremin.com, 2015. Accessed August 21, 2015. http://rcatheremin.com.
Barthel, Ernst. "Mechanischer und organischer Naturbegriff." *Annalen der philosophie und philosophischer Kritik* 5, nos. 3–4 (1925): 57–76.
Becker, Julius Maria. *Syrinx.* Aschaffenburg, Ger.: Viertürmeverlag Hans Volz, 1914.
———. *Syrinx.* 2nd ed. Leipzig: Breitkopf & Härtel, 1918.
Bekker, Paul. "Dream at Twilight." *Modern Music* 12, no. 1 (1934): 8–11.
———. "Hanslick." *Musikblätter des Anbruch* 5, no. 10 (1923): 283–92.
———. *Organische und mechanische Musik.* Stuttgart: Deutsche Verlags-Anstalt, 1928.
———. *Von den Naturreichen des Klanges: Grundriss einer Phänomenologie der Musik.* Stuttgart: Deutsche Verlags-Anstalt, 1925.
Bell, Alexander Graham. "The Photophone." *Science* 1, no. 11 (1880): 130–34.
Bense, Max. "Technisches Bewußtsein." In *Aesthetica: Einführung in die neue Aesthetik,* 126–33. Baden-Baden: Agis Verlag, 1965.
Bergson, Henri. *The Two Sources of Morality and Religion.* Translated by R. Ashley Audra and Cloudesley Brereton. London: MacMillan, 1935. First published as *Les deux sources de la morale et la religion* (Paris: F. Alcan, 1932).
Bernhard, Paul. "Mechanik und Organik." *Der Auftakt* 10, no. 11 (1930): 238–40.
Berthold, Franz. "Verschiedenes." *Zeitschrift für Musik* 105, no. 7 (1938): 830–32.
Besseler, Heinrich. "Grundfragen des musikalischen Hören." In *Aufsätze zur Musikästhetik und Musikgeschichte,* 29–53. Leipzig: Verlag Philipp Reclam, 1978.
Beyer, Robert. "Elektronische Musik." *Melos* 21 (1954): 35–39.
———. "Die Klangwelt der elektronischen Musik." *Zeitschrift für Musik* 113 (1952): 74–79.
———. "Musik und Film." *Die Musik* 21, no. 6 (1929): 447–49.
———. "Musik und Technik." In *Darmstadt-Dokumente I,* Musik-Konzepte Sonderband, edited by Heinz-Klaus Metzger and Rainer Riehn, 45–48. Munich: Edition Text + Kritik, 2007.
———. "Musik und Tonfilm." In Kestenberg, *Kunst und Technik,* 365–94.
———. "Das Problem der 'kommenden Musik.'" *Die Musik* 20, no. 12 (1928): 861–66.
———. "Tonfilm." *Die Musik* 21, no. 10 (1929): 747–50.
———. "Zur Frage der elektrischen Tonerzeugung (nach Art der thereminschen Apparatur)." *Die Musik* 21, no. 5 (1929): 358–59.
———. "Zur Situation der elektronischen Musik," *Zeitschrift für Musik* 117 (1955): 452–56.
Bijsterveld, Karin. "A Servile Imitation: Disputes about Machines in Music, 1910–1930." In *Music and Technology in the Twentieth Century,* edited by Hans-Joachim Braun, 121–35. Baltimore: Johns Hopkins University Press, 2002.

Blotkamp, Carel. *Mondrian: The Art of Destruction*. New York: Harry N. Abrams, 1995.
Blumröder, Cristoph von. *Der Begriff 'neue Musik' im 20. Jahrhundert*. Munich: Musikverlag Emil Katzbilcher, 1981.
Bowdery, Francis. "Music for Player Piano: A Study of Seventeen Selected Examples." PhD diss., Loughborough University of Technology, 1995.
Braun, Hans-Joachim, ed. *Music and Technology in the Twentieth Century*. Baltimore: Johns Hopkins University Press, 2002.
Brecht, Bertolt. "Alienation Effects in Chinese Acting." In *Brecht on Theater*, edited by John Willett, 91–99. New York: Hill and Wang, 1964.
Breßler, Eva Susanne. *Von Der Experimentierbühne zum Propagandainstrument: Die Geschichte der Funkausstellung von 1924 bis 1939*. Cologne: Böhlau, 2009.
Brown, Barclay. "The Noise Instruments of Luigi Russolo." *Perspectives of New Music* 20, no. 1–2 (1981–1982): 31–48.
Brummett, Barry. *Rhetoric of Machine Aesthetics*. Westport, CT: Praeger, 1999.
Buchner, Alexander. *Mechanical Musical Instruments*. Translated by Iris Urwin. London: Batchworth Press, 1959.
Bürger, Peter. *Theory of the Avant-Garde*. Translated by Michael Shaw. Minneapolis: University of Minnesota Press, 1984.
Burkhard, Heinrich. "Anmerkung zu den 'Lehrstücken' und zur Schallplattenmusik." *Melos* 9, no. 5–6 (1930): 230.
Busoni, Ferruccio. *Entwurf einer neuen Ästhetik der Tonkunst*, 2nd ed. Edited by Martina Weindel. Reprint, Wilhelmshaven: Noetzel, Heinrichshofen-Bücher, 2001. First published 1916 (Leipzig: Insel Verlag).
———. *The Essence of Music and Other Papers*. Translated by Rosamond Ley. New York: Dover, 1965.
———. *Sketch of a New Aesthetic of Music*. Translated by Pamela Johnston. London: Precinct, 2012.
———. *Von der Einheit der Musik*. Berlin: Max Hesses Verlag, 1922.
Butterfield, Herbert. *The Whig Interpretation of History*. Reprint, London: Penguin, 1973. First published 1931 (London: Bell).
Cage, John. *Silence: Lectures and Writings*. Middletown, CT: Wesleyan University Press, 1961.
Canguilhem, Georges. "Machine and Organism." In *Incorporations*, edited by Jonathan Crary and Sanford Kwinter, 45–69. New York: Zone Books, 1992.
Cardwell, Donald. *The Norton History of Technology*. New York: Norton, 1995.
Carnap, Rudolf, Hans Hahn, and Otto Neurath. "The Scientific Conception of the World: The Vienna Circle." In Scharff and Dusek, *Philosophy of Technology*, 86–95.
Casella, Alfredo. "Tonmaterial und Klangfarbe." *Melos* 2, no. 2 (1921): 29–31.
Cassirer, Ernst. "Form und Technik." In Kestenberg, *Kunst und Technik*, 15–61.
Chadabe, Joel. *Electric Sound: The Past and Promise of Electronic Music*. Upper Saddle River, NJ: Prentice Hall, 1997.
Channell, David F. *The Vital Machine: A Study of Technology and Organic Life*. New York: Oxford University Press, 1991.

Cherney, Brian. "The Bekker-Pfitzner Controversy (1919–1920): Its Significance for German Music Criticism during the Weimar Republic (1919–1932)." PhD diss., University of Toronto, 1974.
Chessa, Luciano. *Luigi Russolo, Futurist: Noise, Visual Arts, and the Occult*. Berkeley: University of California Press, 2012.
Coeuroy, André. "The Esthetics of Contemporary Music." *Musical Quarterly* 15, no. 2 (1929): 246–67.
Cook, Susan C. "George Antheil's *Transatlantic:* An American in the Weimar Republic." *Journal of Musicology* 9, no. 4 (1991): 498–520.
Cooke, Mervyn. *A History of Film Music*. Cambridge, UK: Cambridge University Press, 2008.
Cowell, Henry. "Music of and for the Records." *Modern Music* 7, no. 3 (1931): 32–34.
Cramer, Alfred. "Schoenberg's *Klangfarbenmelodie*: A Principle of Early Atonal Harmony." *Music Theory Spectrum* 24, no. 1 (2002): 1–34.
Crispin, Judith Michelle. *The Esoteric Musical Tradition of Ferruccio Busoni and Its Reinvigoration in the Music of Larry Sitsky*. Lewiston, NY: Edwin Mellen Press, 2007.
Cuomo, Glenn R., ed. *National Socialist Cultural Policy*. New York: St. Martin's, 1995.
Dahlhaus, Carl. "Neo-Romanticism." *19th-Century Music* 3, no. 2 (1979): 97–105.
———. *Schoenberg and the New Music*. Translated by Derrick Puffett and Alfred Clayton. Cambridge, UK: Cambridge University Press, 1987.
Dammert, Hansjörg. "Grammophon-Konzerte." *Musikblätter des Anbruch* 8, no. 8–9 (1926): 406–7.
Daniels, Dieter. "Artists as Inventors and Invention as Art: A Paradigm Shift from 1840 to 1900." In Daniels and Schmidt, *Artists as Inventors*, 19–53.
Daniels, Dieter, and Barbara U. Schmidt, eds. *Artists as Inventors / Inventors as Artists*. Ostfildern, Ger.: Hatje Cantz, 2008.
Davies, Hugh. "Electrophone." In *Grove Music Online*. Oxford Music Online. Oxford University Press, 2007–. Accessed May 5, 2010. http://www.oxfordmusiconline.com/.
Davis, Erik. *TechGnosis: Myth, Magic and Mysticism in the Age of Information*. London: Serpents Tail, 1999.
De Forest, Lee. *Father of Radio*. Chicago: Wilcox & Follett, 1950.
De Lauretis, Teresa, Andreas Huyssen, and Kathleen Woodward, eds. *The Technological Imagination: Theories and Fictions*. Madison, WI: Coda Press, 1980.
De Schloezer, Boris. "Man, Music, and the Machine." *Modern Music* 12, no. 2 (1935): 3–9.
Dennis, David B. *Inhumanities: Nazi Interpretations of Western Culture*. Cambridge, UK: Cambridge University Press, 2012.
Denton, Clifford E. "The Trautonium: A New Musical Instrument." *Radio-Craft* 4, no. 9 (1933): 522–24, 572.
Dessauer, Friedrich. *Philosophie der Technik: Das Problem der Realisierung*. 3rd ed. Bonn: F. Cohen, 1933.

———. "Technology in Its Proper Sphere." In Mitcham and Mackey, *Philosophy and Technology*, 317–34.
Dewar, Andrew Raffo. "Handmade Sounds: The Sonic Arts Union and American Technoculture." PhD diss., Wesleyan University, 2009.
Doflein, Erich. "Die neue Musik des Jahres." *Melos* 5, no. 10 (1926): 332–38; nos. 11–12 (1926): 369–81.
———. *The Orchestral Revolution: Haydn and the Technologies of Timbre*. Cambridge, UK: Cambridge University Press, 2013.
Dolan, Emily I., and John Tresch. "Toward a New Organology: Instruments of Music and Science." *Osiris* 28 (2013): 278–98.
Donhauser, Peter. *Elektrische Klangmaschine: Die Pionierzeit in Deutschland und Österreich*. Vienna: Böhlau, 2007.
———. "KlarinettenBassgeigenTrompete im Holzkoffer." In Institut für Medienarchäologie, *Zauberhafte Klangmaschine*, 144–45.
Dunn, David. "A History of Electronic Music Pioneers." In *Eigenwelt der Apparatewelt: Pioneers of Electronic Art*. Linz, Austria: Ars Electronica, 1992. Exhibition catalog.
Ebbeke, Klaus. "Paul Hindemith und das Trautonium." *Hindemith Jahrbuch* 11 (1982): 77–113.
Edgerton, David. *The Shock of the Old*. Oxford: Oxford University Press, 2007.
Eggert, John, and Richard Schmidt. *Einführung in die Tonphotographie: Photographische Grundlagen der Lichtton-Aufzeichnung*. Leipzig: S. Hirzel, 1932.
Eimert, Herbert. "Electronic Music." Translated by D.A. Sinclair. Technical Translation TT-601. Ottawa: National Research Council of Canada, 1956.
———. "Elektronische Musik." *Die Musik in Geschichte und Gegenwart*. Kassel: Bärenreiter (1954): 1264–68.
———. "How Electronic Music Began." *Musical Times* 113, no. 1550 (1972): 347–49.
———. "So begann die elektronische Musik." *Melos* 39, no. 1 (1971): 42–44.
———. "What Is Electronic Music?" *Die Reihe* 1, English edition (1960): 1–10.
Einstein, Alfred. "Art and Technology." *Modern Music* 12, no. 2 (1935): 55–61.
Eisenstein, Sergei, Vsevolod Pudovkin, and G.V. Alexandrov. "Statement on the Sound Film." In Sergei Eisenstein, *Film Form*, edited and translated by Jay Leyda, 257–60. New York: Harcourt Brace, 1949.
"Elektrizität und Musik." *Zeitschrift für Instrumentenbau* 8, no. 4 (1887): 46–48.
"Elektroakustische Hausorgel." *Zeitschrift für Instrumentenbau* 53, no. 2 (1932): 25.
"Elektro-akustische Parsifalglocken." *Zeitschrift für Instrumentenbau* 51, no. 23 (1931): 598.
"Elektromusikinstrumente auf dem Weimarer Tonkunstlerfest." *Zeitschrift für Instrumentenbau* 56, no. 19 (1936): 322.
Ellul, Jacques. *The Technological Society*. Translated by John Wilkinson. New York: Vintage Books, 1964.
Elste, Martin. "Die abendländlische Musik zwischen Mensch und Maschine." In *Maschinen und Mechanismen in der Musik*, edited by Boje E. Hans Schmuhl, 183–201. Augsburg: Wissner, 2006.

---. "Hindemiths Versuche 'grammophonplatteneigener Stücke' im Kontext einer Ideengeschichte der Mechanischen Musik im 20. Jahrhundert." *Hindemith-Jahrbuch* 25 (1996): 195-221.

Engramelle, Marie-Dominique-Joseph. *Tonotechnie ou l'Art de noter les cylindres, et tout ce qui susceptible de notage dans les instruments de concerts mécaniques.* Reprint, Paris: Hermann éditeurs des sciences et des arts, 1993. First published 1775 (Paris: P.M. Delaguette, Libraire Imprimeur).

Ermen, Reinhard. *Ferruccio Busoni.* Reinbek bei Hamburg: Rohwohlt, 1996.

Evans, Edwin. "The Foundations of Twentieth-Century Music." *Musical Times* 58, no. 894 (1917): 347-51.

---. "Pianola Music." *Musical Times* 62, no. 945 (1921): 761-64.

Evens, Aden. *Sound Ideas: Music, Machines, and Experience.* Minneapolis: University of Minnesota Press, 2005.

Eyth, Max. *Lebendige Kräfte: Sieben Vorträge aus dem Gebiete der Technik.* Berlin: Julius Springer, 1905.

Felber, Erwin. "Entwicklungsmöglichkeiten der mechanischen Musik." *Die Musik* 19, no. 2 (1926): 77-83.

---. "E.T.A. Hoffmann und die Nachwelt." *Die Musik* 24, no. 10 (1932): 742-45.

Fischer, Lucy. "*Enthusiasm:* From Kino-Eye to Radio-Eye." In *Film Sound: Theory and Practice,* edited by Elisabeth Weis and John Belton, 247-64. New York: Columbia University Press, 1985.

Forman, Paul. "Weimar Culture, Causality, and Quantum Theory, 1918-1927: Adaptation by German Physicists and Mathematicians to a Hostile Intellectual Environment." *Historical Studies in the Physical Sciences* 3 (1971): 1-115.

Foster van Duren, GloryLynn. "René Bertrand's Dynaphone; 'Roses de Metal' by Arthur Honegger." Thesis, California State University, Hayward, 1983.

Galison, Peter. "Aufbau/Bauhaus: Logical Positivism and Architectural Modernism." *Critical Inquiry* 16, no. 4 (1990): 709-52.

Gay, Peter. *Weimar Culture: The Outsider as Insider.* New York: Harper and Row, 1968.

Gayou, Évelyne. *Le Groupe de Recherches Musicales: Cinquante ans d'histoire.* Paris: Fayard, 2007.

Geist, Edwin. "Bedeutung und Aufgabe der elektrischen Musikinstrumente." *Melos* 12, no. 2 (1933): 49-52.

Gell, Alfred. "Technology and Magic." *Anthropology Today* 4, no. 2 (1988): 6-9.

---. "The Technology of Enchantment and the Enchantment of Technology." In *Anthropology, Art and Aesthetics,* edited by Jeremy Coote and Anthony Shelton, 40-66. Oxford: Clarendon Press, 1992.

Gernsback, Hugo. "Electronic Music." *Radio-Craft* 4, no. 9 (1933): 521.

Gershwin, George. "The Composer in the Machine Age." In *Classic Essays on Twentieth-Century Music,* edited by Richard Kostelanetz and Joseph Darby, 43-46. New York: Schirmer Books, 1996.

Gethmann, Daniel, ed. *Klangmaschinen zwischen Experiment und Medientechnik.* Bielefeld: Transcript Verlag, 2010.

Gilfillan, Daniel. *Pieces of Sound: German Experimental Radio.* Minneapolis: University of Minnesota Press, 2009.
Gilliam, Bryan, ed. *Music and Performance during the Weimar Republic.* Cambridge, UK: Cambridge University Press, 1994.
Glinsky, Albert. *Theremin: Ether Music and Espionage.* Chicago: University of Illinois Press, 2000.
Goergen, Jeanpaul, ed. *Walter Ruttmann: Eine Dokumentation.* Berlin: Freunde der deutschen Kinemathek, 1989.
Gouk, Penelope. *Music, Science, and Natural Magic in Seventeenth-Century England.* New Haven, CT: Yale University Press, 1999.
Grant, M.J. *Serial Music, Serial Aesthetics: Compositional Theory in Post-War Europe.* Cambridge, UK: Cambridge University Press, 2001.
Grosch, Nils. *Die Musik der neuen Sachlichkeit.* Stuttgart: Metzler, 1999.
Gronostay, Walter. "Die Klingende Elektrizität und der Komponist." *Die Musik* 24, no. 11 (1932): 808–11.
———. "Die Möglichkeiten der Musikanwendung im Tonfilm." *Melos* 8, no. 7 (1929): 317–18
———. "Die Technik der Geräuschanwendung im Tonfilm." *Die Musik* 22, no. 1 (1929): 42–44.
Gropius, Walter, ed. *The Theater of the Bauhaus.* Translated by Arthur S. Wensinger. Middletown, CT: Wesleyan University Press, 1961. First published as *Die Bühne im Bauhaus* (Munich: Albert Langen Verlag, 1925).
Guderian, Dietmar, ed. *Technik und Kunst.* Düsseldorf: VDI Verlag, 1994.
Grus, H., E. Kruttge, and E. Thalheimer, eds. *Von neuer Musik: Beiträge zur Erkenntnis der neuzeitlichen Tonkunst.* Cologne: F.J. Marcan, 1925.
Gutman, Hanns. "Der töndende Film." *Melos* 7, no. 1 (1928): 6–9.
Haass, Hans. "Über das Wesen mechanischer Klaviermusik." *Anbruch* 9, no. 8–9 (1927): 351–53.
Hagen, Wolfgang. "Busonis 'Erfindung': Thaddeus Cahills Telefon-Telharmonium von 1906." In Gethmann, *Klangmaschinen,* 53–71. ———. "Busoni's Invention: Phantasmagoria and Errancies in Times of Medial Transition." In Daniels and Schmidt, *Artists as Inventors,* 86–107.
———. "Walter Ruttmanns Großstadt-Weekend: Zur Herkunft der Hörcollage aus der ungegenständlichen Malerei." Wolfgang Hagen: Vortraege. 2003. Accessed October 24, 2012. http://www.whagen.de/vortraege/2003/RuttmannWeekend/ruttmann.pdf.
Hagmann, Peter. *Das Welte-Mignon-Klavier, die Welte-Philharmonie-Orgel und die Anfänge der Reproduktion von Musik.* Vol. 10, *Musikwissenschaft.* Series 36, Europaïsche Hochschuleschriften. Bern: Lang, 1984.
Handlin, Oscar. "Science and Technology in Popular Culture." In *Science and Culture: A Study of Cohesive and Disjunctive Forces,* edited by Gerald Holton, 184–98. Boston: Beacon Press, 1965.
Hankins, Thomas L., and Robert J. Silverman. *Instruments and the Imagination.* Princeton: Princeton University Press, 1995.
Harper, Adam. *Infinite Music: Imagining the Next Millennium of Human Music-Making.* London: Zero Books, 2011.

Häusler, Josef. *Spiegel der neuen Musik: Donaueschingen: Chronik, Tendenzen, Werkbesprechungen*. Kassel: Bärenreiter, 1996.
Hausmann, Raoul. *La sensorialité excentrique (1968–69), précédée de: Optophonétique (1922)*. Cambridge, UK: Blackmoor Head Press, 1970.
———. "Vom sprechenden Film zur Optophonetik." *G: Material für elementaren Gestaltung* 1 (1923): unpaginated.
Heinitz, W. "Die Sprechmaschine im Dienste der Musikwissenschaft und der Ästhetik." *Musikblätter des Anbruch* 8, no. 8–9 (1926): 371–73.
Helmholtz, Hermann von. *On the Sensations of Tone*. Translated by Alexander Ellis. New York: Dover, 1954. First published as *Die Lehre von den Tonempfindungen als physiologische Grundlage für die Theorie der Musik* (Braunschweig: Friedrich Vieweg und Sohn, 1863).
Henkel, Hubert. "Die Entwicklungsgeschichte des künstlich erzeugten Tons." In Guderian, *Technik und Kunst*, 92–102.
———. "Die Technik der Musikinstrumentenherstellung am Beispiel des klassischen Instrumenariums." In Guderian, *Technik und Kunst*, 67–91.
Hensheimer, Hans. "Kontra und Pro." *Musikblätter des Anbruch* 8, no. 8–9 (1926): 353–56.
Herf, Jeffrey. "The Engineer as Ideologue." *Journal of Contemporary History* 19, no. 4 (1984): 631–48.
———. *Reactionary Modernism: Technology, Culture, and Politics in Weimar and the Third Reich*. Cambridge, UK: Cambridge University Press, 1986.
Hindemith, Paul. *Aufsätze, Vorträge, Reden*. Edited by Giselher Schubert. Zurich: Atlantis, 1994.
———. *Organ Concertos / Suite for Mechanical Organ*. Koch Schwann CD 312022. 1995.
———. "Zur mechanischen Musik." In Hindemith, *Aufsätze, Vorträge, Reden*, 19–28.
———. "Zu unserem Programm." In Hindemith, *Aufsätze, Vorträge, Reden*, 16–18.
Hinton, Stephen. *The Idea of Gebrauchsmusik: A Study of Musical Aesthetics in the Weimar Republic (1919–1933) with Particular Reference to the Works of Paul Hindemith*. New York: Garland Publishing, 1989.
———. "*Lehrstück*: An Aesthetics of Performance." In *Music and Performance in the Weimar Republic*, edited by Bryan Gilliam, 59–73. Cambridge, UK: Cambridge University Press, 1994.
Hochman, Elaine S. *Bauhaus: Crucible of Modernism*. New York: Fromm International, 1997.
Hocker, Jürgen. *Faszination Player Piano: Das Selbstspielende Klavier von den Anfängen bis zur Gegenwart*. Bergkirchen, Ger.: Edition Bochinsky, 2009.
Hoffmann, E.T.A. "Die Automate." *Allgemeine Musikalische Zeitung* 16, no. 6 (1814): 94–102. English version in *Best Tales of Hoffmann*, edited by E.F. Bleiler, 71–103. New York: Dover, 1967.
Holl, Karl. "Musik und Maschine." *Der Auftakt* 6, no. 8 (1926): 173–77.
Holmes, Thom. *Electronic and Experimental Music*. 2nd ed. New York: Routledge, 2002.

Hong, Sungook. *Wireless: From Marconi's Black-Box to the Audion.* Cambridge, MA: MIT Press, 2001.
Hughes, L.E.C. "Electronic Music." *Nature* 145 (1940): 170–74.
Hughes, Thomas P. *Human-Built World: How to Think about Technology and Culture.* Chicago: University of Chicago Press, 2004.
Hüneke, Andreas. "Musik am Bauhaus." In *Musikkultur in der Weimarer Republik*, edited by Wolfgang Rathert and Giselher Schubert, 189–97. Mainz: Schott, 2001.
Huth, Arno. "Elektrische Tonerzeugung: Zu den Erfindungen von Jörg Mager und Leo Theremin." *Die Musik* 21, no. 1 (1927): 42–45.
———. "Mechanische Musik." 1926. Reprinted in "Zehn Jahre Novembergruppe," special issue, *Kunst der Zeit* 3, no. 1–3 (1928): 48.
Huynh, Pascal. *La musique sous la République de Weimar.* Paris: Fayard, 1998.
Ihde, Don. *Existential Technics.* Albany: State University of New York Press, 1983.
———. "A Phenomenology of Technics." In Scharff and Dusek, *Philosophy of Technology*, 507–29.
———. *Philosophy of Technology: An Introduction.* New York: Paragon House, 1993.
———. *Technics and Praxis.* Dordrecht: D. Reidel, 1979.
———. "Technologies—Musics—Embodiments" In *Embodied Technics*, 17–36. N.p.: Automatic Press / VIP, 2010.
Institut für Medienarchäologie, ed. *Zauberhafte Klangmaschine: Von der Sprechmaschine bis zur Soundkarte.* Mainz: Schott, 2008.
Ircam. *Cahiers de l'Ircam (Recherche et Musique).* No. 7, Instruments. Paris: Editions Ircam, 1995.
Isacoff, Stuart. *Temperament: The Idea that Solved Music's Greatest Riddle.* New York: Alfred A. Knopf, 2001.
Jackson, Myles W. *Harmonious Triads: Physicists, Musicians, and Instrument Makers in Nineteenth-Century Germany.* Cambridge, MA: MIT Press, 2006.
James, Richard S. "Avant-Garde Sound-on-Film Techniques and Their Relationship to Electro-Acoustic Music." *Musical Quarterly* 72, no. 1 (1986): 74–89.
Jemnitz, Alexander. "Antiphonie (Glossen)." *Musikblätter des Anbruch* 8, no. 8–9 (1926): 350–53.
Jewitt, Clement. "Music at the Bauhaus, 1919–1933." *Tempo*, New Series, 213 (2000): 5–11.
"Jörg Mager †." *Zeitschrift für Instrumentenbau* 59, no. 14 (1939): 240.
"Jörg Magers Elektroton-Orgel." *Zeitschrift für Instrumentenbau* 54, no. 2 (1933): 26–27.
Kaes, Anton, Martin Jay, and Edward Dimendberg, eds. *The Weimar Republic Sourcebook.* Berkeley: University of California Press, 1994.
Kahn, Douglas. *Noise, Water, Meat: A History of Sound in the Arts.* Cambridge, MA: MIT Press, 1999.
Kahn, Douglas and Gregory Whitehead, eds. *Wireless Imagination: Sound, Radio, and the Avant-Garde.* Cambridge, MA: MIT Press, 1992.
Kallenberg, Siegfried. "Elektrische Musik." *Zeitschrift für Musik* 94, no. 10 (1927): 557–59.

Kaminski Heinrich. "'Mechanisierung' der Musik?" *Pult und Taktstock* 2, no. 3 (1925): 36–37.

Kapp, Ernst. *Grundlinien einer Philosophie der Technik*. Braunschweig: Georg Westermann, 1877.

Kappelmayer, Otto. "Klingende Elektrizität." *Die Musik* 24, no. 11 (1932): 817–22.

Kartomi, Margaret J. *On Concepts and Classifications of Musical Instruments*. Chicago: University of Chicago Press, 1990.

Kassák, Ludwig, and László Moholy-Nagy, eds. *Buch neuer Künstler*. Reprint, Baden, Switz.: Verlag Lars Müller, 1991. First published 1923 (Vienna: *Ma*).

Katz, Erich. "Mechanische Orgel." *Die Musik* 21, no. 11 (1929): 816–21.

Katz, Mark. "The Rise and Fall of *Grammophonmusik*." In *Capturing Sound: How Technology Has Changed Music*, 99–113. Berkeley: University of California Press, 2004.

Keil, Werner. "The Voice from the Hereafter: E.T.A. Hoffmann's Ideal of Sound and Its Realization in Early Twentieth-Century Electronic Music." In *Music and Literature in German Romanticism*, edited by Siobhain Donovan and Robin Elliott, 143–61. Rochester: Camden House, 2004.

Kellogg, Edward W. "History of Sound Motion Pictures, First Installment." *Journal of the SMPTE* 64 (1955): 291–302.

Kestenberg, Leo, ed. *Kunst und Technik*. Berlin: Wegweiser-Verlag, 1930.

Keyserling, Hermann. "Neue Möglichkeiten der Musik." *Zeitschrift für Instrumentenbau* 53, no. 8 (1933): 128–29.

Kiening, Christian, and Heinrich Adolf, eds. *Der Absolute Film: Dokumente der Medienavantgarde (1912–1936)*. Zurich: Chronos Verlag, 2012.

Kirchmeyer, Helmut. *Kleine Monographie über Herbert Eimert*. Leipzig: Verlag der Sächsichen Akademie der Wissenschaften zu Leipzig, 1998.

"Klavier mit vierteltöniger Tonleiter." *Zeitschrift für Instrumentenbau* 13, no. 29 (1893): 685.

Kleist, Heinrich von. "On the Marionette Theatre." Translated by Thomas G. Neumiller. *Drama Review* 16, no. 3 (1972): 22–26.

Kliemann, Helga. *Die Novembergruppe*. Berlin: Gebr. Mann Verlag, 1969.

Kluitenberg, Eric, ed. *Book of Imaginary Media*. De Balie: NAi Publishers, 2006.

Koetsier, Teun. "On the Prehistory of Programmable Machines: Musical Automata, Looms, Calculators." *Mechanism and Machine Theory* 36 (2001): 589–603.

König, Werner. "Über frühe Tonaufnahmen der Firma Welte und die Werke für das Welte-Mignon-Reproduktionsklavier." *Jahrbuch des Staatlichen Instituts für Musikforschung Preußischer Kulturbesitz 1977*, 31–44. Kassel: Verlag Merseburger Berlin, 1978.

Kool, Jaap. "Geräuschinstrumente." *Musikblätter des Anbruch* 8, nos. 3–4 (1926): 167–69.

———. "Neue Instrumente (I. Glasharmonika)." *Melos* 3, no. 2 (1922): 84–88.

Kowar, Helmut. *Mechanische Musik: Eine Bibliographie und eine Einführung in systematische und kulturhistorische Aspekte mechanischer Musikinstrumente*. Vienna: Vom Pasqualatihaus, 1996.

Krannhals, Paul. *Der Weltsinn der Technik als Schlüssel zu ihrer Kulturbedeutung.* Munich: R. Oldenbourg, 1932.

———. *Das organische Weltbild: Grundlagen einer neuentstehenden deutschen Kultur.* Munich: Bruckmann, 1928.

Krasnopolski, Paul. "Klänge von gestern." *Melos* 7, no. 1 (1928): 10–12

Krenek, Ernst. "Künstliche Stimmen." *Die Musik* 23, no. 8 (1931): 592–94.

———. "Der schaffende Musiker und die Technik der Gegenwart." In Kestenberg, *Kunst und Technik,* 141–55.

Krojanker, E. "Der Tonfilm." *Melos* 8, no. 4 (1929): 182–84.

Kubler, George. *The Shape of Time: Remarks on the History of Things.* New Haven: Yale University Press, 1962.

Kuivila, Ron, and David Behrman. "Composing with Shifting Sand: A Conversation between Ron Kuivila and David Behrman on Electronic Music and the Ephemerality of Technology." *Leonardo Music Journal* 8 (1998): 13–16.

Kuznitzky, Hans. "Neue Elemente der Musikerzeugung." *Melos* 6, no. 4 (1927): 156–60.

———. "Neue Elemente der Musikerzeugung." *Melos* 6, no. 11 (1927): 489–90.

———. "Neues vom Sphärophon." *Melos* 6, no. 6 (1927): 282.

László, Alexander. *Die Farblichtmusik.* Leipzig: Breitkopf & Härtel, 1925.

Laurendeau, Jean. *Maurice Martenot, luthier de l'électronique.* Montreal: Louise Courteau, 1990.

Lauterbach, Ulrich, ed. *Zauberei auf dem Sender und andere Hörspiele.* Frankfurt: Verlag Waldemar Kramer, 1962.

Le Corbusier, *Towards a New Architecture.* Translated from 13th French edition by Frederick Etchells. Reprint, New York: Dover, 1986. First published as *Vers une architecture* (Paris: G. Crès, 1923).

Léger, Fernand. "The Aesthetic of the Machine." In *Theories of Modern Art: A Source Book by Artists and Critics,* edited by Herschel B. Chipp, 277–79. Berkeley: University of California Press, 1968.

Leichtentritt, Hugo. "Some New Mechanical Instruments." *Musical Times* 72, no. 1065 (1931): 1037.

Lertes, Peter. *Elektrische Musik: Eine gemeinverständliche Darstellung ihrer Grundlagen, des heutigen Stand der Technik und ihrer Zukunftsmöglichkeiten.* Dresden: Theodor Steinkopff, 1933.

Lessing, Lawrence. *Man of High Fidelity: Edwin Howard Armstrong.* Philadelphia: J.B. Lippincott, 1956.

Levin, Thomas Y. "For the Record: Adorno on Music in the Age of Its Technological Reproducibility." *October* 55 (1990): 23–47.

———. "'Tones from out of Nowhere': Rudolf Pfenninger and the Archaeology of Synthetic Sound." In *New Media, Old Media: A History and Theory Reader,* edited by Thomas Keenan and Wendy Hui Kyong Chun, 45–81. New York: Routledge, 2005.

Lewer, S.K. *Electronic Musical Instruments.* London: Electronic Engineering, 1948.

Lindner, Gerhard. "Graphomusik." *Die Musik* 24, no. 4 (1932): 265–66.

Lion, A. "Elektrische Musik." *Zeitschrift für Instrumentenbau* 50, no. 22 (1930): 776.

———. "Das elektrische Musikinstrument 'Trautonium.'" *Zeitschrift für Instrumentenbau* 53, no. 5 (1932): 78–80.
———. "Die technische Grundlagen von Theremins Ätherwellen-Musik." *Die Musik* 21, no. 5 (1929): 357–58.
———. "Das Trautonium." *Die Musik* 24, no. 11 (1932): 833–34.
Lodder, Christina. *Russian Constructivism*. New Haven, CT: Yale University Press, 1983.
Luedtke, Hans. "Das Oskalyd." *Musikblätter des Anbruch* 8, no. 8–9 (1926): 385–87.
Mager, Jörg. "Biographisches zum 'Sphärophon.'" *Musikblätter des Anbruch* 8, no. 8–9 (1926): 391–92.
———. "Einführung der elektrischen Klangerzeugung." *Zeitschrift für Instrumentenbau* 52, no. 3 (1931): 45.
———. "Elektro-akustische Musikinstrumente." *Zeitschrift für Instrumentenbau* 51, no. 15 (1931): 418–20.
———. *Eine neue Epoche der Musik durch Radio*. Berlin: Self-published, 1924.
———. "Das 'Partiturophon'—Eine Hausmusik-Lösung." *Zeitschrift für Instrumentenbau* 54, no. 21 (1934): 329–30.
———. "Eine Rundfunkprophezieung." *Der deutsche Rundfunk* 2, no. 29 (1924): 2952–54.
———. *Vierteltonmusik*. Aschaffenburg, Ger.: Franz Kuthal, n.d. [1915].
Manning, Peter. *Electronic and Computer Music*. Oxford: Oxford University Press, 2004.
———. "The Influence of Recording Technologies on the Early Development of Electroacoustic Music." *Leonardo Music Journal* 13 (2003): 5–10.
Marx, Leo. *The Machine in the Garden: Technology and the Pastoral Ideal in America*. Reprint, New York: Oxford University Press, 2000. First published in 1964 (New York: Oxford University Press).
Matzke, Hermann. "Ein Rundgang durch die Entwicklung der Elektromusik." *Zeitschrift für Instrumentenbau* 56, no. 11 (1936): 175–77.
Maul, Andreas. "Die Idee einer 'mechanischen Musik': Über Experimente von Hindemith und Toch mit dem Welte-Mignon-Klavier und der Welte-Philharmonie-Orgel." *Neue Zeitschrift für Musik* 9 (1984): 4–7.
Mersmann, Hans. "Dr. Trautweins elektrische Musik." *Melos* 9, no. 5–6 (1930): 228–29.
———. "Grenzwerte." *Melos* 6, no. 1 (1927): 30–32.
Metzger, Heinz-Klaus, and Rainer Riehn, eds. *Musik der anderen Tradition: Mikrotonale Tonwelte*. Munich: Edition Text + Kritik, 2003.
Meyer, Erwin. "Technische Grundlage und Bedingungen in der mechanischen Musik." In Kestenberg, *Kunst und Technik*, 97–114.
Meyer, Kathi, ed., *Katalog der Internationalen Ausstellung Musik im Leben der Völker*. Frankfurt: Hauserpresse, 1927.
Meyer-Eppler, Werner. *Elektrische Klangerzeugung: Elektronische Musik und synthetische Sprache*. Bonn: Dümmlers Verlag, 1949.
Mitcham, Carl. *Thinking through Technology: The Path between Engineering and Philosophy*. Chicago: University of Chicago Press, 1994.

———. "Three Ways of Being-With Technology." In Scharff and Dusek, *Philosophy of Technology*, 490–506.
Mitcham, Carl, and Robert Mackey, eds. *Philosophy and Technology: Readings in the Philosophical Problems of Technology*. New York: Free Press, 1972.
Moholy-Nagy, László. "Musico-Mechanico, Mechanico-Optico: Geradlinigkeit des Geistes—Umwege der Technik." *Musikblätter des Anbruch* 8, no. 8–9 (1926): 363–67.
———. "Neue Gestaltung in der Musik: Möglichkeiten des Grammophons." *Der Sturm* 14, no. 7 (1923): 102–6.
———. *Painting, Photography, Film*. Translated by Janet Seligman. Cambridge, MA: MIT Press, 1973. First published as *Malerei, Fotographie, Film* (Munich: Albert Langen Verlag, 1925).
———. "Probleme des neuen Films." In Schneede, *Künstlerschriften der 20er Jahre*, 313–21. First published in *Die Form: Zeitschrift für gestaltende Arbeit* 7, no. 5 (1932). Translated by F.D. Klingender and P. Morton Shand as "Problems of the Modern Film," in *Moholy-Nagy: An Anthology*, edited by Richard Kostelanetz (New York: Da Capo, 1970), 131–38.
———. "Produktion—Reproduktion." *De Stijl* 7, no. 5 (1922): 98–100.
Moles, Abraham. *Les musiques expérimentales: Revue d'une tendance importante de la musique contemporaine*. Paris: Éditions du Cercle d'Art Contemporain, 1960.
Möllendorff, Willi. *Musik mit Vierteltönen: Erfahrungen am bichromatischen Harmonium*. Leipzig: F.E.C. Leuckart, 1917. English translation by Klaus Schmirler, *Music with Quarter Tones*, http://tonalsoft.com/monzo/moellendorf/book/contents.htm.
Mondrian, Piet. "De 'Bruiteurs Futuristes Italiens' en 'Het' nieuwe in de muziek." *De Stijl* 4, no. 8 (1921): 114–18; *De Stijl* 4, no. 9 (1921): 130–36.
———. *Natural Reality and Abstract Reality: An Essay in Trialogue Form*. Translated by Martin S. James. New York: George Braziller, 1995.
———. *Neue Gestaltung*. Munich: Albert Langen Verlag, 1925.
———. *The New Art—The New Life. The Collected Writings of Piet Mondrian*. Edited and translated by Harry Holtzman and Martin S. James. Boston: G.K. Hall, 1986.
Morawska-Büngeler, Marietta. *Schwingende Elektronen: Eine Dokumentation über das Studio für Elektronische Musik des Westdeutschen Rundfunks in Köln 1951–1986*. Cologne: P.J. Tonger, 1988.
Morgan, Robert P. *Twentieth-Century Music: A History of Musical Style in Modern Europe and America*. New York: Norton, 1991.
Moritz, William. *Optical Poetry: The Life and Work of Oskar Fischinger*. Bloomington: University of Indiana Press, 2004.
Motte-Haber, Helga de la. *Die Musik von Edgard Varèse*. Hofheim, Ger.: Wolke Verlag, 1993.
Mumford, Lewis. *Art and Technics*. New York: Columbia University Press, 1952.
———. *Technics and Civilization*. Reprint, New York: Harcourt Brace Jovanovich, 1963. First published 1934 (New York: Harcourt).

Nebeker, Frederik. *Dawn of the Electronic Age: Electrical Technologies in the Shaping of the Modern World, 1914 to 1945*. Hoboken, NJ: Wiley–IEEE Press, 2009.
"Ein neues Instrument von Jörg Mager." *Zeitschrift für Instrumentenbau* 50, no. 24 (1930): 814.
Newman, Ernest. "Piano-Player Music of the Future." *Musical Times* 58, no. 895 (1917): 391–97.
Noack, F. "Die Technik des Tonfilms." *Anbruch 11*, no. 5 (1929): 174–76.
Ord-Hume, Arthur W. J. G. *Clockwork Music*. New York: Crown, 1973.
"'Partiturophon,' ein neues elektro-akustische Musikinstrument." *Zeitschrift für Instrumentenbau* 54, no. 15 (1934): 236.
Passuth, Krisztina. *Moholy-Nagy*. London: Thames and Hudson, 1985.
Peukert, Detlev J. K. *The Weimar Republic: The Crisis of Classical Modernity*. Translated by Richard Deveson. New York: Hill and Wang, 1989.
Pfitzner, Hans. *Futuristengefahr: Bei Gelegenheit von Busonis Ästhetik*. Munich: Süddeutsche Monatshefte, 1917.
———. *Die neue Aesthetik der musikalischen Impotenz: Ein Verwesungssymptom?* Munich: Süddeutsche Monatshefte, 1920.
Piano Music without Limits: Original Compositions of the 1920s. CD. Produced by Reimund Grimm and Werner Dabringhaus; liner notes by Irmlinde Capelle. MDG 645 1404-2, 2007.
Pinch, Trevor, and Wiebe E. Bijker. "The Social Construction of Facts and Artefacts; Or How the Sociology of Science and the Sociology of Technology Might Benefit Each Other." *Social Studies of Science* 14, no. 3 (1984): 399–41.
Pinch, Trevor, and Karin Bijsterveld, "Sound Studies: New Technologies and Music." *Social Studies of Science* 34, no. 5 (2004): 635–48.
Pinch, Trevor, and Frank Trocco. *Analog Days: The Invention and Impact of the Moog Synthesizer*. Cambridge, MA: Harvard University Press, 2002.
Plessner, Maximilian. *Ein Blick auf die grossen Erfindungen des zwanzigsten Jahrhunderts. I. Die Zukunft des elektrischen Fernsehens*. Berlin: Ferd. Dämmlers Verlagsbuchhandlung, 1892.
Poggioli, Renato. *Theory of the Avant-Garde*. Translated by Gerald Fitzgerald. New York: Icon, 1971.
Preussner, Eberhard. "Der Musik-'Tonfilm' war da!" *Melos* 9, no. 10 (1930): 428–30.
———. "Musik und Technik in der Geschichte der Musik." In Kestenberg, *Kunst und Technik*, 117–39.
———. "Neue Ton-Bild-Versuche." *Melos* 10, no. 11 (1931): 368–69.
Prieberg, Fred K. *Handbuch deutsche Musiker 1933–1945*. Self-published PDF e-book, version 1.2–3, 2005.
———. *Musica ex machina: Über das Verhältnis von Musik und Technik*. Berlin: Verlag Ullstein, 1960.
———. *Musik des technischen Zeitalters*. Zurich: Atlantis Verlag, 1956.
Pringsheim, Heinz. "Die Mechanisierung der Musik." *Allgemeine Musik Zeitung* (1925): 289–92.
Raven-Hart, R. "Radio, and a New Theory of Tone-Quality." *Musical Quarterly* 17, no. 3 (1931): 380–88.

Raz, Carmel. "From Trinidad to Cyberspace: Reconsidering Ernst Toch's 'Geographical Fugue.'" *Zeitschrift der Gesellschaft für Musiktheorie* 9, no. 2 (2012). http://www.gmth.de/zeitschrift/artikel/698.aspx.

———. "'Gesprochene Musik': The Lost Movements of Toch's 'Geographical Fugue.'" *Current Musicology* 97 (forthcoming).

Redfield, John. *Music: A Science and an Art*. New York: Tudor, 1935.

Rhodes, Richard, ed. *Visions of Technology: A Century of Vital Debates about Machines, Systems, and the Human World*. New York: Simon and Schuster, 2000.

Richards, Annette. "Automatic Genius: Mozart and the Mechanical Sublime." *Music & Letters* 80, no. 3 (1999): 366–89.

Robertson, Emily D. "'It Looks Like Sound!' Drawing a History of 'Animated Music' in the Early Twentieth Century." MA thesis, University of Maryland, 2010.

Ruhmer, Ernst. "The 'Photographophone.'" *Scientific American* 85, no. 2 (1901): 36.

Russcol, Hebert. *The Liberation of Sound: An Introduction to Electronic Music*. Englewood Cliffs, NJ: Prentice-Hall, 1972.

Russolo, Luigi. *The Art of Noises*. Translated by Robert Filiou. 1913. New York: Something Else Press, 1967. Originally a letter to Francesco Balilla Pratella in 1913, first published as *L'arte dei rumori* (Milan: Edizioni Futuristi de "Poesia," 1916).

Sachs, Curt. "Geist und Technik: Ein Blick in die Geschichte des Schaffens." *Die Musik* 20, no. 1 (1927): 26–31.

———. *The History of Musical Instruments*. New York: Norton, 1940.

———. *Reallexikon der Musikinstrumente*. Berlin: Julius Bard, 1913.

———. "Wandel des Klangideals." *Melos* 9, no. 3 (1930): 114–15.

Sachs, Joel. "Some Aspects of Musical Politics in Pre-Nazi Germany." *Perspectives of New Music* 9, no. 1 (1970): 74–95.

Scharff, Robert C., and Val Dusek, eds. *Philosophy of Technology: The Technological Condition*. Oxford: Blackwell, 2003.

Scheinberg, Erica Jill. "Music and the Technological Imagination in the Weimar Republic: Media, Machines, and the New Objectivity." PhD diss., University of California at Los Angeles, 2007.

Schenck, Emil. *Jörg Mager: Dem deutschen Pionier der Elektro-Musikforschung zum Gedächtnis*. Darmstadt: Städtischen Kulturverwaltung, 1952.

Schenk, Dietmar. "Berliner Rundfunkversuchsstelle (1928–1935): Zur Geschichte und Rezeption einer Institution aus der Frühzeit von Rundfunk und Tonfilm." *Rundfunk und Geschichte* 23 (1997): 124–37.

———. "Paul Hindemith und die Rundfunkversuchsstelle der Berliner Musikhochschule." *Hindemith-Jahrbuch* 25 (1996): 179–94.

———. "Die Rundfunkversuchsstelle." In *Die Hochschule für Musik zu Berlin: Preussens Konservatorium zwischen romantischem Klassizismus und neuer Musik, 1869–1932/33*. Stuttgart: Franz Steiner Verlag, 2004, 257–72.

Scheper, Dirk. *Oskar Schlemmer: Das Triadische Ballett und die Bauhausbühne*. Berlin: Schriftenreihe der Akademie der Künste, 1988.

Schillinger, Joseph. "Electricity, a Musical Liberator." *Modern Music* 8, no. 3 (1931): 26–31.

———. "The Electrification of Music." Undated manuscript (ca. 1918). New York Public Library, JPB 86-8, box 9, fol. 16.

Schlemmer, Oskar. "Ausblicke auf Bühne und Tanz." *Melos* 6, no. 12 (1927): 520–24.

———. "Man and Art Figure." In Gropius, *Theater of the Bauhaus*, 17–46.

———. "Theater (Bühne)." In Gropius, *Theater of the Bauhaus*, 80–101.

Schneede, Uwe M., ed. *Künstlerschriften der 20er Jahre: Dokumente und Manifeste aus der Weimar Republic*. Cologne: DuMont, 1986.

Schoenberg, Arnold. "Mechanical Musical Instruments." In *Style and Idea: Selected Writings of Arnold Schoenberg*, edited by Leonard Stein, 326–30. Berkeley: University of California Press, 1984.

———. *Theory of Harmony*. Translated by Roy E. Carter. Berkeley: University of California Press, 1978. First published 1911 (Leipzig: Universal Edition A-G).

Schoon, Andi. *Die Ordnung der Klänge: Das Wechselspiel der Künste vom Bauhaus zum Black Mountain College*. Bielefeld: Transcript Verlag, 2006.

Schumacher, Fritz. *Der 'Fluch' der Technik*. 2nd ed. Hamburg: Verlag Boysen und Maasch, 1932.

———. *Schöpferwille und Mechanisierung*. Hamburg: Verlag Boysen und Maasch, 1933.

Schünemann, Georg. "Produktive Kräfte der mechanische Musik." *Die Musik* 24, no. 4 (1932): 246–49.

Sethares, William. *Tuning, Timbre, Spectrum, Scale*. London: Springer, 1999.

Shapins, Jesse. "Walter Ruttmann's *Weekend*: Sound, Space and the Multiple Senses of an Urban Documentary Imagination." Unpublished manuscript, January 14, 2008. Accessed March 18, 2012. https://radiotekst.files.wordpress.com/2011/07/walter-ruttmanns-weekend-sound-space-and-the-multiple-senses-of-an-urban-documentary-imagination-by-jesse-shapins.pdf.

Shaw, Debra Benita. *Technoculture: The Key Concepts*. Oxford: Berg, 2008.

Simondon, Gilbert. *On the Mode of Existence of Technical Objects*. 1958. Translated by Ninian Mellamphy. London, Ont.: University of Western Ontario, 1980.

———. "On Techno-aesthetics." *Parrhesia* 14 (2012): 1–8.

Smirnov, Andrei. "Boris Yankovsky: Leben im Klangspektrum. Gezeichneter Klang und Klangsynthese in der Sowjetunion der 30er Jahre." In Gethmann, *Klangmaschinen*, 97–120.

———. *Sound in Z: Experiments in Sound and Electronic Music in Early 20th-Century Russia*. London: Koenig Books, 2013.

Smirnov, Andrei, and Tim Boykett. "Notation und visuelle Musik." In Gethmann, *Klangmaschinen*, 121–26.

Solev, Vladimir. "Absolute Music." *Sight and Sound* 5, no. 18 (1936): 48–50.

Spengler, Oswald. *The Decline of the West*. Abridged edition, translated by Charles Francis Atkinson. New York: Oxford University Press, 1991. First published in 2 volumes as *Der Untergang des Abendlandes*, 1918–1922.

———. *Man and Technics. A Contribution to a Philosophy of Life*. Translated by Charles Francis Atkinson. New York: Alfred A. Knopf, 1932.
Stahl, William A. "Venerating the Black Box: Magic in Media Discourse on Technology." *Science, Technology, and Human Values* 20, no. 2 (1995): 234–58.
Stange, Joachim. *Die Bedeutung der elektroakustischen Medien für die Musik im 20. Jahrhundert*. Pfaffenweiler, Ger.: Centaurus-Verlagsgesellschaft, 1989.
Steege, Benjamin. *Helmholtz and the Modern Listener*. Cambridge, UK: Cambridge University Press, 2012.
Stefan, Paul. "Entgötterung?" *Musikblätter des Anbruch* 10, no. 1 (1928): 4–6.
———. "Musik und Maschine." *Musikblätter des Anbruch* 8, no. 8–9 (1926): 343–44.
———. "Der Sommer." *Musikblätter des Anbruch* 8, no.7 (1926): 295–302.
Stege, Fritz. "Jörg Mager in Berlin." *Zeitschrift für Musik* 103, no. 6 (1936): 728.
Stein, Erwin. "Realisierung der Musik." *Pult und Taktstock* 2, no. 2 (1925): 28–31.
Stein, Richard H. "Elektrische Musik." *Die Musik* 22, no. 11 (1930): 861–62.
———. "Zukunftsmusik im Rundfunk." *Der deutsche Rundfunk* 3, no. 12 (1925): 733–36.
Steinhard, Erich. "Donaueschingen: Mechanisches Musikfest." *Der Auftakt* 6, no. 8 (1926): 183–86.
———. "Maschinen." *Der Auftakt* 6, no. 8 (1926): 169.
Sterling, Bruce. "The Life and Death of Media." In *Sound Unbound: Sampling Digital Music and Culture,* edited by Paul D. Miller, 73–81. Cambridge, MA: MIT Press, 2008.
Sterne, Jonathan. *The Audible Past: Cultural Origins of Sounds Reproduction*. Durham, NC: Duke University Press, 2003.
———. "Media or Instruments? Yes." *Offscreen* 11, no. 8–9 (2007): 2–4.
Stiegler, Bernard. "La lutherie électronique et la main du pianiste." In *Mots/Images/Sons,* 229–36. Paris: Institut de Musicologie, 1989.
Stokowski, Leopold. "New Horizons in Music." *Journal of the Acoustical Society of America* 4, no. 1A (1932): 11–19.
Straebel, Volker. "How Light Is Changed into Sound: Eine kleine Geschichte der Photozelle in Musik und Klangkunst." *Neue Zeitschrift für Musik* 158 (1997), 5. Accessed March 18, 2013. http://www.straebel.de/praxis/index.html?/praxis/text/t-photozellen.htm.
Strassburg, Dietrich von. "Offener Brief an H.H. Stuckenschmidt." *Musikblätter des Anbruch* 8, no. 2 (1926): 81–82.
Stockhausen, Karlheinz. "The Origins of Electronic Music." *Musical Times* 112, no. 1541 (1971): 649–50.
Strobel, Heinrich. "Musik aus dem Äther: Professor Theremin im Berliner Beethoven-Saal." *Musikblätter des Anbruch* 9, no. 10 (1927): 435.
———. "'Neue Sachlichkeit' in der Musik." *Musikblätter des Anbruch* 8, no. 6 (1926): 254–56.
———. *Paul Hindemith*. 3rd ed. Mainz: Schott, 1948.

Strzolka, Rainer. *Abriss zur Geschichte des Hörspiels in der Weimarer Republik.* Hannover: Verlag Clemens Koechert, 2004.

Stuckenschmidt, H. H. "Antwort." *Musikblätter des Anbruch* 8, no. 2 (1926): 82.

———. "Machines—A Vision of the Future." *Modern Music* 4, no. 3 (1927): 8–14.

———. "Mechanische Musik." *Der Auftakt* 6, no. 8 (1926): 170–173.

———. "Mechanische Musik" *Der Kreis* 3, no. 11 (1926): 506–8. English translation in Kaes, Jay, and Dimendberg, *Weimar Republic Sourcebook*, 597–600.

———. "Mechanisierung." *Musikblätter des Anbruch* 8, no. 8–9 (1926): 345–46.

———. "Mechanisierung: Antwort an H.K." *Pult und Taktstock* 2, no. 5 (1925): 82–84.

———. "Mechanisierung der Musik." *Ma* 9, no. 8 (1924): unpaginated.

———. "Die Mechanisierung der Musik." *Pult und Taktstock* 2, no. 1 (1925): 1–8.

———. "Musik." *Die rote Erde* 1 (1920): 338–40.

———. "Musik am Bauhaus." In von Maur, *Vom Klang der Bilder*, 408–13.

———. "Musik und Musiker in der Novembergruppe." In "Zehn Jahre Novembergruppe," special issue, *Kunst der Zeit* 3, no. 1–3 (1928): 94–101.

———. "The Third Stage: Some Observations on the Aesthetics of Electronic Music." *Die Reihe* 1, English edition (1960): 11–13.

———. *Twentieth-Century Music.* Translated by Richard Deveson. New York: McGraw-Hill, 1970.

———. "Under the Swastika." *Modern Music* 11, no. 1 (November 1933): 49–52.

Szendy, Peter. "Pour commencer . . . Suivi de: (Re)lire Bartók (Déjà, Encore)." In Ircam, *Instruments* (Paris: Editions Ircam, 1995), 9–23.

Théberge, Paul. *Any Sound You Can Imagine: Making Music, Consuming Technology.* Hanover, NH: Wesleyan University Press, 1997.

Theremin, Léon. "The Design of a Musical Instrument Based on Cathode Relays." *Leonardo Music Journal* 6 (1996): 49–50.

"369 neue Musikinstrumente in zehn Jahren." *Zeitschrift für Instrumentenbau* 59, no. 11 (1939): 173.

Tiessen, Heinz. "Zur Mechanisierung der Musik." *Pult und Taktstock* 2, no. 4 (1925): 61–62.

Toch, Ernst. "Musik für mechanische Instrumente." *Musikblätter des Anbruch* 8, no. 8–9 (1926): 346–49.

———. "Über meine Kantate 'Das Wasser' und meine Grammophonmusik." *Melos* 9, nos. 5–6 (1930): 221–22.

"Tönende Ornamente: Aus Oskar Fischingers neuer Arbeit." In Kiening and Adolf, *Der absolute Film*, 309.

Trautwein, Friedrich. "Dynamische Probleme der Musik bei Feiern unter freiem Himmel," *Deutsche Musik-Kultur* 2, no. 1 (1937–38): 33–44.

———. "The Electric Monochord." Translated by H. A. G. Nathan. Technical Translation TT-606. Ottawa: National Research Council of Canada, 1956.

———. *Elektrische Musik.* Berlin: Wiedmann, 1930.

———. "Das Klangfarben-Musikinstrument." *Musica* 7, no. 7–8 (1953): 301–5.
———. "Über die Bedeutung technischer Forschung und die Zusammenarbeit von Musikern und Technikern für die Zukunft unserer Musikkultur." *Deutsche Musikkultur* 3, no. 6 (1938–39): 455–59.
———. "Wesen und Ziele der Elektromusik." *Zeitschrift für Musik* 103, no. 6 (1936): 694–99.
Trommler, Frank. "The Avant-Garde and Technology: Toward Technological Fundamentalism in Turn-of-the-Century Europe." *Science in Context* 8, no. 2 (1995): 397–416.
Ungeheuer, Elena. "Imitative Instrumente und innovative Maschinen? Musikästhetische Orientiertungen der elektrischen Klangerzeugung." In Institut für Medienarchäologie, *Zauberhafte Klangmaschine*, 45–58.
———. *Wie die elektronische Musik 'erfunden' wurde . . . Quellenstudie zu Werner Meyer-Epplers Entwurf zwischen 1949 und 1953*. Mainz: Schott, 1992.
Varèse, Edgard. *Écrits*. Edited by Louise Hirbour. Paris: Christian Bourgois Éditeur, 1983.
Vierling, Oskar. "Elektrische Musik." *Elektrotechnische Zeitschrift* 53, no. 7 (1932): 155–59.
Volmar, Axel. "Auditiver Raum aus der Dose: Raumakustik, Tonstudiobau und Hallgeräte im 20. Jahrhundert." In Gethmann, *Klangmaschinen*, 153–74.
von Maur, Karin, ed. *Vom Klang der Bilder: Die Musik in der Kunst des 20. Jahrhundert*. Munich: Prestel, 1985.
Wagner, Karl Willy. "Die Frequenzbereich von Sprache und Musik." *Elektrotechnische Zeitschrift* 45, no. 9 (1924): 451–56.
Walther, Gerrit. *Julius Maria Becker, 1887–1949: Ein Dichter zwischen den Weltkriegen*. Baden-Baden: Battert-Verlag, 1989.
Warschauer, Frank. "Musik im Rundfunk." *Musikblätter des Anbruch* 8, no. 8–9 (1926): 374–79.
———. "Was die Funkausstellung dem Musikfreund brachte." *Melos* 11, nos. 8–9 (1932): 295–98.
———. "Die Zukunft der Technisierung." In Kestenberg, *Kunst und Technik*, 409–46.
Weber, Max. *The Rational and Social Foundations of Music*. Translated by Don Martindale, Johannes Ridel, and Gertrude Neuwirth. Carbondale: Southern Illinois University Press, 1958.
———. "Science as a Vocation." In *From Max Weber: Essays in Sociology*, edited by H.H. Gerth and C. Wright Mills, 129–56. New York: Oxford University Press, 1958. First published as "Wissenschaft als Beruf" (Munich: Duncker and Humblot, 1919).
Weidenaar, Reynold. *Magic Music from the Telharmonium*. Metuchen, NJ: Scarecrow Press, 1995.
Weil, Irving. "The Noise-Makers." *Modern Music* 5, no. 2 (1928): 24–28.
Weill, Kurt. "Möglichkeiten absoluter Radiokunst." In *Musik und Theater: Gesammelte Schriften*, edited by Stephen Hinton and Jürgen Schebera, 191–96. Berlin: Henschelverlag Kunst und Gesellschaft, 1990. First published in *Der deutsche Rundfunk* 3, no. 26 (1925): 1625–28.

Weiskopf, Herbert. "Das Sphärophon." *Musikblätter des Anbruch* 8, nos. 8–9 (1926): 388–90.
———. "Sphärophon, das Instrument der Zukunft." *Der Auftakt* 6, no. 8 (1926): 177–78.
———. "Sphärophon, das Musikinstrument der Zukunft." *Der deutsche Rundfunk* 32 (1926): 2203–4.
Weiss, E. "Nouveaux instruments de musique radioélectriques." *La Nature* 58 (1930): 258–67.
Weissmann, Adolf. *Music Come to Earth*. Translated by Eric Blom. New York: E. P. Dutton, 1930. First published as *Die Entgötterung der Musik* (Stuttgart: Deutsche Verlags-Anstalt, 1928).
Wellek, Albert. "Viertelton und Fortschritt." *Zeitschrift für Musik* 92, no. 6 (1925): 352–57.
Westheim, Paul. "Maschinenromantik." *Das Kunstblatt* 7, no. 2 (1923): 33–40.
White Jr., Lynn. *Machina ex Deo: Essays in the Dynamism of Western Culture*. Cambridge, MA: MIT Press, 1968.
Whitney, John. "Bewegungsbilder und elektronische Musik." *Die Reihe* 7 (1960): 62–73.
Willett, John. *Art and Politics in the Weimar Period: The New Sobriety 1917–1933*. New York: Da Capo, 1996.
Winckel, Fritz. "Musik in optischer Gestaltung." *Melos* 10, no. 11 (1931): 365–68.
Winckelmann, Joachim. *Das Trautonium—Ein neues Radio-Musikinstrument*. Berlin: Deutsch-literarisches Institut J. Schneider, 1931.
Wingler, Hans Maria, ed. *The Bauhaus*. Translated by Wolfgang Jabs and Basil Gilbert. Cambridge, MA: MIT Press, 1969.
Wong Doe, Henry. "Musician or Machine: The Player Piano and Composers of the Twentieth Century." DMA diss., The Juilliard School, 2006.
Zeller, Hans Rudolf. "Ferruccio Busoni und die musikalische Avantgarde um 1920." In Metzger and Riehn, *Musik der anderen Tradition*, 9–21.
Zielinski, Siegfried. *Deep Time of the Media: Toward an Archaeology of Hearing and Seeing by Technical Means*. Translated by Gloria Custance. Cambridge, MA: MIT Press, 2006.
———. "Modelling Media for Ignatius Loyola: A Case Study on Athanasius Kircher's World of Apparatus between the Imaginary and the Real." In Kluitenberg, *Book of Imaginary Media*, 29–55.
Zoll, Paul. "Jörg Magers 'Partiturophon': Eine umwälzende, elektro-akustische Erfindung." *Zeitschrift für Musik* 102, no. 12 (1935): 1333–34.
Zschimmer, Eberhard. *Philosophie der Technik*. Berlin: Ernst Siegfried Mittler und Sohn, 1917.
"Zum Inhalt." *Melos* 9, no. 3 (1930): 113.

Index

Adorno, Theodor, 162
Ananiev, Nikolai. *See* Sonar
Andreae, Volkmar, 64
Antheil, George, 22, 90; *Ballet méchanique*, 90, 143, 175n31; "Musico-Mechanico Manifesto," 143
Armstrong, Edwin Howard, 59–60, 76. *See also* radio: regenerative amplification
Avraamov, Arsenii: *Symphony of Sirens*, 142–43, 200n96
acoustics, 9, 71–72; additive synthesis, 70–72, 186n80; formants, 118–20; overtones, 118–20, 157, 162; subtractive synthesis, 73–74; tuning, 55–57. *See also* Heinrich Hertz Institute; Helmholtz, Hermann von; Hermann, Ludimar; heterodyne principle; microtonality; photoelectric cell; Scheibler, Johann Heinrich
Aeolian Pianola: music for, 28, 30, 175nn25,29
Audion Piano, 60, 61fig.8
Audion triode, 16, 59
automata, 24–25, 174n12
automatic instruments, early: music box, 11–12, 24–26; music for, 24–25, 174n14; orchestrion, 24–25. *See also* automata

Bagier, Guido, 50, 188n2; "The Talking Film," 82–83

Bauhaus, 6, 21–22, 37–38, 42. *See also* Gropius, Walter; Meyer, Hannes; Moholy-Nagy, László; Schlemmer, Oskar
Becker, Julius Maria, 56, 150; *Syrinx*, 56–57
Beethoven, Ludwig van, 78, 81, 136–37, 148, 157. *See also* automatic instruments, early: music for
Behrens-Senegalden, G. A. *See* bichromatic piano
Bekker, Paul: aesthetic of, 37, 156, 177n57, 178n64; and Hanslick, 37
Bell, Alexander Graham. *See* Photophone
Bergson, Henri, 11, 153
Berlin Academy of Music (Hochschule für Musik). *See* Radio Research Section
Bernhard, Paul, 51
Berzelius, Jakob, 93–95
Besseler, Heinrich: and Gebrauchsmusik, 128, 201n100
Beyer, Robert, 99, 159, 162–63, 205n31; collaboration with Eimert, 161–62; concept of *Raumton*, 100, 205n31; critique of electric instruments, 104, 206n45; and optical sound film, 99–104, 106, 111; "The Problem of the 'Music to Come'," 103; and the Studio for Electronic Music (Cologne), 159–62, 206n45. *See also* Melochord
bichromatic piano, 55
Bischoff, Friedrich, 98–99, 193n74

230 | Index

Brecht, Bertolt: and "alienation effect," 100, 192n57; collaboration with Hindemith, 128–29
Buchla, Don, 166
Busoni, Ferruccio, 13–17, 54, 74, 97, 120–21, 137, 163, 167; as composer, 28, 36, 175n25; "Für die Pianola," 28; "The Future of Music," 15; *Sketch of a New Aesthetic of Music (Entwurf einer neuen Ästhetik der Tonkunst)*, 1, 13–14, 16, 28, 63, 103, 152, 158; and Mager, 57, 63–64; and the Telharmonium, 13–14, 63, 74, 184n45; as teacher, 58, 192n52

Cage, John, 157–58; "For More New Sounds," 157; "The Future of Music: Credo,"157–58, 203n17; collaboration with Fischinger, 157, 204n19; and gramophone music, 157
Cahill, Thaddeus. *See* Dynamophone; Telharmonium
Casella, Alfredo, 30
Cassirer, Ernst, 6, 15, 136, 152–53, 171n17
Cathodic Harmonium, 115
Clair, René, 96, 98–99
computer, 2, 4, 165–66
Coupleux, Edouard. *See* Radio-Tone Organ
Cowell, Henry, 62, 115, 190n29; and *Modern Music* magazine, 157

de Forest, Lee, 59–60, 76. *See also* Audion Piano; Audion triode
de Schloezer, Boris, 155
Dessauer, Friedrich, 136; *Philosophy of Technology*, 153
diode, 59, 182n28
Disney, Walt: *Silly Symphonies*, 111
Doflein, Erich, 41
Donaueschingen Festival, 50, 134; in Baden-Baden, 188n2; in Berlin, 38, 90–91, 123; July 1926, 18–20, 36, 39, 42, 44, 48–49, 52–53, 64–65, 72, 82
Dynamophone, 180n107

Edgerton, David, 165
Edison, Thomas, 59–60, 191n43. *See also* phonograph
Eggeling, Viking, 42, 88, 99, 193–94n81
Eimert, Herbert: aesthetics of, 160–62, 205n34; collaboration with Beyer, 161–62; *Fünf Stücke*, 162; and serialism, 161–62; and the Studio for Electronic Music (Cologne), 160–63; *Der weisse Schwann* (The white swan), 160; "What Is Electronic Music?" 160–61. *See also* Melochord
Einstein, Alfred, 155
Eisenstein, Sergei: and "Statement on the Sound Film," 96
Eisler, Hanns: collaboration with Ruttmann, 50

electric instruments, 54, 59–60, 68, 114–17, 137–41, 148; ease of playing, 66–68, 116, 137–39; imagery and associations, 52–54, 61–63, 66, 68–69, 73–74, 78, 150–51; vs. mechanical instruments, 67–68, 115; music for, 52–53, 60–61, 80–81, 115, 131–32; sound of, 60, 73–74, 80, 104, 148–49, 157–58; vs. traditional instruments, 114–15, 148, 157–58. *See also* Audion Piano; Cathodic Harmonium; Hellertion; KdF-Großtonorgel; Keyboard Spherophone; Mager, Jörg; Ondes Martenot; *Partiturophon*; Radiophonic Organ; Rhythmicon; Sonar; Spherophone; synthesizer; Telharmonium; Terpsiton; Theremin; Theremin, Léon; Trautonium; Trautwein, Friedrich
electric music (pre-WWII), 58–60, 67–68, 114–15, 120, 141–43, 148; ease of playing, 66–68, 121, 129, 137–39; as "electro-music," 115; imagery and associations, 53–54, 60, 63, 66, 68–69, 73–74, 78; vs. mechanical music, 116; research on, 120–21; and the Third Reich, 135–36–37, 139–40. *See also* Mager, Jörg; Radio Research Section; Society for Electroacoustic Music; Theremin, Léon; Trautwein, Friedrich
electronic music (post-WWII), 3–4, 159–64
Elektrochord, 115–16
Engramelle, Marie-Dominique-Joseph: *La Tonotechnie ou l'Art de noter les cylindres*, 25
Enkel, Fritz, 161
Evans, Edwin, 28, 30, 32, 175n29
expressionism, 35–36, 53, 177n54
Eyth, Max, 9–10

Fessenden, Reginald, 62–63
Finke, Fidelio: and the New Objectivity, 36
Fischinger, Oskar, 154, 193n81, 197n32; "Absolute Sound Film," 108; aesthetics of, 6, 109–110, 110fig.16, 194n93; collaboration with Cage, 157, 204n19; compositional process of, 108–109,

110fig.16, 194n94; and creative
autonomy, 108–109; and optical sound
film, 7, 98, 108–11; *Studies*, 108
Fleming, John Ambrose. *See* diode
Flesch, Hans, 98–99, 193n74
Ford, Henry, 20
Furtwängler, Wilhelm, 32, 135

Galison, Peter, 38, 177n49
Gay, Peter, 11
Gebrauchsmusik, 128–29, 152; and
Hindemith, 128; and Trautwein, 142;
and the Volkstrautonium, 128–29
Genzmer, Harald, 141; Concerto for
Trautonium and Orchestra, 141;
Der Läufer (The runner)141; Second
Concerto for Trautonium and Large
Orchestra, 158
Germany: economy of, 31, 129–30, 133–35;
industrialization of, 9, 20, 35. *See also*:
Third Reich, Weimar Republic, World
War I, World War II
Gernsback, Hugo: "Electronic Music," 125,
197n39; *Radio-Craft* magazine, 125
Gershwin, George, 155
Givelet, Armand. *See* Radio-Tone Organ
Glinsky, Albert, 66
Goebbels, Joseph, 134–36, 141; and electric
instruments, 136, 140, 150; and Nazi
aesthetics, 136
Goethe, Johann Wolfgang von: *Faust*,
80, 154
Goldberg, Georg Julius, 66, 149
gramophone, 2, 11–12, 25–27, 116, 155,
191nn36,37; gramophone music, 90–92,
104, 157, 190n29; as media instrument,
31–32, 40, 50, 83, 87–90, 97, 107,
123, 157, 190n28. *See also* Moholy-
Nagy, László; Prinsgheim, Heinz;
Stuckenschmidt, Hans Heinz
Gronostay, Walter, 152; and Gebrauchsmusik,
129; taxonomy of noise, 101
Gropius, Walter: "Art and Technology: A
New Unity," 21; and the Bauhaus, 21

Haass, Hans, 21fig.1; *Capriccio Fugue*,
19; "Über das Wesen mechanischer
Klaviermusik," 48–49; and the Welte-
Mignon, 19, 49, 180n100
Hába, Alois: and Mager, 62, 64–65, 81,
182n26; and microtonality, 58
Hanslick, Eduard, 37
Hartlaub, Gustav: and the New Objectivity,
35–36

Haydn, Joseph, 44. *See also* automatic
instruments, early: music for
Heinsheimer, Hans, 49
Heinrich Hertz Institute for Oscillation
Research, 121, 134. *See also* Wagner,
Karl Willy
Helberger, Bruno, 139–40, 142. *See also*
Hellertion
Hellertion, 137, 140, 196n11
Helmholtz, Hermann von, 9, 12–13; and
experimental acoustics, 9, 70, 72, 119, 162,
171n26, 185n62, 185n63, 186n80; *On the
Sensations of Tone*, 9, 55, 62, 70–71
Hermann, Ludimar. *See* acoustics: formants
heterodyne principle, 62–63, 76
Hindemith, Paul: collaboration with Brecht,
128–29; collaboration with Schlemmer,
44–46, 52, 82; collaboration with
Gräff/Richter, 50; collaboration with
Trautwein, 121–22; *Concertino for
Trautonium and String Orchestra*, 125;
The Craft of Musical Composition,
159; and Gebrauchsmusik, 128–29;
and gramophone music, 90–92, 104,
123, 157; *Des kleinen Elektromusikers
Lieblinge* (The little electro-musician's
favorites), 123, 124fig.20; and the
machine aesthetic, 22; and mechanical
music, 18, 20, 22, 39–40, 44–46,
46fig.7, 48–50, 84, 92; and the New
Objectivity, 36–37; *Piano Suite op. 26*,
22; "Song over Three Octaves," 91; and
the Spherophone, 52–53, 65, 81, 121,
186n80; and the Third Reich, 134–35,
154; and the Trautonium, 104, 123,
124fig.20, 125, 132–33, 141; *Triadic
Ballet*, 44–46, 52, 82, 179n88; and
the Welte-Mignon, 50, 90–91; and the
Welte-Philharmonie, 44–46; post-WWII
aesthetic of, 159; "Xylophone," 91
Hitchcock, Alfred: *The Birds*, 159
Hitler, Adolf, 133, 135–36, 139–41, 149, 159
Honegger, Arthur, *Pacific 231*, 22
Huth, Arno, 68

Ihde, Don, 112
instruments, new, 1–8, 11–17, 22; critique
of, 14–17, 154–56; and perfection,
1, 5–6, 13–14. *See also* electric
instruments; mechanical instruments;
media instruments
instruments, traditional: critique of, 1–3, 5,
13, 22; refashioning of, 4
intonarumori (Russolo), 4, 85–87, 189n16

Kaminski, Heinrich, 33
Kapp, Ernst, 171n26; *Principles of a Philosophy of Technology,* 9, 171n26
KdF-Großtonorgel, 140
Kestenberg, Leo: *Kunst und Technik,* 152–53
Keyboard Spherophone (Klaviatur-Sphärophon): design of, 76, 122; music for, 80–81, 148; in performance, 76–77, 160. *See also* Partiturophon, Spherophone
Keyserling, Hermann, Count, 145; *Travel Diary of a Philosopher,* 145
Kircher, Athanasius, 24
Klee, Paul, 7, 40
Kleist, Heinrich von: "Über das Marionettentheater," 47–48, 179n94
Krannhals, Paul, 136; *The Organic Worldview,* 136
Krenek, Ernst, 37, 135, 152, 155–56
Kuivila, Ron, 167
Kulbin, Nikolai, 62
Kuznitzky, Hans, 54, 180n6

Le Corbusier: *Vers un architecture,* 20
Lertes, Peter: *Elektrische Musik,* 51, 114–15, 119, 146, 187n91, 197n36. *See also* Hellertion
Levin, Thomas, 93, 191n37, 194n91, 195n101
Lindner, Gerhard, 84
loudspeaker, 126fig.21; and Mager's instruments, 52, 72–73, 80, 145, 149; and optical sound film, 95, 191n43; and regenerative amplification, 59–60; and the Studio for Electronic Music (Cologne), 103, 161, 205n31; and the Third Reich, 140

Mager, Jörg, 67fig.10, 69fig.11, 151fig.27; early life, 54, experiments in tuning, 54–55, 57–58; experiments in electric tone generation, 58–63, 62fig.9, 69–70, 72–75, 78–79; and Hindemith, 121, 134; illness and death, 149–50; and *Klangfarbenmusik,* 72; legacy of, 160–61, 163, 165–66; "Little Christmas Lullaby" ("Weihnachts-Wiegenliedchen"), 148–49; and microtonality, 52, 63–64, 77fig.12, 117, 183n39, 185n62; *A New Epoch of Music through Radio,* 60, 70, 72; and patronage, 64–65, 78, 80–81, 145–46, 149; patents of, 62fig.9, 73–75, 150, 166, 181n11, 186nn83,87,89,90, 187n93, 196n11, 201nn102,109,110;

personality of, 144–45, 150–51; politics of, 58, 149; *Quarter-Tone Music,* 55; "Radio Prophecy," 60, 70; and stage music, 80, 143–44, 158–59; and Theremin, 62–63, 66–68; and Trautwein, 116–17, 120, 125, 134, 137, 144–45, 150. *See also* Keyboard Spherophone; Partiturophon; Society for Electroacoustic Music; Spherophone
Mager, Siegfried, 161
magnetic tape 3, 101, 159–60, 165
Mann, Thomas, 145, 199n72
Martenot, Maurice. *See* Ondes Martenot
mechanical organ, 18, 41–42, 44–45, 50, 174n14, 179n88. *See also* Welte-Philharmonie
mechanical instruments: critique of, 48–50; vs. electric instruments, 67–68; vs. human performance, 18, 28–34, 36, 39; and other media, 50; in performance, 18–20, 30, 38–42, 44, 47–49; music for, 18–20, 24–25, 28, 30–34, 39–40, 44–46, 48–49, 68; and reproduction, 49, 68. *See also* Aeolian Pianola; automata; automatic instruments, early; Busoni, Ferruccio; Donaueschingen; Dynamophone; Evans, Edwin; Newman, Ernest; Haass, Hans; Hindemith, Paul; Maholy-Nagy, László; mechanical organ; Münch, Gerhart; *Musikblätter des Anbruch*; player piano; Schlemmer, Oskar; Schoenberg, Arnold; Stravinsky, Igor; Stuckenschmidt, Hans Heinz; Toch, Ernst; Welte-Mignon; Welte-Philharmonie
mechanical music, 27–28; aesthetics of, 30; critique of, 33, 39, 42 (& in b/w?), 46(?), 48–51; and other media, 42–50; and production, 39–41, 68; as "recorded music," 25; and reproduction, 39–41, 49, 68. *See also* Antheil, George; Bekker, Paul; Busoni, Ferruccio; Haass, Hans; Hindemith, Paul; Honegger, Arthur; Mosolov, Alexander; Münch, Gerhart; *Musikblätter des Anbruch*; New Objectivity; Richter, Hans; Schlemmer, Oskar; Schoenberg, Arnold; Sousa, John Philip; Stravinsky, Igor; Stuckenschmidt, Hans Heinz; Toch, Ernst; Weimar Republic: machine aesthetic
media instruments: 2, 8, 50, 82–85, 88–89, 97, 103, 107. *See also* Bagier, Guido; Beyer, Robert; Cage, John; Fischinger, Oskar; gramophone; Hindemith, Paul; Moholy-Nagy, László; Mondrian, Piet; *Musikblätter des Anbruch*; optical sound

film; Pfenninger, Rudolf; Stuckenschmidt, Hans Heinz; Toch, Ernst
Melochord, 161
Meyer-Eppler, Werner, 160–61, 205n34
Meyer, Hannes, 38; "Die neue Welt" ("The New World"), 38
microtonality, 55–56, 58, 62, 64–65. *See also* Hába, Alois; Mager, Jörg; Möllendorff, Willi; Schoenberg, Arnold; Stein, Richard; Wyschnegradsky, Ivan
Moholy-Nagy, László: aesthetic of, 7–8, 87–88, 92, 192n50; anti-romanticism of, 6, 37, 87, 108; and the Bauhaus, 7, 90, 109, 190n18; experimentation in the arts, 7, 87–88, 90; and gramophone music, 87–88, 90, 92, 160, 166, 190n28; and media instruments, 32, 87–88, 97, 107; and Mondrian, 87–88, 190n18; "Neoplasticism in Music: Possibilities of the Gramophone," 87; and optical sound film, 92, 97–99, 105–7, 113; and Pfenninger, 112–13, 195nn100,101; "Production-Reproduction," 7–8, 87, 92, 97, 102, 157–58, 178n61; and Stuckenschmidt, 32, 88, 90, 92, 166; *Tönendes ABC (Sound ABC)*, 113
Moles, Abraham, 163
Möllendorf, Willi, 58, 181n11
Mondrian, Piet, 85, 99, 107, 188n8; and Moholy-Nagy, 87–88, 190n18; neoplasticism in music, 85–88, 188n7, 189n11,14,15,16
Moog, Robert, 164, 166
Moritz, William, 109
Mosolov, Alexander: *Zavod*, 22
Mozart, Wolfgang Amadeus, 44, 132, 137, 175n25; K. 608, 41. *See also* automatic instruments, early: music for
Mumford, Lewis, 153–54
Münch, Gerhart: *Six Polyphonic Etudes*, 18–20
music box. *See* automatic instruments, early
Musikblätter des Anbruch: and electric instruments, 82; and mechanical instruments, 35fig.4, 82; and mechanical music, 35fig.4, 37, 39; and media instruments, 82–83

Neo Bechstein Grand Piano, 116, 125
Nernst, Walther. *See* Neo-Bechstein Grand Piano
Newman, Ernest, 28, 32; "Piano-Player Music of the Future," 28
New Objectivity *(neue Sachlichkeit)*, 6, 35–38, 177n51, 177n54; in music, 36, 53. See also Strobel, Heinrich

New Sobriety. *See* New Objectivity.
November Group, 38, 99, 178n64

Ondes Martenot (M. Martenot), 115, 155, 186n81
orchestrion. *See* automatic instruments, early
optograph, 94

Partiturophon, 115, 147fig.26, 150; design of, 78–79, 144–48; mass production of, 144–45, 147; music for, 78, 80–81, 147–48; in performance, 150; sound of, 78–79. *See also* Keyboard Spherophone, Spherophone
People's Radio (Volksempfänger), 130
Pfenninger, Rudolf, 6–7, 98, 108, 111fig.17; compositional process of, 109–112; critical reaction to, 112; and Moholy-Nagy, 112–13, 195nn100,101; *Pitsch und Patsch*, 111; and timbre, 111–112
Pfitzner, Hans: aesthetics of, 14–16, 155; *The Danger of Futurism (Futuristengefahr)*, 14
phonograph, 11–12, 25, 93–94, 166. *See also* gramophone
photoelectric cell, 93–95, 95fig.14, 96fig.15, 107, 110, 191n43
Photographophone, 94–95, 191n42
Photophone, 94–95, 191n42
Pinch, Trevor, 164
player piano, 2, 21fig.1, 25–27, 46fig.7, 84; and reproduction, 8; and production, 8, 28. *See also* Aeolian Pianola; Antheil, George; Evans, Edwin; Newman, Ernst; Stuckenschmidt, Hans Heinz; Welte-Mignon
Plessner, Maximilian. *See* optograph
Podovkin, Vsevolod: and Ruttmann, 106; "Statement on the Sound Film," 106
Preussner, Eberhard, 45
Pringsheim, Heinz, 32–33, 89–91, 102, 176n43

Quantz, Johann Joachim. *See* automata

Raabe, Peter, 149
radio: and electric instruments, 61, 65, 116; and electric music, 8, 58–63; and the "radio play" *(Hörspiel)*, 98–99; regenerative amplification, 59–60, 76. *See also* Mager, Jörg; People's Radio; Radio Corporation of America; Radio Research Section (Berlin Academy of Music); Trautonium; Trautwein, Friedrich; Volkstrautonium; Weill, Kurt

Radio Corporation of America (RCA): and the Theremin, 115, 130, 144, 195n3
Radio Research Section (Rundfunkversuchsstelle), Berlin Academy of Music, 120–22, 122fig.19, 124–25, 129, 134, 198n59. *See also* Schünemann, Georg; Stein, Fritz; Trautwein, Friedrich
Radio-Tone Organ, 115, 148, 188n5, 195n5
Ray, Man, 88, 179n73
Redfield, John, 1
Reger, Max, 36, 136
Reich Radio Society (Reichsrundfunkgesellschaft), 133
Rhythmicon, 115
Richter, Hans: *Vormittagsspuk* (Ghosts before breakfast), 50, 88, 99, 105–6, 193n81
Ruhmer, Ernst. *See* Photographophone
Russolo, Luigi, 4, 85, 152, 167; *The Art of Noises*, 1. See also *intonarumori*
Ruttmann, Walter, 7, 88, 98–99, 108, 193n81; *Berlin: Die Symphonie der Großstadt (Berlin: Symphony of a Metropolis)*, 105; collaboration with Eisler, 50; *Melodie der Welt*, 104; *Opus I-IV*, 105; and sound montage, 105–6; *Weekend*, 105–6
Rzhevkin, Sergei, 143. *See also* Cathodic Harmonium

Sachs, Curt, 11–12, 36, 64, 156, 164, 183n39; *History of Musical Instruments*, 156
Sala, Oskar, 134, 144, 154, 158–59, 162–63, 199n75; and Trautonium development, 122, 126, 130, 133, 140, 158, 204n25; and Trautonium performance, 123, 125, 132, 136, 140–41, 158, 198n58
Sancristoforo, Giorgio, 165, 207n59
Schaeffer, Pierre, 161–63
Scheibler, Johann Heinrich, 64, 184n49,
Schenck, Emil, 145
Scherchen, Hermann, 78–79, 159
Schirokauer, Arno, 121
Schillinger, Joseph, 1
Schlemmer, Oskar, 6–7, 42–48, 54, 180n97; and the Bauhaus, 6, 42; collaboration with Hindemith, 44–46, 82; *Triadic Ballet*,18, 42–43, 43fig., 44–45, 45fig., 46, 52, 82, 179n88
Schmidt, Rudolf, 123
Schoenberg, Arnold, 36–37, 57, 102, 135, 160, 193n65; *Harmonielehre (Theory of Harmony)*, 55–56, 71; *Klangfarbenmelodie*, 71–72; "Mechanical Musical Instruments," 27–28, 176n35; and microtonality, 55–56, 181n15; *Pierrot Lunaire*, 43
Schad, Christian, 88, 179n73
Schumacher, Fritz, 153
Schünemann, Georg, 92, 120–21, 124–25, 132, 134
serialism, 158, 161–62
silent film, 96–98; vs. sound film, 96–97. *See also* Eisenstein, Sergei; Podovkin, Vsevolod
Simondon, Gilbert, 166
Society for Electroacoustic Music (Gesellschaft für elektro-akustische Musik), 78, 120, 144–46, 149
Sonar (electric instrument), 115, 196n11
sound film, 7; history of, 50, 93–96; as media instrument, 2, 8, 50, 82–84, 88, 92, 96–113; and modernist art, 97; and montage, 96–98, 103–6; and notation, 83–84, 98, 108–11, 110fig.16, 113; and silent film, 96–98; and synthetic sound, 83, 106–12; technology of, 83, 93–95, 95fig.14, 96fig.15. *See also* Bagier, Guido; Beyer, Robert; Fischinger, Oskar; Moholy-Nagy, László; Pfenninger, Rudolf; Ruttmann, Walter
Sousa, John Philip: "The Menace of Mechanical Music," 25
Spengler, Oswald, 80; *Decline of the West*, 10; *Man and Technics*, 153
Spherophone (Sphärophon): critical reaction to 52, 64–66, 150; design of, 52, 61–62, 62fig., 63, 65, 82; music for, 80–81, 148–49; in performance, 52, 65–67, 123, 160; sound of, 52, 61–65, 70, 74, 82; types of, 75–76. *See also* Keyboard-Spherophone, Partiturophon
Spielmann, Emerich. *See* Superpiano
Stege, Fritz, 149, 202n119
Stein, Erwin, 33
Stein, Fritz, 134, 198n59
Stein, Richard, 58, 62, 68, 181n9, 182n26, 182n36, 200n100
Steinhard, Erich, 22–23, 46, 171n17
Sterne, Jonathan, 8
De Stijl: and Moholy-Nagy, 7, 87; and Mondrian, 85–87
Stockhausen, Karlheinz, 161–63, 205n31
Stokowski, Leopold, 101
Strassburg, Dietrich van, 39
Strauss, Richard, 36, 54, 57, 70

Stravinsky, Igor: Concertino for String Quartet, 22; *Étude pour pianola,* 30, 175n29; and mechanical music, 22, 24, 36,
Strobel, Heinrich, 36–37, 67–68; "Neue Sachlichkeit in der Musik," 36
Stuckenschmidt, Hans Heinz, 6–7, 30, 154, 158, 162–63; anti-romanticism of, 6, 31, 38–39, 47–48, 108; as composer, 7, 44, 48; critique of, 32–34, 39, 89; and the gramophone, 89–90, 92, 166, as impresario, 7, 38; and mechanical music, 30–34, 39, 42, 47–48, 51, 54, 88–89, 90, 92, 99–100, 160, 180n107, 197n44; "Mechanization of Music," 30–31; and Moholy-Nagy, 32, 88, 90, 92, 166; and the New Objectivity, 48, 177n54; and the player piano, 30–32, 88–90, 160; "Under the Swastika," 135
Studio for Electronic Music, Northwest German Radio (Cologne), 159–63, 205n38. *See also* Beyer, Robert; Eimert, Herbert; Meyer-Eppler, Werner; Stockhausen, Karlheinz
Superpiano, 115
Synthesizer, analog, 74–75, 164–66

Taruskin, Richard: *Oxford History of Western Music,* 164
technology: critique of, 8–12, 14, 20, 153; sympathy toward, 9–17, 20–21, 34–35, 115, 137, 139, 152–54, 158; and triumphalism, 152–53. *See also* Audion triode; computer; de Forest, Lee; Dessauer, Friedrich; gramophone; loudspeaker; magnetic tape; phonograph; photoelectric cell; Photographophone; Photophone; radio; Schumacher, Fritz; silent film; Spengler, Oswald; sound film; vacuum tube
Telharmonium: Busoni on, 13–14, 63, 74; Mager on, 63–64
Terpsiton, 115
Théberge, Paul, 164
Theremin, Léon, 66–67, 67*fig.*115, 118, 149; "New Trails in Musical Creation," 66. *See also* Rhythmicon; Terpsiton; Theremin
Theremin (electric instrument), 62–63, 76, 97, 125, 140, 143, 200n88; ease of playing, 67–68, 126; critique of, 104, 155, 157–58; mass marketing of, 115, 130, 144, 195n3; playing technique of, 66–68, 67*fig.*10, 145, 148; sound of, 66

Third Reich, 133–35; aesthetics of, 135–36, 141; Kraft durch Freude (Strength through Joy), 140–41. *See also* Genzmer, Harald; Goebbels, Joseph; Hindemith, Paul; Hitler, Adolf; loudspeaker; Trautwein, Friedrich;
Tiessen, Heinz, 33
timbre/tone-color, 2, 28–30, 50–51, 70–72, 155, 162; electric sound, 60, 65, 69, 72–75, 78–79, 104, 118–20, 123, 129–30, 146, 148–51, 161, 205n31; *Klangfarbenmelodie,* 71–72, 75; *Klangfarbenmusik,* 72, 75, 79, 102, 111, 120, 147, 160–61; mechanical sound, 18–19, 23–24, 33–34, 37, 40–41, 45–46, 49–50, 142–43; optical sound film, 84–86, 99–100, 102–3, 105, 107
Toch, Ernst: *Gesprochene Musik,* 91–92; and gramophone music, 90–92, 104, 123, 157; and mechanical music, 18, 40–41, 69, 84; concept of *Nicht-Wärme,* 40
Trautonium, 118*fig.*18; ease of playing, 118, 125–26, 127*fig.*22, 129–31; design of, 117–18, 122–123, 125–26, 147; models of, 133, 138*fig.*25, 140, 158, 205n38; music for, 123, 124*fig.*20, 125, 131–32, 136, 140–41; in performance, 123, 125, 132–33, 136, 140–41; and radio enthusiasts, 125–27, 127*fig.*22; *Trautonium School,* 132; sound of, 117–19, 123, 130–31. *See also* Volkstrautonium
Trautwein, Friedrich, 118*fig.*18; collaboration with Hindemith, 121–23, 134, 159; collaboration with Sala, 122, 126, 132, 134, 136; early life, 117; *Elektrische Musik,* 123–25; experiments, 116–17, 121; legacy of, 165–66; and Mager, 116–17, 120, 125, 134, 137, 144–45, 148, 150, 160; patents of, 117; post-WWII career, 159; and the Radio Research Section, 121–22, 124–25; and Theremin, 118, 137–38; and the Third Reich, 134–37, 139–40, 142, 154, 159. *See also* Trautonium; Volkstrautonium
Trocco, Frank, 164

Universum-Film-Aktiengesellschaft (UFA), 50, 82–83, 150. *See also* Bagier, Guido

vacuum tube, 16, 51, 53, 59–60, 95, 166, 182n28; in Radio-Tone Organ, 115, 188n5. *See also* Audion Piano; Audion triode; diode

Varèse, Edgard, 1, 3, 62, 155
Verne, Jules, 15, 184n45
Vertov, Dziga: *Enthusiasm: Symphony of the Donbass*, 106
Vienna Circle, 34–35, 177n49
Vierling, Oskar, 73, 125, 134. *See also* Elektrochord; KdF-Großtonorgel
Volkstrautonium (Telefunken-Trautonium), 128*fig.*23; design of, 126–27; mass marketing of, 126–31, 131*fig.*24, 132; in performance, 129, 132; and radio, 127, 129–30; and Telefunken, 126, 129–30. *See also* Gebrauchsmusik, Trautonium

Wagner, Karl Willy: and the Heinrich Hertz Institute, 121, 134; and subtractive synthesis, 73–74, 196n16
Wagner, Richard, 57, 70, 78, 137; *Parsifal*, 80, 158
Warschauer, Frank, 15–16
Weber, Max, 10, 56; "Science as a Vocation," 10
Webern, Anton, 135, 162
Weill, Kurt, 99, 135, 192n52
Weimar Republic, 2, 21, 114, 133, 135, 158; culture of, 2, 37–38, 47, 134–36, 153, 160; and the "machine aesthetic," 21–34, 41, 48, 53; and music, 7, 15, 20, 50, 82, 85, 92, 104–5, 114, 141; musical legacy of, 141, 160–63
Weiskopf, Herbert: and Mager's instruments, 52, 65, 68–69, 72, 185n68
Weissmann, Adolf: *Die Entgötterung der Musik (Music Come to Earth)*, 12, 172n37
Welte-Mignon mechanical piano: critique of, 49; design of, 18, 26–27, 29*fig.*3; music for, 18–19, 49–50, 82, 90–91, 123; in performance, 18–20; and reproduction, 26–27, 31, 49, 82; virtuosity of, 19, 49, 111–12
Welte-Philharmonie mechanical organ: design of, 45–46; music for, 44–45
World War I, 2, 10, 12, 20, 53, 58
World War II, 3, 27, 140–41, 158, 162–63, 197n32
Wyschnegradsky, Ivan, 58

Xenakis, Iannis, 162, 204n21

Zschimmer, Eberhard, 10

www.ingramcontent.com/pod-product-compliance
Lightning Source LLC
Chambersburg PA
CBHW021701230426
43668CB00008B/697